Fantasyland

INSIDE the REIGN of BILL VANDER ZALM

Gary Mason · Keith Baldrey

Fantasyland

INSIDE the REIGN of BILL VANDER ZALM

McGraw-Hill Ryerson
Toronto   Montreal

Fantasyland: INSIDE the REIGN of BILL VANDER ZALM

ISBN 0-07-549868-5

1 2 3 4 5 6 7 8 9 0 D 7 6 5 4 3 2 1 0 9

Printed and bound in Canada

Jacket design and text: Hania Fil
Cover photo: John Douglas Kenny

Canadian Cataloguing in Publication Data
Mason, Gary
Fantasyland: inside the reign of Bill Vander Zalm

ISBN 0-07-549868-5

1. Vander Zalm, William N.   2. British Columbia–
Politics and government–1975-   .*   3. Prime
ministers–British Columbia–Biography.
I. Baldrey, Keith.   II. Title.

FC3828.1.V35M37 1989   971.1′04′0924   C89-095426-7
F1088.V35M37 1989

C O N T E N T S

From the moment Bill Vander Zalm beamed his smile from atop a platform in a muggy convention centre in the mountain resort of Whistler, British Columbia, politics has never been quite the same. Since assuming office on August 6, 1986, Vander Zalm has presided over one of the most tumultuous periods of political turmoil the province—and the Social Credit Party—has ever seen.

He captivated the voters with a promise to end a Socred legacy of confrontation and bitterness left behind by his predecessor, Bill Bennett. But within two years of taking office, he alienated many of the people who had flocked to him in the first place. The promised vision of "open" government and a "fresh start" gave way to a never-ending stream of controversy and scandal.

How did it happen? There are many reasons, but they all centre on one man—Bill Vander Zalm. His personality, his "style," and his ad hoc, free-wheeling method of governing have created an almost constant state of crisis for his government. An insistence on imprinting his religious zealousness and moral view on fellow British Columbians has triggered a lasting resentment among many people.

While British Columbia was in an uproar, the one place he found peace and contentment was amid the flowers and cobblestones of his Fantasy Garden World. He was still king there, in the castle home kept by his wife, Lillian. Here, he could gather strength and confidence. The real world didn't exist. It was a fantasyland, and he felt right at home.

We felt the story of Bill Vander Zalm's rise to power and his chaotic years in the premier's office was simply too good a tale to leave in the columns of newspapers. It finally became apparent that we had an unequalled and unbeatable seat from which to write it.

From the day Bill Bennett announced his intention to retire on a May morning right through to the present, we have chronicled the Vander Zalm phenomenum for the Vancouver *Sun*. Rarely did he leave his legislative office without one or both of us dogging his every step. His open style with reporters allowed us a level of access that provided many of the insights and much of the information needed to write this book.

In the writing of this book, we interviewed nearly 100 people both inside and outside of politics, all of whom were in some way connected to this story. A handful of people spoke on the condition that they not be identified for fear of retribution. We have respected their wishes. Nearly everyone we spoke to was extremely generous with their time and very patient with nagging queries that meant, in some cases, interviewing the same person more than a dozen times. Some of those we spoke to deserve special thanks. They include Bill Vander Zalm, David Poole, Grace McCarthy, Brian Smith, Bill Kay, Stephen Rogers, Rita Johnstone, Bill Reid, and Bob Ransford.

Acknowledgments

There are many people without whose assistance this book would never have been written. Denise Schon and Don Loney for shepherding this project through at McGraw-Hill Ryerson and our agent Denise Bukowski, who helped turn an idea into a book, rank high on the list. Our editors, Rosalyn Steiner and Don Stanley, brought unparalleled skills to the project as well as a reservoir of patience that stood them well when dealing with two authors more used to filing newspaper stories than book chapters. Our researcher, Sheila Hill, saved us untold time and headaches through her steady and immaculate work.

Our friend and colleague, Vaughn Palmer, was an immense help. His columns for the Vancouver *Sun* help define political debate in British Columbia, and his advice and insight helped shape parts of this book. The insights and suggestions of another colleague at the *Sun*, the veteran political writer Tom Barrett, were also of great assistance.

Other co-workers at the Vancouver *Sun* provided support and assistance whenever required. Managing editor Gordon Fisher and city editor Scott Macrae showed remarkable patience and encouragement in letting their two provincial political reporters take extended leaves of absence in completing this book. Head librarian Shirley Mooney and her hard-working staff were also of tremendous assistance, as were photo editor Nick Palmer and the *Sun*'s many talented staff photographers and technicians. A small sampling of their work can be found in this book.

Finally, the most gratitude goes to Barbara Mason and Anne Mullens. Barbara, an accomplished writer and mother of Gary's two sons, offered never-ending support and invaluable advice. So did Anne, a fellow *Sun* reporter and author, who convinced us to write the book back in the winter of 1988 and who provided constant encouragement during some trying times. To both of them go our utmost thanks.

Keith Baldrey
Gary Mason
Victoria, British Columbia
July 1989

The Enemies

It was Friday, July 8, 1988. Bob Ransford was working in the Vancouver cabinet offices of the B.C. government. He had returned from Victoria the night before, uneasy about the future of the man he was there to serve–Premier Bill Vander Zalm.

It had been a tough week, and Ransford was relieved to see it end. He thought he would do some paperwork, make a few calls, have lunch, and then take the afternoon off. His golf clubs were in the trunk of his grey Honda Accord. But shortly after 11:00 a.m. a telephone call changed his plans.

"Bob, David would like you to return to Victoria immediately."

It was Jennifer Stevens, personal secretary to David Poole, Vander Zalm's principal secretary and chief adviser. Poole wanted his executive assistant to return for an emergency meeting with the premier.

Ransford's mind whirled. An urgent meeting could only mean trouble. He wondered who had quit this time. Within an hour Ransford was on an Air B.C. Twin Otter float plane for the thirty-minute southwest flight across the Strait of Georgia to Victoria's Inner Harbour.

Bill Vander Zalm's administration was in crisis. Three days earlier, on July 5, his most senior member, Grace McCarthy, had quit

1

the cabinet, citing unacceptable interference by Vander Zalm and his deputy David Poole in the operations of her ministry. McCarthy's resignation had shocked the Social Credit Party. She was no average minister; she was "Amazing Grace," the party's grande dame and biggest cheerleader, whose interminable optimism and dedication to the cause of free enterprise had brought her a following second in loyalty only to Vander Zalm's.

Ten days earlier, the province's staid attorney-general, Brian Smith, had stood in the legislature to announce that he too could no longer tolerate interference by Vander Zalm in his ministry's affairs and had no choice but to resign from cabinet.

Since January there had been a ceaseless string of controversies. Members of Vander Zalm's own caucus had publicly attacked him for his rigid stand against abortion. Party members said that the premier was running a one-man show and that his cabinet ministers were becoming irrelevant.

Vander Zalm's numerous embarrassing public statements had made him a regular target for cartoonists, who portrayed him as a wild man or a clown. Editorials called for his resignation. Polls put his support at a previously undreamed-of low of 19 per cent.

By July, panic had gripped the premier's Victoria office and Vander Zalm had become increasingly isolated from his staff, with the exception of David Poole. The once-talkative premier would now brush past reporters when he arrived for work. Entering the back door of the premier's wing, he would walk across the office's blue carpeting, past four secretaries, past the spiral staircase leading to the cabinet chamber, to David Poole's corner suite, where he would generally step in and say hello. He would then continue on eight more steps, past his secretary's office, to his own oak-panelled office overlooking the legislative lawns and the ornate Empress Hotel. Poole would follow and close the door. Lunch would be brought in. Appointments would be cancelled. Sometimes Vander Zalm and Poole would sequester themselves for eight hours.

The pall that hung over the premier's office was made worse by the daily media musings that the resignations of Smith and McCarthy, the abortion controversy, and the revelations in April that Vander Zalm had tried to help his friend Peter Toigo buy the valuable government-owned Expo 86 site had left the Socreds no choice but to dump their premier or risk losing the next election. Commentators said that the Social Credit Party, a coalition of liberals and conservatives, could disappear into political oblivion if Vander Zalm remained at the helm.

Ransford's plane splashed down shortly after one o'clock. Decked out in pink golf shirt, blue blazer, brown slacks, and maroon penny loafers, he decided to enjoy the sunshine and walk to the legislature, ten minutes away. With short, tightly curled brown hair and a large, round, cherubic face, Ransford looked younger than his twenty-seven years. But that afternoon, as he entered his corner office overlooking the legislature's rose garden, he felt much older. The pressures of the last few months had been hard on everyone in the premier's office.

Just before two o'clock, Ransford and the other aides took their seats across from the premier.

Poole began the meeting.

"The premier wanted to meet with you guys to discuss some of your concerns," he said. "There's no denying we've got a lot of political problems, and so we have to make some decisions."

He was seated directly across from Vander Zalm, who was leaning back in his chair behind a huge oak desk. To Poole's left was Ransford. On Poole's right were two other advisers, Brian Battison and Bill Bachop. Bachop was also Vander Zalm's press secretary.

Poole told the group about a disturbing conference call among Social Credit Party directors that had occurred two days earlier, on July 6. During the call, Party president Hope Rust had reported that headquarters had received five hundred phone calls since McCarthy's resignation, with only fifteen of them supporting the premier. During the same call, the Socred caucus chairman, Carol Gran, had hung up on the premier over his handling of a cabinet shuffle. The directors had expressed their concern about the growing dissent in the party and had said emphatically that something had to be done fast.

Vander Zalm looked solemn as he listened to Poole. He lit his pipe. The sweet, pungent smell of his own special blend of tobacco filled the room.

The premier's office wall displayed reminders of better times. His favourite in a gallery of photos from the 1986 Socred leadership convention showed him cheek to cheek with his wife, Lillian, her trademark headband in place, their high-voltage smiles lighting up the Whistler convention centre. The picture had been taken moments after he captured his party's top prize. Fifty-two years old at the time, he looked younger in the picture. Now he looked tired and worn.

Vander Zalm took the floor. His indefatigable optimism had been tested in recent months, but it remained irrepressible. He told the group to hang tough.

"I don't think the problems are as bad as they're being made out," he said. "I think we can turn things around if we just make a few changes."

The aides, however, knew it was time to go on the offensive against Vander Zalm's enemies; they just had to convince their boss.

Bob Ransford pointed out the window, toward the glorious view of Victoria's Inner Harbour. "Look, Premier," he said, "I don't want to be standing out there packing boxes and wondering what happened.

"Premier, number one, you've got to change your style and part of changing that style is changing the office and part of changing the office is for us to leave."

Ransford, Poole, Bachop, and Battison knew they were all being blamed for the premier's problems–particularly Poole.

His nineteen months in the job had gained him a reputation for being arrogant and power hungry. Not content with being Vander Zalm's chief political adviser–the traditional role filled by a principal secretary–he had seized control of the supposedly non-partisan bureaucracy.

Poole loved his job. He often arrived for work at seven in the morning and didn't leave until eleven at night. Poole was short, with dark hair, a round face, and a small, upturned nose, but the long hours had left him often looking haggard, with an ever-widening mid-section that tested the buttons of every shirt he put on.

Along with the job's challenge, he also relished the attention that it focused on him. His counterparts in other provinces would never have dared to assume so public a persona. A principal secretary was supposed to be a quiet adviser, neither seen nor heard. That wasn't Poole's style. He was constantly quoted in the press. When Vander Zalm was out of town, Poole appeared on the evening news responding to political crises, acting like a minister.

Old-line Socred ministers were appalled, particularly Grace McCarthy. She and Poole engaged in public slanging matches, showdowns that ultimately undermined the premier's authority.

By July, Poole had beome a symbol of everything that was wrong with Vander Zalm's administration. Members of the Socred caucus wanted him fired. He knew it. Vander Zalm knew it, too, but the last thing he wanted was to let his most trusted and faithful adviser go. Poole and Vander Zalm had forged an uncommon bond during the 1986 general election. Since then Vander Zalm had refused to turn to anyone else for political advice. In return, he received total reverence from Poole, who kept a framed picture of Vander Zalm hanging in his master bedroom.

Looking directly at Vander Zalm, Ransford suggested that he, Bachop, and Battison leave immediately and Poole leave within a few months, thus avoiding the impression of a mass desertion.

Vander Zalm couldn't believe what he was hearing. Imbued with a macho view of responsibility, he felt that men should always confront their problems rather than trying to elude them.

"You guys are overreacting. What are you, a bunch of quitters? Are you going to run away from the problem?"

The discussion turned to other matters—the premier's enemies, mainly McCarthy.

Her resignation hurt. Like the departed Brian Smith before her, she had been made to look like a martyr, sacrificing her cabinet post to sound the alarm about problems in the premier's office, doing it all for the greater good of the party.

As the minister in charge of selling the Expo site, a valuable piece of property in downtown Vancouver, she had cast herself as the heroine, protector of the public trust. The premier was portrayed as the villain, attempting to thwart the legitimate public bidding process in order to assist an outside bidder, his millionaire friend Peter Toigo, who had helped raise funds for Vander Zalm's leadership bid.

Poole and Ransford felt that McCarthy didn't deserve her pristine image. The premier's office was the receptacle for rumours of every sort, and there was no shortage of them concerning McCarthy.

While Vander Zalm listened, Ransford and Poole described how McCarthy had filled the ranks of her economic development ministry through some of the most blatant patronage appointments ever seen in the Social Credit Party. They said Grace's friends were everywhere.

They also talked about rumours that she had cut a private deal during the Expo land sale that was supposedly beneficial to McCarthy's developer husband, Ray. (McCarthy told the authors: "I haven't benefitted financially and neither has my husband [from the Expo land sale]. There is nothing this family has gained in all of the years I've been in politics.")

A month earlier, someone had leaked the embarrassing details of a $1-million renovation and redesign of McCarthy's legislative and Vancouver offices to the media. Getting more dirt on McCarthy would take a certain kind of professional digging. The man they had in mind was the former head of the RCMP in B.C., Peter Bazowski.

Bazowski, ostensibly retired, had been brought into the premier's office two days earlier, on July 6, as part of a reorganization aimed at stifling criticism that Vander Zalm's aides were incompetent and that he needed the aid of professional bureaucrats. After his RCMP days Bazowski became a deputy minister with a legendary reputation as a tough hatchet man but also as a highly skilled administrator. His job in the premier's office wasn't strictly defined, but Bazowski's understanding was that he would talk to people in the premier's office and throughout the bureaucracy and make recommendations for salutary changes.

He could never have imagined what the premier and his aides were dreaming up for him.

To get information on McCarthy's alleged patronage spree, Ransford wanted Bazowski to go into McCarthy's old ministry, interview people, get job descriptions, and search her files for anything incriminating. (The day McCarthy quit, Ransford wanted the premier's office to change the locks on her office door to prevent her from retrieving files that might contain information that could one day be used against her. That idea was vetoed.)

The group also discussed having Bazowski look into McCarthy's role in the Expo lands deal. But Vander Zalm wasn't entirely comfortable with the plan his advisers were developing to get McCarthy, whom he still considered a friend.

"I don't want to be too negative," he said. "Grace has a lot of support in the party."

It wasn't a matter of being too negative, the premier's aides argued, it was a case of Grace getting some of her own medicine. They knew that some of her supporters were quietly campaigning to unseat the premier through a leadership review at the party's upcoming fall convention. And the aides weren't about to forgive McCarthy for the trouble she and officials at the B.C. Enterprise Corp. (BCEC), which was responsible for the Expo deal, had given Vander Zalm.

The aides believed that BCEC's chairman, Peter Brown, a high profile Vancouver stock promoter and prominent Socred supporter, and the corporation's president, Kevin Murphy, were working with McCarthy to unseat Vander Zalm so that she could assume the Socred throne.

During one BCEC board meeting in May, Brown went on a twenty-minute tirade about the efforts of Poole, Vander Zalm, and Toigo to disrupt the Expo sale. Brown's rant—in front of the entire board—included every rumour he'd heard swirling around town about the premier, Poole, and Toigo.

Poole was furious. In the meantime he had heard a rumour of his own: Hong Kong billionaire and real estate magnate Li Ka-shing, who eventually purchased the Expo lands, had promised Murphy a job in one of his companies upon completion of that sale. There was absolutely no truth to the rumour.

Poole and others in the premier's office believed that a thorough investigation of the Expo lands sale by an impartial person might unearth some disturbing revelations about the people at BCEC. At the same time, Poole believed that any report into the matter would vindicate himself, the premier, and Toigo.

This, in short, was another job for Bazowski.

The final enemy was the former attorney-general.

"We've got something on Brian Smith," David Poole said, looking at the premier. "He's overstepped his bounds and we've got the evidence."

Vander Zalm nodded agreement. Neither Poole nor Vander Zalm would tell the others what they meant. The aides glanced at each other with curiosity.

What the premier and Poole knew was that, a few months earlier, Smith had initiated an RCMP investigation into the premier's relationship with Peter Toigo. The investigation had been prompted when Kevin Murphy and Keith Mitchell, BCEC's lawyer, went to Smith with allegations against Toigo of influence peddling.

Vander Zalm knew through the RCMP that its investigation had turned up nothing incriminating. That's what they had on Brian Smith. How to deal with it was one more job for Peter Bazowski.

In the space of three hours, the premier's aides had devised a strategy to get back at Vander Zalm's enemies. It involved turning a highly respected former civil servant, Peter Bazowski, into an undercover cop whose task would be to ferret out dirt on the premier's adversaries.

It was now nearly 5:00 p.m., and the premier was going to be late for the Government Air shuttle to Vancouver that was due to leave the government hangar near the Victoria airport in minutes. He was often behind schedule, holding up the blue-and-white executive Citation jet and all the ministers aboard.

The group decided that Ransford, Battison, and Bachop would draft a detailed strategy memo to be presented to Poole on Monday.

Outside the premier's office, a small group of reporters had been waiting for more than an hour for the premier to emerge. Finally, Bill Kay, Vander Zalm's trusty driver and aide de camp, descended the stairs with a briefcase and other items that he put in the premier's waiting white Ford LTD.

The premier appeared minutes later, squinting against the sun. After answering a few questions, he was drawn aside by the Vancouver *Province*'s Brian Kieran, who had a question he didn't want any other reporter to hear. A minute later, Kay wheeled the car out of the driveway.

The premier's car had just reached the highway to the airport when the black phone between Kay and Vander Zalm began beeping. Kay answered. It was a reporter.

"How the hell did you get this number?" barked Kay. "We're going to have to get it changed now."

Vander Zalm grabbed the phone. The reporter wanted to know whether Kieran's private question to the premier was going to set off any bombs.

"Oh, no, it was just something silly about some guy I used to know," said Vander Zalm.

"You're sure it's nothing?" asked the reporter.

"Absolutely. You've got nothing to worry about."

On Sunday morning Kieran's story broke. On the front page of Vancouver's morning tabloid was a full-page picture of one Jud Cyllorn, accompanied by a huge headline: "Zalm's Fortune Teller." The story said that Vander Zalm had hired a numerologist friend to do a $1500 study for the government on entrepreneurial immigration.

In follow-up radio reports, the premier quickly distanced himself from Cyllorn, who had worked on Vander Zalm's leadership campaign and was one of a handful of campaign workers who shared a fascination with numbers and fate.

Vander Zalm told reporters that Cyllorn was an acquaintance, nothing more. David Poole said there was absolutely no truth to the story. What the reporters did not know was that the premier and Poole had had dinner with Cyllorn at the Union Club in Victoria four nights before the story broke. It was there that initial arrangements were made for Cyllorn to do the immigration study.

Links to the dubious world of numerology weren't what Vander Zalm needed. He spent most of Monday denying the Cyllorn story, while inside his office Bachop, Battison, and Ransford put the final touches on their memo to David Poole.

The memo included strategy recommendations to diminish Poole's role by splitting his duties with another person who would take over Poole's responsibilities for the civil service. It also included tactics for dealing with the upcoming leadership test at the fall party convention. A third item outlined assignments for Peter Bazowski, who had barely settled into his coveted corner office, directly above Vander Zalm's.

Poole reviewed the memo, and two days later the aides met with

Vander Zalm to go over the action plan. He agreed to a special two-day Socred caucus meeting to be held the following month in Courtenay, a Vancouver Island resort community, but no one in the room was confident that at that meeting Vander Zalm would be tough enough on the outlaws in his ranks. He simply wasn't as concerned as his aides were about a possible challenge to his leadership.

As for his enemies, Vander Zalm said that he would talk to the designated hit man, Peter Bazowski. Desperate times had provoked desperate measures.

Garden Fresh

Bill Vander Zalm was in his garden, engaged in his favourite pastime: watering plants and sweeping dust off the walk. The soil, the smell of the flowers, the care that went into their survival—these all spelled relaxation to the fifty-two-year-old career politician and gardener.

His biblical garden theme park, Fantasy Garden World, was just getting off the ground, and Vander Zalm and his wife, Lillian, were working sixteen hours a day at the complex in Richmond, a suburb on the Fraser River flatlands south of Vancouver.

Two garden visitors walked up to him. "Have you heard the news?" one asked. "Bill Bennett says he's quitting."

Vander Zalm raised his eyebrows. "Why no, I hadn't heard that," he replied, and hurried to the front shop.

It was May 22, 1986, and Bill Bennett had just announced that, after almost eleven years as premier, he was retiring. There had been rumours but, even so, Vander Zalm was as shocked as most British Columbians by the actual news.

"By the time I got back to the booth . . . the media were phoning to find out if I knew, and what my reaction was—would I be seeking the leadership," Vander Zalm recalls.

"My first response was: I've always had some interest in this sort of thing, but given the circumstances now with [Fantasy Gardens], I don't think I will."

Not many people believed him.

Vander Zalm had been out of government since quitting the cabinet in 1983, less than one year after calling his cabinet colleagues "gutless" for not supporting one of his pet pieces of legislation on land use. Speculation at the time had him convinced the Socreds would lose the next election, setting the stage for his taking over the leadership. But Bennett and the Socreds won, and Vander Zalm returned to cultivating his garden.

He made a disastrous run at the Vancouver mayoralty in 1984. After being trounced by incumbent mayor Mike Harcourt–later to be the leader of the provincial New Democrats–Vander Zalm was back in the garden park muttering about "communists" beating "Christian businessmen" in the race for city council.

But with Bennett out of the way he once again had a chance at the premier's chair and the limelight he loved. On the other hand, there was his new multi-million-dollar garden park. While Vander Zalm dithered, the B.C. political scene was in an uproar.

Bill Bennett's departure marked the end of a political dynasty that spanned four decades. For the first time in almost thirty-four years, the Social Credit Party would not have a leader from the Kelowna hardware merchant family.

Bennett had come a long way from being "daddy's boy," as the New Democrats delighted in calling him when he first came to the legislature in 1973. He had inherited a dispirited, broken-down party from his father, former premier W.A.C. Bennett, who had lost the 1972 election. Together with Grace McCarthy, the flame-haired queen of Social Credit, Bill set out to rebuild it.

McCarthy travelled the province, using her irrepressible positivism to sign up thousands of members. In the legislature, she enthusiastically supported Bennett when the NDP taunted him mercilessly. Bill Bennett wooed some sitting Liberal MLAs and a few "name candidates" (including the colourful Surrey mayor, Bill Vander Zalm) into his party, and the free enterprise coalition was reborn.

Once in power, Bill Bennett introduced his party to the modern age of politics, bringing in help from Ontario's fabled Big Blue

Machine that had kept the Conservatives in power for so long there. The Social Credit Party, already stunningly successful at winning elections, became a fine-tuned political machine. Government advertising campaigns became the order of the day, particularly for the 1983 election's key issue, "restraint," which led to Bennett's demise and Vander Zalm's opportunity.

There had been a sudden drop in resource revenues during the recession of the early 1980s. In a province where the resource industries–forestry, mining, and fishing–drive the economy and provide much of the employment, the government suddenly faced large deficits and mounting debt.

Much of the blame could be laid directly on Bennett. His government was vulnerable partly because of its uneconomic megaprojects that were financed on borrowed money and future taxes. But in the 1983 election, the voters bought his call for economic restraint and gave the Socreds another chance.

Armed with an election-victory mandate for restraint, Bennett's government plunged ahead with a vengeance. In one dizzying budget, he introduced twenty-seven bills that "undid" many things British Columbians had come to take for granted: many of the bargaining rights of civil servants were eliminated, for example. The rentalsman's office–which protected tenants–and the human rights branch were simply dismantled.

In October 1983, some 60 000 marchers surrounded the Hotel Vancouver, where the Socreds were holding their annual convention. Under the banner of "Solidarity," a giant coalition of labour and community groups did its part to undo the Socreds' populist legacy.

As for Bennett himself, his "tough guy" Clint Eastwood image, though successful in the 1983 election campaign, had by 1986 become a liability. The polls, however, showed that voters were not necessarily fed up with a Social Credit government, just with the man leading it. Bennett was determined not to inflict the damage his father had by overstaying his welcome; the result in 1972 had been an NDP government and the collapse of the Social Credit Party.

So Bill Bennett resigned. It was better than losing an election, and losing elections is something the Social Credit Party is not very good at. Holding power is a big part of what Social Credit is all about.

Aside from a commitment to "free enterprise," it is a party based less on ideology than on the cult of personality.

And now, in the spring of 1986, Social Credit was once more looking for that personality: a dynamic new leader, a charismatic populist perhaps, another messiah in the W.A.C. Bennett mould. British Columbian voters gravitated toward such personalities.

While Vander Zalm hemmed and hawed, the party executive was in a state of confusion. The Socreds had had only one leadership convention in almost thirty-five years, and the party's constitution contained just two vague paragraphs dealing with such an event. But at least Bennett had helped with one key task: choosing the date and location of the leadership convention. It would be held July 28–30 in the ski resort town of Whistler, 100 kilometres north of Vancouver.

By mid-June, no less than eleven candidates had entered the race, an indication that there was no heir apparent to Bennett. The aspirants included the queen of Social Credit, Grace McCarthy. Adored by the party faithful, ridiculed by her political enemies, McCarthy had more political savvy than most of her opponents put together. She had served under W.A.C. Bennett and held various cabinet portfolios for more than fifteen years.

Her trademarks: sunny smile, constant optimism, boundless energy, and flaming red hair. A resident of Shaughnessy, one of Vancouver's wealthy neighbourhoods, McCarthy had once turned all her expensive rings around on her fingers while announcing a cut to welfare rates.

"Gracie," Social Credit personified, became an immediate front runner. Only Vander Zalm could match her strong personal following in the party.

One of her chief rivals was Bud Smith, a lawyer from the Interior city of Kamloops. As Bennett's principal secretary, Smith had helped hone Bennett's "gunslinger" image during the 1983 campaign. He was a devout disciple of the U.S. Republican school of politics. Bright, tough, arrogant, and experienced in running a political machine, he liked to wear cowboy boots and checked shirts. His chief problems: he had never held political office and hardly anyone knew him.

The other Smith was Brian, the province's attorney-general, a true-blue, tweed-suited conservative. Dour, stuffy, and a little reserved, the pipe-smoking Smith resembled a pompous professor. It would be an uphill battle to try to change his image into something more upbeat; Smith found it hard even to clap spontaneously.

Each of the "Smith brothers," as they came to be called, was seen as a natural extension of the other. Many observers imagined the two forming an alliance, dubbed the "cough drop conspiracy," but there was just one problem with the scenario: the two men loathed each other.

Two other Socred veteran cabinet ministers also jumped in: Jim Nielsen, whose uncanny resemblance to a teenage biker earned him the nickname "The Fonz," and Stephen Rogers, a charming and irreverent former airline pilot who was also a member of B.C.'s wealthy Rogers family of B.C. Sugar fame.

Both men had recently suffered a run of bad luck and bad press. Nielsen sported a black eye from the fist of a jealous husband. Rogers, who possessed the image of a rich playboy and the reality of a vast stock portfolio, couldn't seem to stay away from conflict-of-interest allegations.

Then there was John Reynolds, a former MP and radio hot-line host. He was also a stock promoter who had suffered from some well-publicized allegations that he had connections to organized crime–allegations that were never proved and that he strongly denied.

There were also two candidates from the Fraser Valley, B.C.'s bible belt. Bill Ritchie, a loud bull moose of a politician, was not likely to appeal to bible belt voters, having just left his wife for his executive assistant. Bob Wenman, a sitting Conservative MP with strong Christian ties who had once been a Socred MLA, was not well known outside the valley.

Kim Campbell, a bright conservative Vancouver lawyer and the only other woman in the race, had a big handicap: young female lawyers from Vancouver didn't go over well with the rural rubes in Social Credit.

A few lesser-knowns made pitches hoping to give their fledgling provincial political careers a boost. They were Mel Couvelier, the mayor of a Victoria suburb and a former provincial Liberal candidate, and Cliff Michael, an ex-millworker from the southern Interior.

By mid-June, all the candidates were in. All, that is, except the gardener from the Vancouver suburb of Richmond. Most of the candidates assumed Vander Zalm would run; his ambition had always shone brightly.

But there was some speculation that Bennett himself did not think Vander Zalm would run. The potential for conflict-of-interest allegations involving Fantasy Gardens seemed enormous, and some thought Bennett had timed his resignation with that in mind.

Bill Bennett did not want Vander Zalm anywhere near the premier's chair.

Vander Zalm was the potential candidate whom Bennett and his government colleagues feared–and loathed–the most. Vander Zalm's popularity among the faithful was formidable; no one got bigger ovations at party conventions, not even Bennett. Anyone who had ever worked with Vander Zalm in cabinet considered him to be inept at administering anything. They worried that if he won he could tear the party apart with his right-wing policies and his unorthodox way of doing just about everything. And there was widespread resentment against him among his former cabinet colleagues, who felt he was a renegade because he had deserted them when the going got tough in the bitter restraint years. But there wasn't much they could do except watch and see if he ran.

A college journalism instructor, Charlie Giordano, began to lobby Vander Zalm heavily to join the race. Giordano's association with Vander Zalm went back almost twenty years. He had played a major role in almost every Vander Zalm political campaign since his first run for the Surrey mayoralty.

Socred supporters across the province phoned Fantasy Gardens and pleaded with Vander Zalm to run. Jack Davis, the maverick Socred MLA who had been shunted to the political wilderness because of his inability to get along with Bennett and because of his involvement with scandal in the late 1970s, dropped by the Gardens to try to convince Vander Zalm to get in the race. So did Dave Mercier, the former mayor of the Vancouver suburb of Burnaby; he was considering becoming a Socred candidate after failing to get the moribund provincial Conservative Party off the ground. Two other long-time associates, Surrey MLAs Rita Johnston and Bill Reid, also tried their best to convince him.

Media speculation was intense. Vander Zalm's dithering became almost a daily story, and he milked it for all it was worth. He got more coverage outside the race than most of the declared candidates.

A man who would later come to wield influence over Vander Zalm also began pressuring him to join the race. Peter Toigo, a millionaire restaurateur from Powell River, visited the Gardens in mid-June. Toigo, who had gotten to know Vander Zalm a year earlier when Toigo was considering putting a catering operation in Fantasy Gardens, first advised Vander Zalm not to run and to concentrate on his business. Later, he changed his mind and promised to look after Vander Zalm's fundraising.

Finally, Grace McCarthy—worried that the Smiths could forge a two-pronged attack against her candidacy—phoned Vander Zalm herself.

"Grace phoned and said, 'Look, you have got to run. You are a good candidate and I think you should be in there with the rest of them running.' And I had a long, long talk with Grace. And then Grace sort of convinced me that I should go in," Vander Zalm recalls.

"Sort of convinced" is correct, because still Vander Zalm hesitated. There were family pressures: his youngest daughter, Lucia, had been relieved when he dropped out of politics in 1983. His wife, Lillian, said she would support whatever decision he made, but he knew she preferred to have him concentrate on Fantasy Gardens.

Finally, on Thursday, June 20, he instructed Giordano to prepare a news release saying he was not going to run. Giordano scheduled a news conference for the next day.

Then Vander Zalm thought about it some more. He phoned an exasperated Giordano back and told him to prepare an entirely new release saying that he *would* run. Vander Zalm also phoned Toigo for a last-second shot of encouragement.

The news conference was held in the gleaming white atrium at Fantasy Gardens. It was only 10:00 a.m., but the temperature in the atrium was over 100 degrees. It would not be the last time Vander Zalm deliberately gave his garden park some free publicity. Reporters, waiting for the chronically late Vander Zalm, sweated profusely in the humid room and wondered aloud what he would say. Even at this point, there was some speculation he would not run.

Jack Davis sat quietly, waiting for Vander Zalm. His presence was the first sign that Vander Zalm was indeed getting back into politics. A worried John Plul, one of Grace McCarthy's campaign managers, hovered in the background, trying to figure out whether or not Gracie's chief competitor would join the race.

Finally, Vander Zalm arrived and announced his candidacy to bring "true Christian principles" to government–a comment that would prove prophetic in the turbulent months ahead.

The comment was also a direct slap at Bill Bennett. It inferred that such "true Christian principles" were not already being followed by the current government, which was not really a revelation. After all, the recent spate of conflict-of-interest allegations involving three cabinet ministers–Rogers, Tom Waterland, and Hugh Curtis–plus the indiscretions or marital woes of Jim Nielsen and cabinet minister Bob McClelland (whose name turned up on a credit card receipt in the course of a prostitution investigation) had already demonstrated that the Socred administration was no Boy Scout troop.

Vander Zalm, knowing that the conservative Socred faithful were offended by such goings-on, was quick to make the break with the current regime. His campaign would soon evolve into one aimed not at the NDP, but at Bill Bennett himself.

In another attempt to foster the image of a common, decent man trying to put ethics back into government and power back into the hands of the people, Vander Zalm told reporters he considered his rivals' high campaign budgets "immoral."

He also displayed his unyielding optimism and confidence. "I've been very up-front and I've been with the people of this province. I have great support among people who hold various philosophies. In short, I have the greatest appeal," he said that day.

After the news conference he huddled with Giordano and his other advisers and asked, "What do we do now?"

There were four clear front runners: Vander Zalm, McCarthy, and the two Smiths. The race almost immediately focused on a major theme: the "grassroots" of the party versus its "establishment."

Bill Bennett himself had said it was time for "fresh blood," which didn't help his former ministers Nielsen, Brian Smith, Ritchie, and Rogers. Some read into Bennett's comment a veiled endorsement of Bud Smith, Bennett's former aide, essentially "new" to the party. There was resentment toward Bennett's former aide among his cabinet ministers, summed up by Jim Nielsen's line during the campaign: "I didn't shovel shit in the stables for ten years to have someone else come in and ride the pony."

McCarthy dubbed her campaign "Operation Grassroots" and lashed out at the big-spending "establishment" campaigns of Bud and Brian Smith, both of whom employed seasoned political strategists to run high-tech, sophisticated campaigns.

McCarthy, never one to spend one dollar on campaigns when two will do, was guilty of her own big-spending charge, but both she and Vander Zalm milked the grassroots theme for all it was worth. She refused to speak to a meeting of the so-called "Top Twenty" club, downtown Vancouver financiers who contributed large sums to the party. The stuffy business group was the perfect symbol of the despised establishment, and although Vander Zalm was not actually invited to attend one of their luncheons (as a half-dozen other candidates were), he went out of his way to point out that he had not met with them.

Vander Zalm's campaign was in fact financed largely through small donations from party supporters. A steady stream of envelopes containing $10 or $20 arrived at his Richmond headquarters.

He spent less than his major opponents, and finances were not the only thing separating his campaign from the others.

For one thing, it was totally isolated from the other candidates' campaigns. When Bud Smith's campaign manager phoned the Vander Zalm headquarters one day, no one had a clue who the manager was.

Vander Zalm's delegate tracking and polling systems were not as sophisticated as those used by his biggest rivals. Aside from three MLAs, Vander Zalm's top-level staff consisted of complete amateurs, eccentrics, or people whose experience was mostly in municipal politics.

His co-campaign managers were Charlie Giordano and Bill Goldy, who met Vander Zalm when the two were active in the B.C. Chamber of Commerce after Vander Zalm left politics in 1983. Goldy, who had never run any kind of political campaign before, was also into numerology, and two other so-called numerologists and mysterious self-described "philosophers" were active on the campaign: Allan Robertson and Jud Cyllorn. (Goldy spelled his name "Goldie" at the time of the leadership campaign, but changed it two years later using a numerology formula.)

Cyllorn lurked in the background, discussing proposed policies with Vander Zalm and Robertson. In the opinion of many campaign workers, he made a nuisance of himself. "He didn't get along with too many people. He was always telling people what to do and how to do it," Goldy remembers.

Other core staff were lawyer Al Basile; Richmond video maker Robbie Robertson; Roberta Kelly, a close friend of Jack Davis's who ran the Richmond campaign office; and Larry Fisher, a Surrey businessman who had worked on almost every Vander Zalm political campaign since the 1960s.

The only politicians active on the campaign were three Socred backbenchers: Jack Davis, who helped Vander Zalm formulate policy statements; Bill Reid, who took care of polling and delegate tracking; and Rita Johnston, who ran the Surrey campaign office and looked after the campaign outside the Lower Mainland.

The campaign strategy consisted of one basic principle: get Vander Zalm in contact with as many voting delegates as possible. His optimistic advisers were convinced that getting their man to spend mere minutes with any delegate would be enough to woo that person's vote.

"Strategy? Just letting him be himself, that was the key," remembers Goldy. "His own charisma and his knowledge of people was tremendous. Anywhere that I got him in, he knew so many people, he knew their families, he had been there before."

The party's leadership campaign itself consisted mostly of the candidates visiting the delegate-selection meetings in the province's various ridings, where the selection process was quite simple: each riding, no matter what its population or number of party members, got twenty-five delegates, plus one more for every hundred memberships past a certain mark. Sitting MLAs got automatic delegate status. That was it. No automatic status for party executives, interest groups, or anyone else. You joined the party, went to the meeting, and either ran for delegate status or voted for your favourite twenty-five people.

This unique process worked to Vander Zalm's advantage. It meant that rural ridings (his strongest base of support) had just as many, if not more, delegates as the urban ridings (his weak spots). It also penalized Grace McCarthy, the heavy favourite of delegates in the big city of Vancouver.

More important, the process robbed the party establishment of any base among voting delegates. With no automatic delegate selection—a feature of almost every other political party in Canada—entrenched party machine professionals stood no better chance than quiet, anonymous party members when it came to landing delegate status. The "outs" of the party would have more power than the "ins."

That was just fine for Vander Zalm, who was running against the party establishment anyway. But it was fatal to the other candidates, particularly the two Smiths, who could not compete with Vander Zalm and McCarthy for those many grassroots votes.

And so the candidates travelled the province, sometimes dropping into several ridings a week. There would be about 1300 voting delegates at Whistler, and their support was all that mattered.

Vander Zalm's drawing power was considerable. Whenever he walked into a room, all heads turned toward him. He never had to search out delegates; they looked for him.

He went into Jim Nielsen's back yard in the Vancouver suburb of Richmond and stole almost every delegate. (Nielsen said later that he knew he was in trouble when anti-abortionist Socred members showed up at the meeting in force.) That same night Vander Zalm picked up almost every delegate in Surrey, the Vancouver suburb where he had once been mayor. In Burnaby's three ridings, McCarthy strongholds, Vander Zalm was everyone's second choice.

McCarthy had most of Vancouver to herself, Vancouver Island

was pretty much Brian Smith territory, and Bud Smith had most of the Interior locked up. But Vander Zalm, whose main base of support was the Fraser Valley and much of the suburbs, also had pockets of support all over the province. Most of the Socred delegates considered themselves fairly right-wing, and Vander Zalm was easily the most right-wing candidate in the race. By the first week of July, it was clear he would top the first ballot.

As Vancouver *Sun* newspaper columnist Vaughn Palmer pointed out at the time, the arguments against the front runners were that McCarthy was too old, Brian Smith too dull, Bud Smith too inexperienced, and Vander Zalm too crazy.

A "fifth man" scenario developed, with the bottom candidates agreeing to support a compromise candidate, namely whoever finished fifth on the first ballot, behind the front runners.

Then an extraordinary event occurred, one that sent shudders through Vander Zalm's opponents. In early July, he hosted a giant cocktail party at Fantasy Gardens for any and all delegates who wanted to attend, plus his campaign workers. More than 400 people showed up at the lavishly catered affair. His daughter, Juanita, unveiled the campaign song she had written for her father: "Vander Zalm, He's Our Man."

More important, television cameras attended and recorded the event, catching a slightly tipsy Vander Zalm loudly singing in an impromptu barbershop quartet and hamming it up. Guests were invited to ride on the garden's kiddie train, and the wine and food lasted all night.

The province's powerful number-one television station, BCTV, ran an extended report on the cocktail party, and a media love-in with Vander Zalm began. Patrick Kinsella, Brian Smith's campaign manager, later said he considered the race over when he saw the broadcast: "The media had chosen its candidate."

With Vander Zalm the man to beat, the other candidates began taking shots at him. Both Nielsen and Rogers expressed doubts about being able to serve under him in cabinet if he became premier, a tactic that had little effect except to put their own political futures in doubt.

A Vancouver *Sun* poll two days before the convention opened showed Vander Zalm was far and away the most popular leadership candidate in the province. Only Grace McCarthy came close.

It was essentially a name-recognition poll—not a poll of the delegates, who were going to pick the next premier—but it had quite an impact at Whistler. "Thanks a lot! Thanks a whole lot! I could kiss you guys," Vander Zalm told two *Sun* reporters the night before the convention. The poll had fuelled Vander Zalm's momentum.

The Eastern media got into the act, too, albeit unwittingly. When the *Globe and Mail* published an editorial endorsing Bud Smith, Brian Smith's supporters gleefully made and distributed hundreds of copies of the article. Gaining the favour of the Eastern establishment press was the kiss of death in the eyes of many suspicious Socreds.

For three days, the little mountain town of Whistler was turned into a giant tacky Socred playground. Many of the more than 1300 voting delegates, plus almost an equal number of alternate delegates, campaign workers, and hangers-on, wore the traditional Socred army dress: the "full Nanaimo" (white shoes, white belt, and white tie). A lot of alcohol was consumed.

The alpine village, normally the haven of youngish, swinging skiers, now became the home of middle-aged up-country right-wingers. Village buildings and lamp poles were plastered with pictures of the candidates, many of whom based their headquarters in, appropriately enough, one of the many village pubs. As well, each candidate—except Bob Wenman, who was broke and couldn't afford the $5000 fee—erected a huge tent on a neighbouring golf course.

Bud Smith's was the biggest by far, and he even had a giant helium balloon with his name emblazoned on it tied up outside just in case people didn't know who he was.

The insides of the tents varied from candidate to candidate. Some candidates were running out of money and simply stocked their tents with campaign literature and booze. Kim Campbell and Mel Couvelier were forced to share a tent, while Cliff Michael used his to sell campaign buttons and raise some money.

The interior of McCarthy's tent, however, resembled a cluttered frontier museum. Thrown inside was any object even remotely connected to B.C.—stuffed animals, wagon wheels, barbed wire, Expo 86 posters.

Bud Smith, still trying for the cowboy image, spread sawdust around, put up a podium surrounded by chairs, and made folksy speeches to his supporters.

Vander Zalm had the strangest tent of all. It was a cross between Appalachia and the Swiss Alps, with a dash of a prayer revival meeting. Some inhabitants were dressed like hillbillies, others like Swiss goat herders. Accordion players vied with barbershop quartets. Polkas clashed with bluegrass. A giant organ played circus music, and there was even a popcorn maker on the go all day long.

Occasionally, Bill and Lillian would take the stage and lead a sing-along of some European drinking song. There were Fraser Valley fundamentalists to tell all who would listen about the evils of abortion and other sins. Several times a day, the Vander Zalms would suddenly gather the whole crowd and go for an impromptu march past the other tents, through the village square, and back to their own tent.

The circus atmosphere attracted saturation media coverage. Each television station had several crews there, while the Vancouver *Sun* sent no less than twelve reporters–one for each candidate. Radio stations issued hourly bulletins, and the CBC planned to carry day-long live television coverage of the balloting. For three days, most British Columbians turned their attention to Whistler.

The convention opened with a first-night tribute to Bill Bennett. It was a typically tacky Socred affair. There were plenty of gushing speeches about the man few people really knew. The tribute focused on his last few years in office and defended the restraint program. Speakers blamed the media and the public for giving Bennett a raw deal.

It was clear that Bennett would be remembered, even by his own party and supporters, for the bitter restraint experience. The party's big reward to Bennett for his eleven years as leader was paying off the 1975 Chevrolet he had used in office and buying him a new speedboat. It didn't seem like much for a man who had rebuilt the party and guided it for more than a decade. He would soon discover just how completely the Socred party had turned against him.

The speeches that would really count at this convention occurred the next evening, July 29, one day before the voting began. For almost five hours, the delegates sat in stifling heat to listen to the candidates, who exposed some of the underlying tensions.

The normally stiff and formal Brian Smith–accompanied by a Kinsella-produced eye-popping modern laser light show that fit his personality poorly–made his best speech of the campaign, while McCarthy again emphasized her "operation grassroots" theme.

The most thoughtful speech was given by Kim Campbell, who knew she had absolutely no chance of winning. Articulate, intelligent, and analytical, Campbell also got off the best line of the evening, a direct hit on Vander Zalm: "Charisma without substance is a dangerous thing."

Vander Zalm, who spoke last, almost bombed. His delivery was uncharacteristically stiff and awkward, he made a few weak attacks on the grubby Easterners–a traditional Socred target–then a revealing appeal for first-ballot support. He had expressed worries earlier that too many people who promised to support him would not do so on the first ballot, and would instead cast their vote for a "favourite son or daughter." If that happened, Vander Zalm could lose momentum to McCarthy or even to one of the Smiths.

Talk of deals and backroom intrigue dominated conversations leading up to the vote, but no deals came to fruition. The two Smiths' managers–Kinsella and Laschinger–were still hoping to forge an alliance among their delegates should one of them falter, although both knew that Vander Zalm almost had it wrapped up and that their candidates disliked each other. A desperate Kinsella even tried to plant the idea of an "anyone but Zalm" movement in reporters' minds at a news conference the second day of the convention.

Despite his worries, however, Vander Zalm was supremely optimistic. At a dinner the night before with his advisers, Vander Zalm had made it clear that there would be no deals with any candidate. He would win on his own.

How confident was Vander Zalm? Just after he settled down in the chair on his small platform on one side of the hall, before the balloting started, Vander Zalm pulled out some papers and showed them to a Vancouver *Sun* reporter. One piece of paper contained some scrawled notes: "Stress party unity, fresh start, naming new bridge after Alex Fraser."

"It's for my victory speech," he confided to the reporter. "I think the part about naming the bridge after [veteran Socred minister] Alex Fraser is a nice touch, eh? That will do a lot for party unity." (Fraser, a Bud Smith supporter, had recently been stricken with throat cancer.)

Vander Zalm also pulled out his horoscope, which he had clipped from the newspaper. It showed that the stars were smiling on him this day. He got a kick out of that.

He even predicted that he would get about 500 votes on the first ballot. Making such rash predictions can land a candidate in a lot of trouble if they fall short of their guess, as Vander Zalm's advisers had warned him. But Vander Zalm ignored them.

When the first ballot was announced, Vander Zalm had received just 367 votes. "Gee, that's too low," Vander Zalm said, looking at a reporter's notepad which listed the results: McCarthy next with 244, Bud Smith with 202, Brian Smith closely following with 196, and then a tie for fifth spot between Jim Nielsen and John Reynolds, who each received 54 votes. The rest were well back; Kim Campbell was last with just 14 votes.

Almost two-thirds of the convention had voted against Vander Zalm. Of course, many of those who opted for other candidates considered Vander Zalm their "second choice," but the first ballot showed that even the grassroots were not entirely sold on him as leader.

The results brought any talk of alliances crashing down around the candidates. The two Smiths were much too close for either candidate's delegates to bolt to the other, while the fifth-man theory had been sent reeling because now there were *two* fifth men.

After expressing a bit of disappointment, Vander Zalm regained his smiling optimism and waited for the next ballot. On the floor, his operators–clad in clothes only a Socred could love: shocking-pink suits with white ties, white belts, and white shoes–set about wooing other delegates. They knew their man was the second choice of many delegates, and they used a giant plastic pink flamingo to entice delegates over. "Just follow the flamingo over to us," Bill Reid told wavering delegates. It actually worked.

A huge mob of reporters remained camped around Vander Zalm's platform the whole day. He chatted constantly with them, saying anything that came into his mind, musing aloud about the events around him. He even agreed to their request not to stand up to wave to his supporters after each ballot, and to instead remain seated to field questions. "Whatever you guys want," he told them. "When can I stand? Okay, you just tell me."

The lesser candidates began moving immediately after the first ballot. Campbell went to Brian Smith, while Couvelier–thought to be a Brian Smith backer–joined Vander Zalm. Rogers, his hopes of being the fifth man dashed, joined Brian Smith; so did Ritchie.

Wenman joined Brian Smith's camp. McCarthy, who was godmother to one of Wenman's children, looked shocked.

On the second ballot, Vander Zalm picked up 90 votes to increase his lead to 457. McCarthy's votes increased slightly to 280. Brian Smith moved to 255, while Bud Smith gained some but still dropped to fourth with 219. Reynolds, with 39, and Nielsen, with 30, were well back.

The excitement built. Reynolds, accompanied by Michael, moved to Vander Zalm. Nielsen went to Brian Smith, where most of his cabinet colleagues gathered. By now, the entire Socred cabinet was stacked against Vander Zalm. The still unanswered question: What would Bud do?

Then came the most dramatic moment of the entire convention. Bud Smith, after conferring with his advisers, left his platform and began a slow, laborious walk across the floor through a crush of delegates. For a moment, it looked as if he might be going over to Brian Smith's camp. But it slowly dawned on everyone that he was heading somewhere else: to Vander Zalm. The impact was electric. A surprised Vander Zalm welcomed him onto the platform with a hug and Smith offered an awkward smile.

Smith later explained it was clear that the "will" of the convention wanted Vander Zalm as leader. In the final analysis, Vander Zalm would have won without Bud Smith. Many of Bud's delegates were headed to Vander Zalm anyway, but their candidate's crossing over sealed the fate of the convention. Brian Smith's people were devastated by the one scenario they hadn't figured on.

Desperately, Brian Smith's camp tried to convince McCarthy to join them in an alliance against Vander Zalm, but the Social Credit icon would have none of it. She remained neutral to the end.

Just after six o'clock, the third ballot results were announced: Vander Zalm with 625 (just 12 votes short of a victory), Brian Smith with 342, and Grace McCarthy third with 305.

It was all over. But Smith, ignoring his advisers who told him to bow out gracefully, hung on for one more ballot. When the inevitable was announced–Vander Zalm 801, Smith 454–a deafening roar went up and a beaming Bill and Lillian Vander Zalm hugged each other cheek-to-cheek for the news cameras.

The "outs" had defeated the "ins" hands down. The party had repudiated Bill Bennett's government and his style of governing.

Bill Vander Zalm inherited the torch carried not by Bill Bennett, but by his father, W.A.C. ("Wacky") Bennett, the first messiah of Social Credit. Vander Zalm was Wacky's natural heir: charismatic, populist, and a personality who could woo voters outside his own party. To become heir, Vander Zalm had campaigned successfully against Wacky's son. Such are the ironies of B.C. politics.

It had been a long day and a long two months. Leadership races and conventions are, in many ways, more emotionally draining than general elections, and Whistler was no exception. Many of the delegates, their eyes red from crying, simply hugged each other, sobbing. The Vander Zalm camp, of course, was delirious, but other delegates warned darkly that his win would be a disaster for the party.

All the candidates gathered on stage with Bill Bennett and joined hands. Juanita Vander Zalm came out to sing her father's campaign song, which seemed to momentarily lift the gloom from some of the disappointed delegates' faces. Others simply stared in wonder at the spectacle.

Brian Smith gave a gracious speech, promising, "We will all be together, Bill." He then asked for the vote to be declared unanimous, a traditional request that was approved. But party unity would always be shaky under Vander Zalm, no matter how much handholding there was. Grace McCarthy, still wearing an enormous smile, said: "The NDP must be eating its heart out right now."

And then Bill Bennett stepped up to the microphone. He had never been very good at looking comfortable in front of people, and this night was no exception. He wore a tight smile and looked over at the man he had long feared more than anyone else in the party. Bennett clung to the party unity theme, extolling Vander Zalm's virtues and claiming that Vander Zalm could lead the party and run a government.

Vander Zalm then spoke briefly, touching on the same points contained on the scrawled paper he had shown a reporter hours before. He followed through on his idea of promising to name a new bridge after Alex Fraser and called for party unity. But his first word would become his trademark: "Faaaaaaaantastic!"

The King,
His Queen,
Their Castle

At night, it rises out of the darkness on the Fraser River flatlands like a giant shining cross.

It is actually a huge windmill, an unusual sight outside the Netherlands. Seen after dark from the highway outside Richmond, the windmill seems to come out of nowhere; but during the day, motorists emerging from the monotonous scenery of the flatlands see much more than a windmill. Just a few yards from the highway there is also a castle, a miniature train track, a small petting zoo, and a large parking lot. A high hedge hides other sites. Flags on a dozen poles flutter in the wind.

A highway sign says "tourist attraction." The attraction is Fantasy Garden World, a biblical theme park/children's farm/convention centre/garden complex all rolled into one. And in the middle of it live the premier of B.C. and his wife.

Bill and Lillian Vander Zalm make their home in a large apartment in a brick castle-like structure, just above a drawbridge. There is a moat filled with dirty brown water underneath. Harp music from a tinny sound system echoes outside their window. A second-floor balcony allows the Vander Zalms to step out and wave to visitors in the cobblestone courtyard below.

Off to one side, outside a large replica of a Dutch medieval castle, six winged angels hang suspended from the brick walls. Inside, it is

31

Christmas all year round. More than three dozen Christmas trees of various sizes reside on the castle's three floors. Christmas carols play all day long, and wrapped presents lie under the trees. Even on a scorching July day, there is always a cheery Christmas somewhere at Fantasy Gardens.

The garden complex shuts out the outside world. The roar of the neighbouring highway is barely audible. The castle walls and the high hedge around the site obscure all other buildings. Gentle music wafts over the hundreds of flowers, a sea of reds, yellows, violets, and whites. The lush lawns are immaculate.

Political pressure does not exist at Fantasy Gardens. Instead, there is tranquillity, hard work, cleanliness—and, more important, salesmanship. Many things are for sale here, including trinkets, records, and books autographed by the Vander Zalms.

In the midst of it all, the premier of B.C. can frequently be found walking around, smelling the flowers or deep in thought. He might be greeting visitors or helping out with some replanting. If it's raining, he can be found inside his castle; his queen is often with him.

Gardening is associated with the Dutch, and Vander Zalm is proud of his heritage. He was born in Noordwykerhout, Holland, on May 29, 1934. Before the Second World War started, his large family—he has three brothers and two sisters—enjoyed a relatively prosperous existence; his parents operated a bulb-growing business. But the war ended all that. Vander Zalm's father was in Canada when it broke out; the family would not be reunited until after it was over.

Nazi Germany's forces occupied the Netherlands. Food was scarce, and Vander Zalm says he often had to beg for it. Sugar beets and tulip bulbs, awful-tasting as they were, became dietary staples. Immediately afer the war, the grim conditions continued and claimed the life of Vander Zalm's youngest brother, a tragedy that has haunted him throughout his life. He visits his brother's grave whenever he returns to his home town.

Vander Zalm's work ethic, determination, and eternal optimism sprang paradoxically from that harsh season. He even told author Alan Twigg, in Twigg's book, "From Immigrant to Premier," that his optimism allowed him to see some good things that resulted from the Nazi occupation (order and stability, he said, at least in the early stages).

Vander Zalm arrived in Canada in 1947 and joined his father—who had returned briefly to Noordwykerhout after the war ended—in B.C.'s agricultural garden, the Fraser Valley. The entire family was reunited later that year. His father had maintained a bulb-selling business in B.C. during the war, and the entire family pitched in and soon returned to their pre-war prosperity.

Despite his poor English and his ignorance of Canadian customs, Bill Vander Zalm was a popular student, especially with girls. His graduating class annual said "he likes to be surrounded by beautiful girls" and predicted he would open a modelling agency one day.

He is remembered as a go-getter who liked to keep a neat, well-groomed appearance—a trait he still retains. He also earned a reputation as a hard-working, shrewd businessman. When he was seventeen, his father had a heart attack and young Bill had to take over the family business. With his newly acquired driver's licence, he set out to sell bulbs across western Canada. On one such trip he fell in love.

After more than thirty years of marriage, Bill and Lillian Vander Zalm still act like newlyweds. In a crush of people, Bill will often shout, "Where's Lillian?" and hug her when they are reunited. They hold hands constantly.

When the couple went to Europe together in early 1987, they behaved like lovesick doves. Lillian held his hand while he drove, and they looked into each other's eyes for long stretches, even while the car was whizzing through the Dutch countryside.

"I couldn't believe that two people their age could still be as kissy-kissy. It used to almost embarrass me when I first met them," Bill Kay recalls.

Their courtship and marriage was the stuff of a romance novel.

Wearing a pink shirt and blue suede shoes, he comes across her photo in the window of a shop in the town of Kelowna. "That's the girl I'm going to marry," he declares.

Minutes later, he meets her in a corner malt shop. Only fifteen, she is still in pigtails. He, a handsome lad of eighteen, simply stares at her. She has to pick up some flowers. He does it for her.

"It was love at first sight," Lillian would recall later. "He was a dreamboat."

Vander Zalm spent the next year writing love letters to her while flogging flower bulbs shop-to-shop across the Prairies and B.C. They started going steady. Their favourite record was "Melody of Love," and they still play it to each other. He proposed by letter and could not afford an engagement ring. Their white wedding in 1956 was held in glorious sunshine; it rained the day before and the day after.

They raised a family—two boys (Wim and Jeffrey) and two girls (Juanita and Lucia)—and all of them helped out at the family's gardening shop. Lillian kept all of Bill's love letters, all of her children's teeth, pieces of hair, little foot and hand prints, swimming badges, and report cards. She put them in boxes and gave them to each child when the child grew up.

The Vander Zalms lived according to traditional, conservative family values—the husband is the breadwinner; the wife cooks and rears the children. They were like a 1950s sitcom family: the pipe-smoking sweater-clad dad and the cheerful, sunny mom.

Bill Vander Zalm had made his first big deal in 1955, when he purchased a garden business called Art Knapp's Nurseries. There was no store; Vander Zalm auctioned plants off the back of a truck in supermarket parking lots. Soon after, he bought a piece of land in south Burnaby, a suburb of Vancouver. There, he built the first Art Knapp's Nurseries gardening store.

Together with his brothers and friends, Vander Zalm built the business into a well-known province-wide chain of independent outlets. Lillian and he worked long and hard at making it a success. He is an expert on gardening, and people came from miles around to receive free gardening tips.

He did a thriving business, he met a lot of people, and his reputation grew. One day, in 1964, a group of people approached him. They were upset about Surrey council turning a park near his home into a gravel pit. "They said, 'You know something about lawns; why don't you help us fight this thing?' " he recalls. His political career had begun.

He was defeated on a first try for a seat on Surrey's municipal council, in 1964. In 1965 he finished second in the polls and won a two-year council seat. He topped the polls two years later, and in December 1969, at the age of thirty-five, he became Surrey's youngest-ever mayor.

Surrey has long been referred to as the redneck capital of the Lower Mainland. As the joke goes, its difference from yogurt is its lack of culture. But the "ape hills" of Surrey–a sprawling municipality and B.C.'s third most populous town–have been home to some of the most bitter and colourful politics in the province.

Vander Zalm started making headlines early on. The "big city" media, notably the Vancouver *Sun*, realized he was good copy and started making him front-page news in the early 1970s, particularly when he was cooperative enough to provide outlandish statements against "hippies" and "welfare bums"–two groups that he blamed for most of society's ills.

In the meantime, Vander Zalm started looking beyond Surrey to expand his political career. He had already run unsuccessfully as a federal Liberal candidate in 1968, and in 1972 he decided to run for the leadership of the provincial Liberal Party, which at that time was still able to elect a few members to the legislature. It was a two-person race: Vander Zalm against Vancouver Island Liberal MP David Anderson.

Vander Zalm, wearing a white suit, cut quite a figure at the Penticton convention. His supporters passed out campaign literature that vowed he would "whip-lash drug pushers, cut off welfare deadbeats, update education, crack-down on wife-deserters and provide government-financed dental care." Vander Zalm lost by a vote of 388 to 171, but he made some valuable political contacts in the process, notably Jack Davis, who played a vital role in his 1986 leadership campaign, and Mel Couvelier, a 1986 Socred leadership candidate who switched to Vander Zalm after the first ballot and later became his finance minister.

During his days as Surrey mayor, Vander Zalm made a name for himself by taking on the welfare system. At that time, municipalities, not the provincial government, controlled welfare payments. He was convinced that there was widespread welfare fraud, even when a special investigation by his own office turned up little evidence.

In 1974, his council took all welfare recipients under thirty-five years of age off the welfare rolls and turned them into farmworkers, paying them as little as $25 a day.

Vander Zalm could be credited for improving recreational facilities, garbage pickup, and sewers. He built more senior citizens' homes.

But while he was mayor, Surrey also became a real estate speculator's dream. The RCMP ended up investigating several land deals that occurred in that era. Some land developments resulted in the principals being sent to jail. Fractious council members warred with each other, and accusations of conflict-of-interest and ethical misconduct were common. Vander Zalm wasn't spared: the council once voted to investigate him on conflict-of-interest charges that sprang from a messy land transaction in the Newton area.

Vander Zalm had urged the provincial government to launch an inquiry into the transaction; when the inquiry broadened to include a look at each civic party's finances and membership rolls, Vander Zalm tried to put the brakes on it. His own financial holdings eventually were dragged into the affair, and the council thought enough questions had been raised to warrant a more in-depth look at his holdings. A fellow alderman had accused him of voting in favour of a mobile home development in exchange for campaign contributions.

But Vander Zalm, having read the Municipal Act, knew that only he, as mayor, had the power to subpoena witnesses in any council-ordered investigation. He said he would cooperate with an outside, independent inquiry; otherwise, no go. The council eventually reversed its position after the principals involved in the mobile home development made it clear that Vander Zalm had played no improper role.

Just when that controversy was dying down, another land deal made headlines. The owner of a property in the Bridgeview area, one of Surrey's poorest, was rumoured to be in financial difficulty. Following a meeting between Vander Zalm, an alderman, and a municipal land agent, Surrey prepared to buy the site. The agent dutifully went about securing a feasibility study. Less than a week after the agent submitted his report to Vander Zalm, it was revealed that Vander Zalm's brothers had bought the property a few months earlier. Vander Zalm's years as a Surrey politician are examined in a National Film Board documentary, *Some People May Have to Suffer.*

By 1974, Vander Zalm had again started looking beyond Surrey to further his political career. Having failed twice as a Liberal, he looked to the provincial Socreds, who were then reorganizing in the wake of their 1972 election defeat. In May 1974, fledgling Social Credit leader Bill Bennett announced that Vander Zalm had joined his party. His days as the redneck mayor of the redneck town were almost over. But his biggest headlines were still ahead of him.

Bennett put together a motley crew of car dealers, retreads from the Liberal and Conservative parties, and incumbent Socreds to oust the NDP's Dave Barrett in the pre-Christmas election of 1975. Bennett gave the new boy from Surrey one of the toughest and most thankless portfolios–human resources. Bill Vander Zalm would now dictate provincial policy for one of his least favourite groups: welfare recipients.

Just after the cabinet swearing-in ceremony in January 1976, Vander Zalm uttered one of his most famous lines: "If anybody is able to work, but refuses to pick up a shovel, we will find ways of dealing with him."

He turned the shovel into his trademark, with his uncanny knack of converting bad publicity into good. Gold shovel lapel pins are worn by Vander Zalm supporters. Vander Zalm still auctions off shovels at party functions. He signs his gardening books "Happy shovelling." (Of course, the shovel trademark has also helped promote his gardening business.)

Over the next seven years, Vander Zalm became B.C.'s best-known politician. His willingness to make outrageous redneck comments kept him in the news more than anyone else. He became addicted to controversy and to publicity. It was during this time that he learned how to exploit the media's thirst for controversy. Reporters and editors had a sure-fire solution to slow news days, particularly on weekends: phone Vander Zalm at home and ask him to comment on a timely subject.

He created one controversy after another, sometimes as a result of his actions, but more often simply by opening his mouth. He took pride in saying how he felt, all the time. To him, that was honesty. "The things I say are probably what a lot of people are thinking," he told an interviewer in 1982.

And, shortly after becoming premier: "If I always thought before I spoke in detail, perhaps I wouldn't say some of the things I did and people wouldn't respond."

(Eventually, in 1988, his many utterances found their way into a "little red book" entitled "Quotations from Chairman Zalm," a best-selling take-off on Mao Tse-Tung's collected wisdom.)

He held three cabinet portfolios in Bennett's government and created a steady stream of controversies in each one. He fought with welfare recipients, teachers, school administrators, municipal councils, and the labour movement. He even fought with his own cabinet colleagues, calling them "gutless" in 1982 when they would not support one of his pieces of legislation. Less than a year after saying that, he was out of politics.

His years in cabinet and on Surrey council revealed the foundation of his own political philosophy, one that would re-emerge when he became premier. It is grounded in his experiences as a small businessman and small-time developer. He has an intense dislike for government, seemingly odd for a person who has spent so much of his life as an elected politician. Ideally, he feels, there should be a minimum of rules, regulations, and laws. Governments and bureaucracies hold things up, he believes, rather than allowing anything to get done; and government intervention and participation can only lead to bad results.

"For twenty-five years I've been in government in some way and I've never learned to like government," he told the authors. "If I have a philosophy, it's one of individualism rather than government. I suppose it comes about from my war years as a kid. We had to stick together as a family. We really couldn't go around crying about things or complaining."

But there are some inconsistencies in that philosophy. For example, he has shown great enthusiasm for retaining as much power as possible for himself in whichever office he occupies.

When he was Surrey mayor, his council scrutinized many land development proposals and exerted tremendous control over the development process. He spent much of his time in cabinet removing local autonomy from regional governments and municipalities, and putting that power in his office. He cut down on the planning authority of municipalities and tried hard to change the school system, going around locally elected school boards and the teachers; he warred with regional districts.

In a way, the moves fit his philosophy: eliminating whole programs or departments does reduce the size of government. But he did not necessarily reduce the government's power; he merely shifted much of it to his own office. He took that individualistic attitude with him when he moved to the premier's office.

Democracy is a time-consuming process that creates headaches and delays for people trying to get something done. It is an inherent feature of the system that when everybody gets a say, it takes some time to let them say it. Vander Zalm has never been comfortable with that process. Getting things done is the most important part, he feels, not the process that leads up to it.

"The application of democracy sometimes gives me trouble," he told a Vancouver *Sun* reporter in 1982. "Democracy requires that you set up a lot of committees and commissions."

As for the parliamentary system, Vander Zalm had this to say to the Kamloops Chamber of Commerce in March 1986: "It is totally antiquated. It is really a bit of a farce. Most elections mean another dictator for three or four years."

The first comment was made when he was a cabinet minister, trying to "get things done." The second statement was made when he was out of politics and playing the role of small business-man again.

Fantasy Gardens, with its fairy-tale feeling and its bizarre mixture of beauty and kitsch, is a representation of how the Vander Zalms would like to view the world. Everything should be nice, clean, and orderly, like an enchanted kingdom.

Soon after winning the Surrey mayoralty in 1969, Vander Zalm announced a few grand plans for Surrey's many districts. He wanted to turn Cloverdale into a "Dodge City"; Crescent Beach would have a Spanish architectural motif and palm trees lining its beach-front; another area would be built, from scratch, into an

"Olde English"-style town; Newton would get a "space-age" industrial park.

None of those dreams were realized, but they indicated that
Vander Zalm's ideal world would have—like Disneyland—many
"theme worlds" within it.

He and Lillian developed their gardening store in Burnaby this
way; they created "specialty shops" within the store, each with its
own architectural theme; Tudor, Old West, Gothic. . . .

The same formula has been used at Fantasy Gardens. There are
four areas within the complex. The drawbridge leads directly to the
park's "European Village," a brick courtyard housing a dozen or so
shops and restaurants. Staff—mostly young women—wear European
costumes (Dutch, German, and Swiss are particular favourites)
whether they serve ice cream, candy, beer, or fish and chips.

There is the Dutch Coevordon castle, with its year-round
Christmas motif, and also a children's "farm" area, complete with
kiddie rides, a petting zoo, and a replica of Noah's Ark (complete
with washrooms labelled "Billy" and "Lilly"). Then there is
the biblical garden, off by itself in a quiet corner designed for
quiet meditation. One can also get married at the Gardens, in a
private chapel.

It is a matter of debate whether Fantasy Gardens turns a profit,
but if not, it is not for lack of trying. Commercialism reigns
supreme. The park's many gift shops sell the usual B.C. and
Canadian souvenirs—lots of T-shirts with West Coast Indian
patterns, salmon figurines, and a variety of dogwood-flowered
products—and they also stock some unique items. For instance, one
can buy a song recorded in Dutch by Bill Vander Zalm, and a
Christmas record by his daughter Juanita.

There are also several gardening books, including two by the
owner himself. There is a guide to Fantasy Gardens, the text written
by Vander Zalm. And, of course, there are the headbands made
famous by Lillian.

Bill Vander Zalm is, if nothing else, a top-notch salesman. The
sales techniques he learned during his years of flogging flower bulbs
across the West have not left him, and he sees one of his main
responsibilities as premier as "selling" B.C. to developers and
potential investors.

As he told author Alan Twigg: "Politics is marketing. Promoting British Columbia. Getting economic development. That's marketing. Running a Fantasy Gardens is marketing. Much in life is marketing. Even a strong marriage involves a degree of marketing. Life is marketing."

The politician-as-salesman image is appropriate for Vander Zalm. He retains the salesman's method of idealizing the good points of a product and overlooking the bad ones. He loves everyone and needs them to love him back. He is also very charming and very smooth.

Fantasy Gardens was built the same way Vander Zalm built his own political career: a few rules bent here, some corners cut there. For example, Richmond council bent its by-laws to allow the Dutch Coevordon castle to be moved to the site. The building had too much of an overhang, but it was allowed to stay.

Vander Zalm was able to take a chunk of valuable agricultural land and turn it into a mini-shopping centre by realizing something basic about municipal bureaucracy: smaller projects are more easily approved than larger ones. It was a lesson he had learned well in Surrey, and he knew Richmond would not be much different.

Vander Zalm has maintained that there was never really a large, well-thought-out plan for Fantasy Gardens; it just happened. A Richmond alderman once said the project "grew like topsy" without the municipal council ever being told of its full extent. Vander Zalm does not deny that it just grew and grew, but he insists he did nothing wrong.

Vander Zalm, through one of his companies, purchased the 8.5 hectare site in 1984 for $1.7 million (by this time, he had amassed a fair-sized fortune from his many real estate transactions through the years). A small botanical garden already existed on the site, but since the property was in the agricultural land reserve–a government-administered body designed to protect farmland–its commercial potential appeared limited.

Vander Zalm, however, quickly received a zoning change that allowed him to add buildings that were not part of the Gardens themselves–a key step toward steering the property away from agricultural use and toward commercial development.

And bit by bit the project grew—a $500 000 conservatory was added, then a barn, a parking lot, a replica of Noah's Ark, a minia-ture railway station, and a restaurant. Municipal planners and permit directors were baffled and confused. None of them had ever handed out permits for windmills and arks before.

The Vander Zalms did not take out one big permit for the whole concept—a course that would likely have led to rejection—but instead secured about forty smaller ones along the way. The Vander Zalms were able to convince the permit regulators that each addi-tion was allowed under the new zoning.

Another key hurdle was getting the land out of the agricultural reserve, a touchy subject in B.C.: removing land parcels can lead to huge public outcries. But taking the land out of the reserve meant its value would skyrocket and the Vander Zalms could lease shops in the complex, which was not permitted on agricultural reserves.

No decision was made on Vander Zalm's application until August 1986, less than a month after he was chosen premier. The government-appointed agricultural land commission granted the application, and the land's assessed value soared from $800 000 to $4.9 million.

A premier who owns a giant theme park—particularly one situated on valuable agricultural land controlled by the government—is a prime candidate for conflict-of-interest allegations.

Interestingly, during the leadership campaign, Vander Zalm had been the first to make it an issue. And as he later tried to explain, his acknowledgment of the issue proved he was not in conflict. He had been "honest" with everyone. If the public was aware of it, and if he was worried about it, how could there be a conflict? It was an argument he would repeat steadily over the next two years.

Vander Zalm had, however, told the Vancouver *Sun* editorial board that he would "probably" have to "dispose" of the Gardens should he become premier. And he made it clear that simply transferring ownership into his wife's name would not solve the problem.

"Because whether it's in my name, or my wife's name, it's the same thing. I can't con anybody on that, now would I?" he told the board.

One day after he became premier, he contradicted what he had said less than two months earlier: "Lillian isn't too keen on selling. If there's an apparent conflict-of-interest, I'll have to consider it. But this is not an opportune time. I don't want to take a beating on it."

Soon afterwards, he transferred ownership into Lillian's name. He still owns at least 30 per cent of Fantasy Garden World.

But the conflict allegations did not go away, at least not for a while. Some argued that the land commission would not dare rule against the premier on his own application (and, even if it did, all appeals of its decisions go to the provincial cabinet's environmental land use committee, on which the premier sits).

There was also the fact that Vander Zalm's banker was the Canadian Imperial Bank of Commerce–the major bank for the provincial government. What's more, shortly after becoming premier Vander Zalm had appointed himself finance minister–a position he was determined to hold onto, until he was mercilessly hammered about his apparent conflict by broadcaster Jack Webster on live television one evening. He gave up the finance portfolio in the next cabinet shuffle, in November 1986.

Vander Zalm also shamelessly promoted Fantasy Gardens during speeches he made as premier. Whenever he referred to Fantasy Gardens as "Lillian's place," he got a lot of knowing chuckles from sympathetic audiences.

Less than a month after becoming premier, he referred to the Gardens several times in a speech in the mining town of Trail. He stopped at one point and asked the audience, most of whom were Socred party members, if they thought he was in conflict. Naturally, the crowd replied with a resounding "No!"

Vander Zalm pointed to the media table and yelled: "Well, why don't you tell those people that?" And indeed, after the speech, audience members took reporters aside and chided them indignantly.

At a western premiers' conference in Humboldt, Saskatchewan, in 1987, Vander Zalm made a joke about conflict of interest and then invited everyone to visit him and Lillian at the Gardens. When television reporters come to the Gardens on weekends for quick interviews, he obligingly stands in front of the castle so that its image can be beamed into everyone's homes.

By the time the legislature session finally rolled around six months later, conflict of interest was almost a dead issue. It appeared that Vander Zalm had guessed correctly: the conflict allegations were merely the media's doing; the general public couldn't care less.

By 1989, there was widespread speculation that the Gardens had financial problems. It carried more than $7 million in mortgages. Attendance at the Gardens had reportedly dropped sharply; an unofficial boycott of the place by Vander Zalm's political opponents—notably labour unions and their members—seemed to be hurting business considerably. Rumours of the park being for sale came and went.

But Lillian continued to work her sixteen-hour days. Other than occasionally complaining about the unofficial boycott, Vander Zalm rarely admitted that the Gardens were in trouble.

"I don't like being the bearer of bad news at any time. I prefer good news," he told the authors. "I'm generally optimistic about things. I see the bright sides. When you have to bring bad news it hurts me. . . . That's a weakness perhaps."

He is stubborn as well, and attributes that to his Dutch heritage. "People say how could you take all the flack and keep smiling. I have a great personal philosophy," he says. "I don't let too many outside influences bother me. If I believe what I'm doing is right, I can take a lot of garbage and criticism and I can continue on. I don't get rattled, because I believe in what I do."

Optimist, stubborn, and a positivist. Whether it's day-to-day life or a crucial policy decision, Vander Zalm wears the same rose-coloured glasses.

He had them on in May 1988 when he was trying his best to avoid a group of angry college students in North Vancouver.

The crowd had surrounded his car and was in an ugly mood over a cut in college funding. Inside the car, chauffeured by an increasingly worried Bill Kay, Vander Zalm kept a tight smile on his face, waving as the crowd pressed closer. In the back seat was a Catholic church publication called "You and Your Funeral: How to Plan for Your Family."

A young woman started pounding on the car window, baring her teeth while screaming obscenities. A mystified Vander Zalm looked at her and frowned.

"Roll down the window, Bill, and see what the lady wants," said Vander Zalm.

"Are you out of your mind, Premier?" a disbelieving Kay shouted. "I think it's clear what she wants."

Vander Zalm looked at the woman, then at the crowd, and then at the woman again before it dawned on him that it might not be a good idea to roll down the window. People continued to crowd around the car as Kay tried to manoeuvre gently out of the parking lot.

"Maybe I should just floor it," muttered Kay.

"Oh, no! Don't do that!" Vander Zalm said quickly.

"I was just kidding, Premier," Kay sighed.

Eventually, accompanied by a Vancouver *Sun* reporter in the back seat, they set off for the next stop on the premier's itinerary. There were no advisers, no staff except Kay, no other help. The next step was the official opening of a new office building in Burnaby. During the ride over, Kay and Vander Zalm, like a couple that had been married too long, squabbled continually about which direction to take. When they finally arrived, it wasn't clear just where the opening was to take place.

"I know where we're going. Turn down into that underground parking garage," a confident Vander Zalm ordered. Kay rolled his eyes but did what he was told.

"This doesn't look right. Why would we park down here?" Kay asked. They argued about parking the car for the next few minutes, until Vander Zalm almost grabbed the steering wheel himself to convince Kay to pull into one of the stalls.

"Come on. Park here. There's lots of parking down here," Vander Zalm barked. Finally, after the premier's fifth plea, Kay wheeled the car into a stall.

"I know where we're going. It's just up these stairs," Vander Zalm announced.

His companion was doubtful, but followed him anyway. Vander Zalm opened the door with a flourish and walked triumphantly through it into what he expected to be a large crowd at an official opening. Instead, he found himself in an immense empty outdoor parking lot. The men stared dumbly for a minute, until Kay couldn't resist getting in a few shots at his boss.

"Oh, right. Great. You know where you're going all right," Kay said in a mocking voice.

Vander Zalm was mystified but turned around and dashed up the next flight of stairs. The door there was locked. Kay had visions of being locked in the stairwell for the entire weekend. "I don't like this," he said.

"Well, I'm sure there's a way out of here. Come on," Vander Zalm called, remaining upbeat. They went up the next flight of stairs; the door there was, mercifully, open. Vander Zalm bounded through it, and found himself in the middle of an office complex. He walked through the door of a travel agency. A half-dozen women looked up, startled to see the premier of British Columbia in their office.

"Hi, ladies! It's me! The premier!" he announced with a wide smile. "Is there some sort of opening around here?" Shocked, they didn't answer. "Bye, everybody!"

He suggested they take the elevator. "Hit any floor," a confident Vander Zalm told Kay, who was growing more irritable by the minute. But that didn't help. There was no official opening on the next floor either, or on the one after that.

"Who organized this bloody thing, anyway?" a frustrated Kay asked. "What's going on around here?"

They finally went down to the main floor, walked outside, checked the address, and looked up at the building. And there, looking down at them, were about thirty office workers. The word had evidently gone through the building quickly: the premier is wandering around inside, lost.

Vander Zalm squinted through the sun at the workers looking down at him. A huge grin spread across his face and he began waving. They waved back. That was all the reassurance he needed.

"This has got to be the place. Come on," he said, his confidence restored. With a purposeful stride, he marched back into the building and went back up the elevator. One floor up, a woman got on and told the premier that he was, in fact, in the wrong building.

"You want the building across the parking lot," she said.

Vander Zalm raced to the parking lot. He was running a bit late by now. And there before him was a sea of people, all with their backs to him. He was, of course, supposed to have entered from the other side, where his car was to drive up and be greeted by waiting dignitaries.

"We're waiting for the premier," a man nearby told a reporter, craning his neck to see over the crowd. Little did he know that the premier was right beside him, trying to get to the front of the crowd.

Finally, word got out that the premier had indeed arrived, but not in the right place. And like a giant snake in a birdhouse, the whole crowd slowly turned around as some of the dignitaries ran to the back to welcome the premier. Vander Zalm winked at his companions and smiled at everyone else.

"See, I told you we'd get here."

Bill Vander Zalm has a seemingly endless supply of energy. In the capital, a typical day begins at 7:30 a.m. and ends just before midnight. He lives in a suite at the Harbour Towers, one of the more upscale of Victoria's many hotels.

He is a light eater in the morning; some bran flakes and juice are enough. He usually eats breakfast with Bill Kay, who lives in a hotel suite next door. Vander Zalm will occasionally read *The Globe and Mail*, usually with a "Canada A.M." broadcast on television in the background.

Kay wakes Vander Zalm and even helps dress him. Vander Zalm, rather inept when it comes to doing some things with his hands, needs Kay to fasten his cufflinks for him.

Kay also helps him pick out his suit for the day. Vander Zalm prefers to dress in clothes that went out of style in the 1970s (if they were ever in style at all), such as suede leisure suits and golf course attire. Only reluctantly does he agree to don the dark three-piece suits Kay and others think more appropriate for a provincial premier. He is immaculate about his personal appearance and keeps a comb and razor close by at all times.

Kay drives Vander Zalm the three blocks to the office each morning. A pack of reporters frequently greets Vander Zalm's arrival each day. If he is in an uncommunicative mood, he might put his head down and walk up the back stairs to his office. Often, though, he greets reporters like long-lost friends.

He eats light dinners, usually at the posh, private Union Club near the legislature, or sends out for sandwiches from a nearby restaurant. He spends most weekends at Fantasy Gardens, and frequently tries to leave Victoria on a Thursday night and not return until Tuesday morning, thus maximizing the time spent at home with Lillian. Even at the Gardens, though, the happy couple sometimes see little of each other. Weekends bring the big crowds, keeping Lillian busy, and the premier brings home stacks of papers to work on.

Vander Zalm is a man of few vices. He will drink a glass of wine or two at dinner. He smokes a pipe or cigarillos, though he has been trying to quit for years. He gets little exercise, and since his term began he has developed a small paunch around the middle.

Aside from newspapers, briefing notes, and government reports, he reads very little. He has no time for books; never has. Occasionally, he will thumb through a biography, usually of a world leader. He claims to have seen just one movie in the past ten years–the 1989 film *Cousins*, simply because part of it was shot at Fantasy Gardens. He rarely watches television except for newscasts and the odd western. His favourite sports are soccer and hockey, but he does not get to see many games.

He likes to listen to country music, but doesn't know the names of the bands or the songs. Says Bill Kay: "When we go driving and a song comes on the radio, Lillian and I will start singing. But he will never know the words. He never listened to stuff like that. He was out making his first million."

Vander Zalm's heroes are mostly conservative world leaders: Winston Churchill, Ronald Reagan, and Margaret Thatcher. He also admires John F. Kennedy. But he is not familiar with political ideologies. He does not know the difference between, say, a communist and a fascist. He has never studied political history or theory; his ideas have been formed by his own experiences. During an interview with one of the authors of this book, Vander Zalm pointed to a book his office had just received in the mail. It was part of a Time-Life series on Nazi Germany, and this particular volume was on the notorious S.S. units.

Vander Zalm pointed to the title. "Leftists," he said, lighting his pipe.

"Leftists?" asked his interviewer.

"Well, they were National Socialists, weren't they?" Vander Zalm replied.

"Well, yes, but that was a name. They weren't socialists. They were Nazis, fascists."

"Aaaah, same difference," Vander Zalm said, waving his hand. "They were totalitarians, just like the communists."

He likes to strip problems and concepts down to an easy-to-grasp black-and-white basis, and political and economic theories are no exception. He sees the economic world split into two camps: free enterprisers and capitalists versus everyone else (i.e., mostly socialists and communists). Bill Kay says his boss sees things in "biblical simplicity."

When he speaks of socialism, his voice rises and his eyes narrow. He considers it a dark menace that threatens the very foundations of society.

"It seems to me somewhere someone, somehow took a shortcut in effect by saying, 'Why give them the tools to form an individual opinion, when the consensus should be one basic opinion?' I call that socialism," he said in an 1982 speech. "And of course, from whence I come and where I stand, you can appreciate, I think this is dangerous stuff."

As befits a man who lives in a fantasy castle, there is still a bit of the little boy in Vander Zalm. He often has trouble telling when people are kidding. Sarcasm, irony, and satire go right over his head. "I think he's still naive on some things," says Bill Kay. "He wants to be friendly but doesn't understand you can't trust everybody. He's very rural in that sense. You know, 'Don't latch the door.' Now, maybe he locks the front door but not the back."

Vander Zalm, who is usually willing to listen to almost anyone's story, question, or complaint, is also impressionable. "You know," Vander Zalm told the authors, "what I get into trouble for with Bill

Kay or any of the people who are around me on a regular basis is that I tend to listen to an awful lot of people."

A former aide says: "He will listen to the last person he talked to and act on the last piece of advice he received."

Some of his former aides say he lacks a ruthlessness sometimes necessary for a government leader. He carries few grudges. When Stephen Rogers was harshly critical of Vander Zalm's leadership in the spring of 1989, the premier did nothing. As a matter of fact, he gave Rogers–whom he had fired from cabinet six months earlier–a hearty greeting on his way into a reception just after that spring's throne speech. He would rather avoid dealing with a problem than face it head-on, if dealing with it means getting into a nasty, personal shoving match. He has an innocent trust in people; he simply cannot believe that some of them may want to do him harm. He also has a deep-rooted need to be liked.

"The guy just can't stay mad. He'd rather have everything nice and comfortable," says Kay. That fits with Vander Zalm's optimism and aversion to "bad news"; negative things like anger and grudges are not part of his personality.

Still, he has a nasty streak that shows itself now and then, particularly when things are not going well for him. When he lost the Vancouver mayoralty race in 1984, he gave a particularly bitter concession speech in which he expressed alarm that "communists" could be elected over "Christian businessmen." He also successfully sued a Victoria cartoonist for depicting him gleefully pulling the wings off flies; the judgment was later overturned on appeal. And in the legislature in 1988, at the height of the many crises his government found itself in, he raised allegations against an NDP MLA which he knew were untrue, as he later admitted. Around the same time, he unleashed bitter, harsh denunciations of the media for being unfair to him.

Perhaps the most important thing to Bill Vander Zalm, as important as his family, is his religion. He is a devout Roman Catholic. Rarely does he talk of "the Lord" or "Christ" or the teachings of the Bible. He will often make reference to "Christian principles" and how important they are to society, but he has trouble defining those principles in interviews.

The key, however, seems to be to "influence" others' beliefs. It is something he feels very strongly about. "Should we attempt to influence the morals of the province? The answer is yes. If we don't have committed leaders, we don't have political leaders. We have a bunch of wimps," he said in April 1988, after the controversy that had dogged his government over his stand on abortion.

He attends mass each weekend; if he cannot make it on Sunday—and he frequently can't, because of his own engagements and Lillian's work with the Gardens—then he attends, with Lillian, on Saturday evening. Almost everywhere he goes, he carries a small prayer book. Religious literature—usually a pocket bible or a prayer book—is always in his car. More literature is tucked behind the seats.

"I pray all the time. I pray sitting behind my desk, or maybe in the hallway on my way to a meeting," he told the authors. "It's very important to me. . . . Religion is . . . the bond, partly, between Lillian and I. It's the bond in the family and the extended family."

Fantasy Gardens is filled with references to Jesus and stories from the Bible. The biblical garden is off by itself, separated by a white wall from the rest of the complex. The visitor's first sight upon walking in is a huge bank of flowers that spell out "I Am the Way." The flowers appear to be growing on the open pages of a large concrete Bible.

A small waterway, alternatively labelled the Sea of Galilee and the River Jordan, runs through the garden. (Much of the scenery has been constructed from a unique offering a businessman once made to Vander Zalm: ten tons of rock from Israel and ten large containers of water from the Sea of Galilee and the River Jordan.)

The garden is laid out in a counterclockwise fashion. Every few yards a scene from Jesus Christ's life is depicted, from birth to death. The scenes consist of life-size sculptures of Jesus, his apostles, and other appropriate characters. They include Jesus' baptism, the temptation in the wilderness, and the Last Supper.

The scenes continue relentlessly until Christ appears on the cross, in the middle of the waterway. But optimism and faith reign supreme in this part of the garden complex as well: a few yards further on is the Resurrection. (Fantasy Gardens' only indication that any non-Christian faith exists is a small Buddhist rock garden off to one side.)

The garden is not the park's only reference to the Bible. There is a Noah's Ark in the children's area. As well, little homilies on hanging signs dot the landscape. Some of them are quotations from the Bible; others, simple quotations about the meaning of life: "Your life can be a garden, and a lovely place indeed."

It costs almost six dollars to enter the garden part of Fantasy Garden World; walking across the drawbridge into the European Village is free. There are two dozen or so gift shops, specialty stores, and restaurants in the village square. Cobblestone streets and Bavarian-style buildings dominate the surroundings. The place is spotless.

The tenants squabble sometimes with their landlord, Lillian Vander Zalm. She oversees everything and strides through the complex like a monarch. There is occasional criticism of her management style: that she is too demanding, too inflexible, too frugal. But whatever the criticisms, one thing is clear: she is the boss.

Lillian Mihalic was born near Winnipeg in 1937, the fourth child in a poor family of ten. Her father was Croatian, a house painter and construction labourer who emigrated from Yugoslavia when he was twenty-one. Her mother is a long-time New Democrat, and even voted for the NDP in the 1986 election. Lillian dropped out of school after Grade 7 to contribute to the family income.

Lillian had stayed mostly in her husband's shadow until the leadership race, but the campaign turned her into as much a star as her husband. Almost immediately, she became known for her trademark braided, terry-cloth headbands and gushing smile. Despite the fact that headbands had gone out of style years before, she started doing a brisk business selling them at Fantasy Gardens.

In August 1987, she marked her fiftieth birthday by wrapping what she claimed to be the world's biggest headband around Fantasy Gardens. The headband was made out of leftover Expo 86 fabric and stuffed with foam chips. Balloons, jugglers on stilts, a giant cake, and a prize cow were also part of the festivities.

Lillian has cultivated an image that grew out of her charming ability to smile frequently, say very little, and look good doing it.

Like her husband, she is extraordinarily photogenic and adept at wowing crowds. She is pretty, and her gray hair does not make her look old, only prettier.

Part Jackie Kennedy and part bubbly prom queen, she can be quick to size people up and make instant judgments. Get on the wrong side of her, and it is tough getting back into her good graces. She has vigorously chided journalists who dare to criticize the premier. Crowds often turned out as much to see Lillian as her husband. All she had to do was smile, wave, and chat amiably with a few people. She is usually upbeat and charming. She never makes speeches. She did, however, make several magazine covers.

The couple were often labelled "Kennedyesque"–sometimes sarcastically, sometimes as a compliment–because they evoked that handsome young couple from an earlier, seemingly more innocent political era. Indeed, when "Vander Zalmania" swept B.C. in 1986, voters were looking for something new, an end to bitterness and confrontation. The Vander Zalms–smiling, handsome, and good-natured–seemed to be the tonic.

They made a big splash in March, 1987. Lillian had paid $750 000 for the replica Dutch castle that had sat at the corner of two of downtown Vancouver's busiest streets for the previous year as a commemoration of the city's one-hundredth anniversary. The Coevordon Castle, as it was called (after the Netherlands town that had been the ancestral home of Captain George Vancouver), was to be moved that night to its new home at Fantasy Gardens.

A huge crowd gathered just before midnight. Some had come downtown especially for the event, while others were late-night revellers wondering what all the fuss was about. The streets were cordoned off and a giant tractor rig was moved into position.

Normally, the street corner would have been deserted at that time of night. The huge bright lights, powered by electric generators, plus the noisy crowd and the humid air, gave the scene a surreal quality.

Finally, a shiny white Ford pulled up and Bill and Lillian Vander Zalm leaped out, sending a ripple of excitement through the crowd. It was as if Fred Astaire and Ginger Rogers had just arrived together at the Oscar ceremonies. Television cameras closed in and flash-bulbs went off.

"The whole thing seemed like something off a Hollywood backlot, and the Vander Zalms were like movie stars," remembers Miro Cernetig, who covered the event for the Vancouver *Sun*. "I had never seen anything like it."

Dressed in pullover sweaters and matching, gleaming white running shoes, the couple made their way through the mob and climbed into the cab of the truck that would take their castle home. They waved to the crowd and posed for photographers. Then they walked back onto the street. A guest from one of the nearby hotels suddenly appeared, clutching a bottle of champagne and two goblets. He cracked open the bottle, and the Vander Zalms hoisted their glasses and toasted their good fortune.

More than a dozen Vancouver police officers were present for crowd and traffic control. Several of them watched as the Vander Zalms sipped their champagne. Normally, anyone caught drinking alcohol from a bottle on a downtown Vancouver street at 2:00 a.m. would be ticketed, or tossed in jail, or at the very least forced to pour the bottle's contents down a drain. But the officers simply looked the other way or shrugged their shoulders. (Just a few weeks before, Ontario's attorney-general had been forced to resign because he was caught drinking beer on a private boat with a police officer on board one sunny Sunday afternoon).

There wasn't anything the Vander Zalms weren't up for, especially if it was something they could do together.

At a softball game in 1987 between the legislative press gallery and the premier's office, Bill and Lillian showed up late. They had raced in from the Victoria airport, where they had arrived after a flight from Saskatchewan. Their car could be seen winding its way down a hill toward the playing field with its lights on and flags fluttering on the hood. It drove right out into foul territory in the middle of the game. The action stopped, and all eyes turned toward the car as the Vander Zalms leaped out and ran onto the field, hugging a few of their teammates; the office staffers gave a great cheer. The reporters from the press gallery stared and shook their heads.

Bill wore a safari leisure outfit; Lillian, a white jumpsuit and, of course, a headband. She also displayed her athletic skills during the game, getting more hits than anyone else on her team. Bill, on the other hand, did not know how to hold the bat.

Later that same year, at the annual Social Credit convention in the fall, the two of them attended a 1950s theme dance. He was dressed in a black leather jacket, with greased-back black hair and shades. She wore a white sweater with the letter "L" on her chest, a white shirt, a pony tail and bobby socks. They danced all night and drank beer. The television cameras and photographers surrounded them.

The next morning, on the *Province*'s front page, appeared a picture of Bill: hair slicked back, grinning madly, holding up several bottles of champagne.

In late 1988, at a time when Vander Zalm's relations with the media had soured, the couple agreed to help out at a charity flea market sponsored by a persistent critic, the Vancouver *Sun*. The two of them patiently autographed boxes of Christmas cards to raise money and then helped auction other goods off. A few boos echoed through the barn-like building when they were introduced, but they simply smiled and waved.

On their way to the auction, they had to walk down an aisle past tables of junk, relics, and gadgets. At the back near the exit, a one-metre-high poster caught Lillian's eye. "Oh look! It's Elvis!" she shrieked. "He's one of my heroes! I've got to buy that. I know just the place for it back at the Gardens!"

It was a huge framed colour photo of the King himself, clad in his white jumpsuit with a Hawaiian lei around his neck, crooning into a microphone.

The premier was slow to catch up to his wife. But when he did, he also spotted the picture and his eyes lit up. "Honey, look! It's Elvis!" he shouted with the same enthusiasm. The owner, when found, demanded $15 for it. Vander Zalm offered $10. No sale. Lillian watched nervously, determined not to let the prize get away.

"Fifteen bucks or forget it. You're the premier, you can afford it," said the vendor.

"I like your style," Vander Zalm said, forking over the cash.

Lillian insisted on carrying the poster herself. "Our son once went to Graceland, you know," she confided to a reporter.

At the auction, Bill was able to fetch $50 for a grotesque brass lamp and $45 for an equally ugly fireplace set. People were almost mesmerized by his auctioneering skills. Lillian spent hundreds of dollars on a variety of items. They stayed an extra hour. For a while, the daily headaches and problems of being premier could be ignored and the Vander Zalms could do what they enjoyed most: being celebrities.

Several associates say Vander Zalm would much rather be a movie star than a politician. He has even starred in a made-for-television movie about Christmas. Called "Sinterklaas Fantasy," it tells the story of the fourteenth-century saint of merchants and sailors—Santa Claus to the children of the Netherlands. Vander Zalm is the narrator of the semi-autobiographical tale, which also uses Fantasy Gardens as the "home" of Sinterklaas's cousin, Santa Claus II. Lillian also has a starring role.

The film started shooting in 1986, before the Social Credit leadership campaign. For two years rumours circulated that the project had been shelved, but at last report it was scheduled to be broadcast on Canadian television in time for Christmas 1989.

When Bob Hope, a regular visitor to Vancouver, stopped by in the spring of 1989, he paid a visit to Vander Zalm. Hope apparently told Vander Zalm that he had the makings of a true movie star. Vander Zalm was thrilled by the compliment and couldn't wait to tell Lillian. "He likes the attention," says Bill Kay. "He'd rather be a movie star and be shaking hands. He likes all that glamour and excitement."

The glamour eventually wore off. The couple themselves had not changed much—they still smiled constantly and were as flashy as ever. But they were not quite as upbeat as they had been, and neither were their audiences. People who had once been entranced by their presence now just rolled their eyes.

And Lillian, despite her star quality, sometimes proved to be a headache for the premier's office. Like her husband, she was slow to realize that being premier is not like running a small business. Rather than following the conventions of political life, they acted like the suburban Surrey couple, starry-eyed at the situations they found themselves in.

"She only came in on special occasions, and when she did she would often complain to the premier and Bill Kay that our office was too big and that we had too many people and that nobody did any work," remembers a former premier's office staffer.

Once, David Poole insisted that Vander Zalm get a special, private line installed in his apartment at Fantasy Gardens, so his staff could contact him without going through the main business number for the Gardens. The first time Poole phoned there, Lillian picked up the phone.

"Who is this?" she asked.

"David Poole."

"David Poole, you're not supposed to be using this phone. Where did you get the telephone number from?" Lillian said to a disbelieving Poole.

Lillian, never afraid to voice her opinions, occasionally admonished cabinet ministers for using rough language. She once chewed out Finance Minister Mel Couvelier for saying "goddamn." If Vander Zalm swore around the office–as he occasionally did, his favourite epithets being "asshole" and "bastard"–he would immediately catch himself: "Boy, if Lillian heard me say that, I'd be in trouble."

The premier's office staff found that dealing with her on administrative matters such as scheduling events for the premier could be a major headache. On one occasion, in late 1987, a formal government dinner was to be held in Victoria in honour of Queen Beatrix of the Netherlands. Seating plans for such occasions are, needless to say, drawn up well in advance. One week before the event, Lillian still had not decided how many members of her family would be attending.

"She complained that it cost a lot of money for them to come to Victoria and rent tuxedos and they weren't sure they wanted to do that," a former office staffer recalls. "Forty-eight hours before the event, Lillian said: 'Tell them at Government House just to have extra plates ready in case the kids want to come.'"

Lillian has also created problems for the Social Credit Party. She and her husband refused to pay her way when she accompanied the premier on his trips to the Far East in 1987 and Europe in 1988.

The B.C. government has strict rules governing a spouse's expenses on such trips: the taxpayers do not pick up the tab. With the Vander Zalms refusing to fork over any money for Lillian's trips, and with the government unwilling to pay her way, there was only one place left to turn: the Social Credit Party.

The party has a limited company, known as the Social Credit Fund, that was set up to collect donations to the party. It also covers "unusual" expenses. Unknown to everyone in the party except for a small circle, that fund paid for some of Lillian's expenses on the two overseas trips, plus her and the premier's expenses on a January 1988 holiday trip to Hawaii—more than $7000 in total. (According to government spending vouchers obtained by the authors the premier's return airfare to Hong Kong via Tokyo was $5141.)

Peter Webster, the party's chief fundraiser and administrator of the fund, has the authority to approve expenditures up to $10 000, but he balked at first, arguing against using party money to pay bills rung up by the premier's wife.

The premier's office was worried, too. If the public learned that the party was picking up Lillian's expenses, the publicity would devastate fundraising efforts and thus put further strain on relations between the premier and many elements of the party.

"As more and more tension built in the party, Webster had become more and more conscious about how it would look if the party were paying Lillian's bills," a party insider familiar with the fund told the authors.

But the frugal Vander Zalms were adamant: Lillian would not pay her own expenses.

The trips included ten days to Japan and Hong Kong, and twelve days in London, Holland, and West Germany. There were immense accounting problems associated with the European trip because Vander Zalm was lax in keeping track which days were spent on government business and which were holidays. It took government accountants months to sort everything out.

Social Credit Party members have never been told what the special fund has paid for. Webster, already upset with Lillian because he did not think she was participating in enough party fundraisers, met with Vander Zalm in the fall of 1987 to complain. But he was fighting a losing battle. It wouldn't be the last time Webster would have to dip into the fund against his wishes.

Lillian also requested that the Canadian embassy in Tokyo assist her in shopping expeditions around the city. She visited wholesalers in efforts to purchase goods for Fantasy Gardens, and in a huge, unfamiliar city like Tokyo, she needed a car and driver.

The fact was, Vander Zalm needed Lillian to travel with him. He relies more on his wife than on anyone else. When they're apart, which is often, they sometimes talk four or five times a day on the phone. She will call him if she has any problems at Fantasy Gardens; during the working week in Victoria, he ends each day with a phone call to her just after 11:00 p.m.

The two generally talk about Fantasy Gardens, but politics is another major topic. Lillian encourages her husband to always do what he thinks is right.

"What Lillian likes to talk about is her day and the things that she's involved with; she doesn't want to hear too much about the heavy politics, but we talk about politics from time to time," Vander Zalm told the authors.

"She's still into politics, too, because she gets all those people dropping by and people want to meet her and talk to her, so she'll relate or relay a lot of information to me. She'll get talking about some of the day-to-day stuff but not the policies per se."

At home in the castle, when they are not working (and Lillian usually is doing something around the Gardens), Lillian will spend evenings ironing his shirts while he reads an endless stack of cabinet briefing notes. The television may be on in the background.

Vander Zalm believes that women should be homemakers. During the 1986 election campaign, he was asked at one stop where Lillian was. "She's washing socks, ironing shirts, and getting me ready for next week. I always wear a clean shirt, thanks to Lillian," he told the audience. "I guess she wants to put a lot of love into the shirt and that's why she wants to do it herself. We're equal partners in everything."

He also believes in "women's intuition." Shortly after becoming premier, he said, "Very often women have extrasensory perception. Women have more of this than men. Women have lots more intuition than men."

Later on in the election campaign, he told one of the authors that Lillian and he possessed a unique talent that allowed them to determine people's problems without actually talking to them. "We can somehow figure out what it is that people really want or like without them telling us," he said.

Despite such comments, and despite their flashy lifestyles, the Vander Zalms astound many people simply because of the fact that, through twenty-five years of politics, they have stayed together and are still, it seems, as much in love as the day they met in the Kelowna malt shop in 1953.

Bill Vander Zalm is proud of Lillian, his family, his religion, his record, and his life.

And he is proud of Fantasy Gardens.

When he was asked by the authors what he thought of the idea of B.C.'s premier living in a castle, above a drawbridge and a moat, surrounded by cobblestone streets and thousands of flowers, he was quick to answer:

"I think it's neat."

The Bill and Lillian Show

On the morning after his victory at Whistler, the remarkably serene premier-elect sat down for breakfast with the man he would be succeeding.

What should have been an awkward encounter—because of Vander Zalm's indirect attacks on Bill Bennett during the leadership campaign—was surprisingly comfortable. The two chatted about the premiers' conference to be held in Edmonton in a week's time, and Bennett told Vander Zalm to get to know Saskatchewan Premier Grant Devine, a helpful and unpretentious veteran among the first ministers. But their amiable banter didn't mean that Bennett lacked reservations about the man across from him.

Bennett didn't consider Bill Vander Zalm a team player; more personally, he could never forgive Vander Zalm for calling him and the cabinet "gutless."

And, as part of the father-and-son team that had built Social Credit, Bennett was concerned for the party's health under Vander Zalm. He didn't feel Vander Zalm understood Social Credit, understood that the party was greater than the leader. Bennett also feared that Vander Zalm didn't understand that the office of premier was greater than the man.

Bennett knew that when Vander Zalm had been a Socred politician from Surrey, he had let party matters in his riding slide while he toured the province promoting himself.

Hence another source of tension between the two men: Despite Bill Bennett's hard work for the party, the people in it loved Bill Vander Zalm more. Shy and bland, Bennett was no match for the political dynamo that was Bill Vander Zalm. When Bill Bennett walked into a crowd of supporters there was always generous applause. When Bill Vander Zalm walked into the same room there was pandemonium.

Breakfast over, Vander Zalm thanked Bennett for his advice. Within a few weeks Vander Zalm would step up his campaign against the Bennett record. In the meantime, Bennett would maintain a diplomatic silence in his home town of Kelowna as he watched Vander Zalm bring the Socred party to the brink of destruction. Unlike Pierre Trudeau, who couldn't resist undermining the leadership of his successor, John Turner, Bennett proved that he was, above all a party man; he held his tongue no matter how many times Vander Zalm attacked him.

"I, William Nick Vander Zalm, do solemnly and sincerely promise and swear that I will duly and faithfully . . . execute the powers and trusts reposed in me."

On August 6, shortly after 1:30 p.m., bible in his right hand, left hand in the air, Vander Zalm took the oath of office as British Columbia's twenty-seventh premier.

The new premier looked awed by the whole exercise. During his speech, he uttered prophetic words: "I must be frank. I cannot—and I will not—promise you perfection. Mistakes will be made, there will be errors. But I tell you now they will be honest errors."

As members of the cabinet, guests, and the media horde mingled at Government House on that sunny afternoon, there was truly a sense that government would be different under Bill Vander Zalm, especially for those covering political events in the capital. (One of his first acts as premier was to personally deliver flowers and beer to members of the legislative press gallery.)

After the swearing-in ceremony, Vander Zalm held a wide-ranging news conference which touched on the potential conflict problem with Fantasy Gardens, even though he had transferred ownership to his wife during the leadership race.

"Let's face it, man and wife are one, so we're together on it and that's something I would want to address in the not-too-distant future," Vander Zalm said. (Three years later he would still own a minimum 30 per cent interest in the Gardens but would continue to insist it was his wife's.)

Vander Zalm also revealed that a new cabinet would be announced in a week. Advance notice for any government announcement, especially a cabinet shuffle, was completely unheard of under Bennett. But Vander Zalm had promised open government, and, besides, the media were his friends.

Vander Zalm was helped in selecting a cabinet by Bennett's principal secretary, Jerry Lampert, who had agreed to stay on with Vander Zalm at least until a general election was called. A former executive director of the Social Credit, Lampert was a slick political operative who had learned the business with Ontario's Big Blue Machine.

Lampert assumed the role that Vander Zalm's leadership campaign manager, Bill Goldy, had aspired to. Like most of the outsiders who had helped Vander Zalm win in Whistler, Goldy would be shut out of Vander Zalm's office. That was another Vander Zalm paradox: he could be fiercely loyal to some people, such as Bill Kay and later David Poole, and show no loyalty at all to others, such as Goldy.

On August 14, Vander Zalm rewarded the only Socred politicians—all backbenchers—who had supported his leadership bid by including them in cabinet: Surrey's Bill Reid and Rita Johnston and North Vancouver's Jack Davis, the cerebral maverick who had languished on the backbench under Bennett.

Vander Zalm assumed the finance ministry himself, a move that gave him absolute control over his government. There was a precedent: W.A.C. Bennett had also held the finance portfolio while premier and so, for a short while, did the NDP's Dave Barrett. Vander Zalm took the post because he didn't trust anyone else's abilities. It wouldn't be long, however, before the obvious conflict of interest in his taking the job would become apparent to the public and the media.

As finance minister, he decided to eliminate a 7 per cent tax on restaurant meals, which had an immediate positive impact on restaurants operating out of Fantasy Gardens and certainly benefited his close friend and fundraiser Peter Toigo, who owned a popular B.C. restaurant chain. As well, Fantasy Gardens' biggest creditor was the Canadian Imperial Bank of Commerce. As finance minister, Vander Zalm was in a position to give that bank lots of government business. In the next shuffle, a few months later, Vander Zalm would drop the finance portfolio.

On the afternoon of his first shuffle, Vander Zalm met alone in his office with a Vancouver *Sun* reporter to discuss his new cabinet and offer his early impressions on being premier. In a line that would come back to haunt him, Vander Zalm said of being premier, "So far, it's a piece of cake."

This was partly, it seems, because of Divine Guidance: "I know this sounds corny, but's it's almost like I'm having some sort of a guiding hand. I considered myself quite capable but I thought I would have some difficulties with it, but I don't." The words echoed those of W.A.C. Bennett, who had insisted that he was "plugged into God."

Vander Zalm behaved typically during his first days in office: he was unguarded but charmingly honest. Unlike most modern-day politicians, Vander Zalm insisted on one-on-one interviews with reporters, with just the reporter recording the comments. He had utter confidence in himself and the media: he didn't need handlers protecting his interest; the media would do that.

In late August, Vander Zalm and Lillian toured the Kootenays, in southeastern British Columbia.

When Vander Zalm and a group of cabinet ministers first arrived in the Kootenays aboard two government jets, Lillian was not present. Vander Zalm decided he missed her, so he asked one of his aides, Jim Arthur, to send a government jet back to get her. Arthur, realizing how bad that would look if it became public, got Socred headquarters to arrange a commercial flight for the premier's wife instead. When Arthur explained to the premier how bad redirecting government jets for his wife would look, Vander Zalm, ominously enough, didn't understand.

The three-day event was one big photo opportunity. The cameras caught it all: the Vander Zalms riding a sled down a twisting track on the side of a mountain; Lillian yanking an accordion out of a man's hands to play it while her husband the premier led an impromptu sing-along of a beer-drinking song; the premier playing bocce with a group of elderly Italian men.

"Are we in some sort of movie?" asked one television cameraman.

Gone were the ways of Bennett, isolated by a wall of bureaucrats and protocol. Vander Zalm phoned reporters at home, staying in scrums sometimes for thirty minutes until every last question was answered. The media ate it up. Each night, British Columbians turned on the television news to catch up on the latest mini-series: "Bill Vander Zalm, Premier."

A bona fide populist, Vander Zalm would phone citizens at home and give them a chance to air beefs directly with the man who could most quickly address their problems. The downside was that Vander Zalm didn't have any elaborate policy plans. In fact, he had no plans at all.

"The head office of the Vander Zalm administration is located in the pocket of the premier's ultra-suede jacket," wrote columnist Marjorie Nichols of the *Sun*.

When Vander Zalm vowed to eliminate the restaurant tax, questions about the benefits it would bestow on Fantasy Gardens faded away unanswered. He set such a frenetic pace during his first days that whatever people were upset over one minute was forgotten the next.

When a friend who owned a fur shop in Prince George snapped a picture of Vander Zalm wearing a $2500 coyote coat and then used the picture to advertise her merchandise, the premier said he was just "having a little fun." He didn't see what all the fuss was about. "If it's of some economic benefit . . . all the better. Am I the new Sylvester [Stallone]? I didn't take off my shirt," he said, referring to ads of the bare-chested movie star modelling fur coats. Vander Zalm shrugged off the story, and the population did too.

Everything was "great" or "fantastic" or "super." Vander Zalm was always up. He was B.C.'s teflon-coated Ronald Reagan. It was morning in British Columbia again.

Imagine the NDP's frustration. Their two-year strategy of focusing on Bennett's hated name had been immensely successful.

When Bennett stepped down, the Socreds trailed the NDP by twelve points. Of all the candidates in the Socred race, the NDP had most feared Vander Zalm, the populist. Of all the candidates in the Socred race, Vander Zalm best understood what moved British Columbians.

Vander Zalmania paralyzed the NDP. The public wasn't responding to the campaign against past Socred scandals, and nobody cared about Vander Zalm's Fantasy Gardens conflict of interest.

Even when the premier asked his health minister to survey the availability of abortions in B.C. hospitals, temporarily resurrecting Vander Zalm's past strident pro-life views, the issue didn't go anywhere.

Slowly, surely, Vander Zalm's folksy charm and promises of cheaper beer for the working man eroded the NDP's blue-collar strength. The public believed in redemption, and for the most part Vander Zalm was acting like a changed man; no confrontation, no evidence of his past radicalism.

Two key events led to Vander Zalm's ultimate victory.

On August 20, the B.C. Government Employees Union and the provincial government agreed on a thirty-three month contract. Vander Zalm, who had promised an end to the government's bitter relationship with its 34 000 unionized workers, was given all the credit, even by the head of the union.

It was a settlement Bennett probably could have achieved before leaving office, but he had decided it would better to "give" it to his successor, who could have been his protégé, Bud Smith. The government's chief negotiator, Bob Plecas, was encouraged to stall the negotiations so that the new administration would have the good news to announce. Thus Vander Zalm had his first major victory handed to him on a silver platter.

"The atmosphere and direction I believe that Mr. Vander Zalm brought to the talks was a catalyst to push the talks to a successful conclusion," union head John Shields said.

John Shields became a very lonely man. The NDP and union leaders across the province were apoplectic. In a single ten-second sound clip, Shields gave Vander Zalm the key victory he needed to take into a general election campaign. So much for the NDP's strategy to portray him as a confrontational flake.

On the same day that Shields anointed Vander Zalm, NDP Leader Bob Skelly helped to demoralize his own supporters.

Skelly was talking with an NDP colleague when a Vancouver *Sun* reporter, Lisa Fitterman, walked in and was invited to sit down. She turned her tape recorder on and Skelly practically conceded the next election to Vander Zalm, saying he couldn't compete with the new premier's "charm and charisma."

"The game was over," recalls a high-ranking NDP official about the Skelly interview.

Such NDP MLAs as Vancouver East's Bob Williams, the Okanagan's Lyle MacWilliam, and Vancouver Island's Colin Gablemann wanted Skelly out. At a special caucus meeting there was a vote to dump him: eleven stuck with him, seven voted against him, and three abstained. Less than two weeks later he had to fight an election.

Meanwhile, Vander Zalm worked to counteract the scandal-tinged image of his predecessor's government.

In the months leading up to Bennett's resignation, there had been a string of conflict-of-interest controversies and the embarrassing peccadilloes involving cabinet ministers Nielsen and McClelland.

Vander Zalm said he expected his new cabinet to be totally discreet. For good measure he announced that he was severing his ties with the Sentinel Group, an umbrella name for several companies owned by well-known political operations—such as Big Blue Machine type Patrick Kinsella—all of whom had played a major role in dispensing advertising and political advice to Bennett.

During the leadership race, members of the highly influential Sentinel Group had backed either Bud Smith or Brian Smith. Grace McCarthy resented that, and she helped plant the bug in Vander Zalm's ear that he should investigate the company. Because of his own suspicions of the group, it didn't take much encouragement for Vander Zalm to launch a probe to see if there were any irregularities in the relationship between Sentinel and Bennett's office.

Vander Zalm's message was clear: goodbye to the slick promoters who operated with Bennett.

And for added emphasis, Vander Zalm sharply criticized Bennett for the way the Socred restraint program had been implemented in 1983—even though Vander Zalm had been a member of Bennett's cabinet when the restraint program was being devised.

On the morning of September 24, Vander Zalm and Bill Kay arrived at the legislature shortly after 9:00 a.m. The premier was resplendent in a blue suit, and his shoes were highly polished. Word was out that Vander Zalm would end the election suspense.

British Columbians were feeling good about themselves and were particularly proud of the success of Expo 86, which was coming to its conclusion. The province was also showing signs of finally emerging from the recession which had knocked B.C. flat three years earlier.

The people were optimistic about their future. It was a perfect time to call an election.

"I wouldn't rule it out," Vander Zalm teased reporters. "I wouldn't go away. Stick around."

Vander Zalm laughed, clasped his hands in delight and bounded up the back stairs to his office. Five hours later he would make a ten-minute trip to Government House to seek dissolution of the legislature in order to hold an election. The vote was set for October 22.

"There's going to be sunshine for the next twenty-eight days," Vander Zalm said. And there would be.

In August, Social Credit headquarters, under the direction of its executive director, David Poole, had begun assembling a campaign organization.

Over the years, with the help of experts from Ontario, the Socred campaign organization had become one of the best in the country. But this time around, there was a feeling that organization didn't really matter. B.C. had fallen for Vander Zalm; all the polling confirmed it.

"I think it's fair to say that the feeling we all had, including the premier, was that we could not lose," remembers Poole. "And . . . it really didn't matter what else we did."

Vander Zalm was so confident that he had wanted to call an election weeks earlier. He had bounded into a meeting with Poole and Lampert and said: "What would you think if I called it tomorrow on the Gary Bannerman show?"

Bannerman was a popular morning-radio talk-show host and a close friend of Vander Zalm's. But the party wasn't ready; the

Socred nomination process was just getting under way across the province.

In mid-September, Vander Zalm, Poole, and Lampert had sat down with Decima polling president Allan Gregg at the Airport Inn in Richmond. Gregg's polling confirmed what Vander Zalm's gut had told him: people loved him and he'd be crazy not to call an election almost immediately. He was twenty points ahead of NDP leader Bob Skelly.

On the afternoon that Vander Zalm finally did call the election, Skelly called a news conference in the legislative press theatre. He stood at the podium for a few nervous moments while the television cameramen got ready. The row of hot lights above him were reflected in his glasses.

He had barely begun his address when his voice began to quiver. Then the quiver became more pronounced. He stopped momentarily, then continued. But by now the quiver had overcome him.

"Can I stop this?" Skelly pleaded.

Reporters exchanged startled glances. Skelly tried again but finally had to halt his speech. He'd had an anxiety attack on the opening day of the campaign.

The incident was painful to watch. For NDP party members, it was a terrible blow. Skelly's leadership was under siege within his own caucus, and this hurt his confidence even more. It made him look weak and uncertain. And juxtaposed on the evening news with Vander Zalm's jaunty, confident first day, it only served to emphasize the differences between the two men.

Skelly was an unlikely politician. He hated public speaking, and during his years as an MLA he had done everything he could to avoid it. As Opposition leader, the election call was his first real test under the harsh glare of the television lights. It was the worst possible moment for a nervous public speaker to have to prove himself.

A day after his disastrous news conference, Skelly made matters worse when, during a radio interview, he responded to a question about the anxiety attack by saying, "I think I went out for lunch and ate the wrong kind of tulip bulbs."

The bizarre comment was ostensibly an attack on Vander Zalm's claim that he and his family were so poor during the war they were forced to eat tulip bulbs. But people saw the comment as petty, and it wiped out any public sympathy over Skelly's display of nervousness.

Unfortunately for Skelly, the jitters would strike twice more, focusing attention on his public speaking problems rather than on NDP policies. A BCTV reporter would refer to covering the Skelly campaign as a "deathwatch."

Vander Zalm, meanwhile, spent the first full day of the campaign visiting a tiny Indian reserve at Kingcome Inlet, a remote fishing village mid-way up the B.C. coast.

The visit had been arranged some time earlier, but Vander Zalm refused to cancel it once the election campaign was underway—even though B.C. native people hated the Socred government because of its refusal to address land claims. But a visit which could have been a public relations disaster turned into a public relations coup.

Vander Zalm stood in a Tsawataineuk longhouse beside a roaring fire which was sending embers through a hole in the roof. Village children tugged at his trousers, begging for his attention. Then, defying every tenet of modern-day politics, Vander Zalm broke into song, the television cameras recording his every word.

"On top of spaghetti, all covered in cheese, I lost my poor meatballs, when somebody sneezed."

The light in the longhouse grew dimmer and Vander Zalm and Lillian were asked to perform in a native dance. The couple emerged from a back room minutes later in full native regalia. The premier's red and blue cloak dragged on the floor. His headdress, adorned with rabbit-fur tails, came close to falling over his eyes. Vander Zalm and Lillian hugged and kissed; the villagers clapped. The provincial election campaign seemed hundreds of years away.

When Vander Zalm returned to Vancouver Island for the real start of his campaign, one of his first stops was Port Alberni, Skelly's riding. Vander Zalm's campaign stopped at a mall, and somebody pulled out a football.

Footballs can make or break election campaigns. The famous picture of Tory leader Bob Stanfield looking daft while fumbling a football was blamed in part for his 1974 election defeat to Pierre Trudeau. Since then, political handlers have usually made sure campaigning politicians don't get near the pigskin.

"Throw me the ball," screamed Vander Zalm, as his aides reeled in horror. The ball spiralled through the air for what seemed an eternity, the television cameras capturing its every spin, before it slipped through Vander Zalm's arms and his legs, which he awkwardly bent together to save it, and bounced on the ground.

"One more time," Vander Zalm screamed. He missed again.

"Come on, one last time," Vander Zalm insisted. The ball went up again, and again spiralled down through Vander Zalm's waiting arms.

"Oh, darn. I guess I'm not going to be a football player." Vander Zalm wasn't afraid of looking stupid. The fact that he had dropped the ball was irrelevant. In the fall of 1986, the public saw Bill Vander Zalm as a good sport, not a bumbling fool.

How accommodating was Vander Zalm to the press? In Nanaimo for a Socred fundraising auction, Vander Zalm and reporters got word that there had been a plane crash in northern B.C., and Socred MLA Al Passarell was believed dead.

CBC television reporter Rick Ouston jumped over a rope keeping the press at bay from the premier. He asked Vander Zalm if he had heard the news about Passarell. Vander Zalm said he had heard about the crash but that Passarell's death had not been confirmed.

"Well, how about if you give us a comment which we will only use if we get it confirmed that Passarell has in fact been killed?" asked Ouston.

The ever-accommodating Vander Zalm agreed. And within minutes he was outside, surrounded by reporters.

"It's a very sad event, obviously, and we're very distressed that it would happen. . . . There's very little we can say except we're going to miss him and his children obviously will be looked after."

(Unfortunately, the news about Passarell was indeed true. The dress rehearsal served as the real thing.)

Vander Zalm's campaign routinely ran ninety minutes to three hours behind. Each time he and Lillian walked off the campaign bus they were mobbed. It would take them an hour to get through a mall as hundreds of autograph seekers crowded around with notebooks, ticket stubs, paper bags, or copies of Vander Zalm's gardening books.

When aides trying to keep the campaign on time tugged at Vander Zalm's sleeve to get him moving, he'd shrug the aide off. There were more hands to be shaken, more autographs to be signed. Lillian was almost as popular as her husband. Women were showing up at campaign stops wearing headbands. The aides were getting hell from head office, which in turn was dealing with Socred event organizers furious that the premier was turning up hours late.

Vander Zalm was annoyed himself about all the people travelling with him. He had by accident found an entourage list in his hotel room. In an interview with the *Sun*, Vander Zalm made his beefs public.

"There's things to be said for it [the campaign] but it's not what I'm accustomed to; it's totally the opposite of Bill Vander Zalm. I could travel in my car instead of a bus and I could travel in a much smaller plane than I'm travelling in."

Vander Zalm believed he could win a campaign from the back of a pickup truck. And it might have been preferable to the campaign bus, on which Bill and Lillian had a private room in the back; they were constantly nauseated by the chemical smell emanating from the toilet in their small room.

(Despite his complaints about extravagance, some major expenses resulted from Vander Zalm's impulses. He was supposed to have a quiet Thanksgiving dinner at the posh William Tell restaurant in Vancouver with his immediate family. The intimate gathering quickly ballooned into a full-fledged party of more than twenty, mostly staff and friends of the Vander Zalms.

(The bill, close to $3000, was treated as election expenses. When the party's comptroller asked campaign tour director Jim Arthur for an explanation, he simply explained that it was Vander Zalm's party.)

Vander Zalm's criticism of the campaign angered party workers. David Poole had to straighten him out.

"I told him: 'Premier, you're one guy but there's sixty-eight other [Socreds] fighting this campaign too. We need to advertise, we need an organization. You don't think one thousand people show up at a campaign stop because they hear you're coming. There's people out there who make sure it happens.' "

Poole didn't mince his words. Vander Zalm liked that. As the campaign progressed, he came to enjoy Poole's company more. He felt Poole possessed a quick mind, but, more importantly, he saw Poole as a doer. Furthermore, he wasn't one of the hated slick old pros. (In fact, Poole had very little political experience: six months earlier he had been a college administrator in Prince Albert, Saskatchewan.)

Vander Zalm sensed that Poole had no hidden agendas and no desperate urge for power and therefore was a person he could trust. He became a permanent fixture at Vander Zalm's side; there was little doubt that he would inherit an important position in his boss's administration.

The Socred campaign strategy was simple: get the Bill and Lillian Vander Zalm Show into every B.C. community possible before election day. The party's tracking showed that wherever Vander Zalm and Lillian went the party's fortunes rose dramatically.

Vander Zalm refused to debate Skelly publicly because Socred strategists felt it would only give Skelly a chance to exploit the fact that the Socreds didn't have a policy platform (which they had decided to postpone developing until after the election).

Vander Zalm's opinion: "The smart candidate avoids detailed policy statements, for they rarely help and can do you harm. Your answers should concentrate on style."

Lillian had urged her husband not to talk about style, saying people wouldn't understand what he meant. This is how he explained it: "It's the openness, it's the availability, it's the willingness to talk about things. It's optimism. Optimism is determination. That's style."

Vander Zalm did have a slogan: "A Fresh Start for B.C." The Socred television ads showed him sitting on a stool in front of a yellow tarpaulin talking about his new style of government. Although Bill Bennett wasn't named, the point was to convince voters that the new premier would be different. Vander Zalm was running as much against his predecessor as against the NDP.

One day Vander Zalm would criticize Bennett's powerful deputy Norman Spector (now deputy of federal-provincial relations in Ottawa) as one reason Vander Zalm left government in 1983. The next day he would criticize Bennett's mining policy, restraint, and years of confrontation.

The inevitable meeting between Vander Zalm and Bennett occurred during a campaign stop in Bennett's home town of Kelowna. The two Bills, who disliked one another, stood side by side smiling for the crowd.

"Do you think this man here was responsible for confrontation in B.C.?" a reporter asked Vander Zalm.

"Well–" Vander Zalm began.

"It's just like EXPO 86, everyone working together," Bennett cut in, quickly ushering Vander Zalm away from the media.

On Monday, October 6, mid-way through the campaign, Vander Zalm's tour of a fish-packing plant in the mid-coast city of Prince Rupert was interrupted by an urgent telephone call from David Poole. Poole told him there was room for a possible settlement in the three-month-old International Woodworkers of America (IWA) dispute.

Vander Zalm had tried earlier to get the IWA to settle with the forest companies. Vander Zalm needed another resolution to go with his victory in the government employees' union settlement: Vander Zalm, the man for cooperation and conciliation.

He interrupted his campaign to fly to Vancouver for a meeting at the Delta River Inn.

Jack Munro, the giant and blustery head of the IWA, recalls that the meeting was set up because Poole told the IWA that the forest companies would make a major concession in the key problem area: the right of companies to contract out work to non-union workers.

"Are you sure, David, that that's what they're saying?" Munro demanded of Poole. Poole checked again and phoned to tell Munro yes, the companies were prepared to move.

Munro began the meeting by saying that he understood there would be concessions on contracting out. No way, the companies shot back. There must have been a misunderstanding.

Munro and chief company negotiator Keith Bennett started arguing, and the two sides were put in separate rooms. Vander Zalm and Poole began shuffling between them, looking for a compromise. The IWA wasn't pleased with Poole's presence. "He had his political campaign manager inside this goddamn meeting trying to resolve the strike. It was fucking unbelievable," recalls the always eloquent Munro.

The IWA leader says Vander Zalm wasn't much better: "He was completely and totally over his head. He didn't fucking understand. What the fuck would a gardener know about heavy-duty forestry industry negotiations? And this was heavy duty. I think I told him this would teach him to leave his goddamn rose garden and come into here for fuck's sake. I said: 'You don't know what you're doing.' "

While negotiations were falling apart, a podium bearing the British Columbia seal was being set up for the announcement that the strike had been resolved. The premier's handlers were proceeding on Poole's assurances that Vander Zalm was about to produce another miracle.

Outside the meeting, weary reporters looked for any scrap to feed to their radio stations or newspapers. But there were only brief clips from Vander Zalm: "Strange business this negotiating."

Around 3:00 a.m., after nearly twelve hours of talks, Vander Zalm emerged to announce that there was no settlement. He was, however, appointing a mediator in the dispute and warned of impending back-to-work legislation.

When Munro watched the television news the next day he was amused to hear Vander Zalm say: "It's amazing how often you think you've almost got it and then all of a sudden it slips away on you." What a joke, Munro thought; they were never even close to getting a settlement.

Vander Zalm and Poole were convinced that Munro had received marching orders from the NDP and the Canadian Labour Congress that under no circumstances was he to allow Vander Zalm to walk away with a victory in the dispute in the middle of an election. Munro didn't want to be the next John Shields.

(However, Munro could hardly have settled when the major issue of contracting out was unresolved).

Vander Zalm's failed intervention in the IWA marked a campaign turning point. The premier was criticized for getting involved in a dispute he knew little about and dragging his political campaign manager along with him. Moreover, the incident shattered Vander

Zalm's aura of invincibility. A less popular leader facing a stronger opponent might have been destroyed by this debacle. As it was, Vander Zalm's momentum came to an abrupt halt and from that point on the Socred challenge was to hang on and win. Fortunately for them, there was a little more than a week left in the short campaign.

Besides the forestry strike, other issues were enlivening the race.

The U.S. lumber industry rejected Canada's–and Vander Zalm's–stumpage increase offer. Vander Zalm had gambled that his decision to review B.C. stumpage rates (the amount forest companies are charged for cutting down Crown timber) would head off a decision by the U.S. commerce department to grant an application by U.S. forest companies for a 36 per cent tariff on Canadian softwood imports.

The forest companies refused to withdraw their application for the tariff. This allowed the NDP to legitimately criticize Vander Zalm for undermining Canada's position against the tariff. Vander Zalm had conceded that B.C.'s low stumpage rates amounted to a subsidy, which was precisely what the U.S. forest companies were arguing in their case before the U.S. commerce department.

There was also the universities issue. Russ Fraser, who was post-secondary education minister at the time, publicly suggested that students should postpone a university education if they couldn't afford it. The comment underlined the NDP's charge that Social Credit was run by a bunch of millionaires who did not represent the average family. Fraser's comment cost him a cabinet position following the election.

With ten days left in the campaign, Skelly was gaining confidence and the twenty-point lead the Socreds had begun the campaign with was quickly evaporating. Part of the NDP's success lay in its highly effective television ad campaign, which showed Vander Zalm's head flipping from side to side as a voice listed all the issues that Vander Zalm had changed his position on since becoming premier.

Bereft of policies, Vander Zalm was asking voters to trust him. The NDP said the man couldn't be trusted.

Vander Zalm's popularity, the only tool the Socreds had to overcome the NDP's edge in organization, was beginning to wear thin.

Lillian's mom told reporters she was going to vote NDP.

Vander Zalm's ad hoc style of governing was beginning to frighten Socred organizers. For example, the premier blurted out in a shopping-mall parking lot that the minimum wage was going to go up. It was the first anyone had heard of such a policy decision.

Other gaffes portended things to come. At one stop near the end of the campaign, Vander Zalm was gladhanding without Lillian. When reporters inquired about her absence, Vander Zalm said his wife was at home, "washing socks, ironing shirts and getting me ready for next week." The female reporters covering the tour were appalled and immediately took Vander Zalm to task. But such pronouncements were nothing new: As a Socred minister Vander Zalm had said, "Women make the best cooks and housewives and should be encouraged in that role." (There would be more such insults by Vander Zalm, and by 1989 Social Credit's standing with many women would be abysmal.)

Vander Zalm was also getting tired and edgy.

During a campaign stop in Nelson, Vander Zalm was taken aside by Mark Schneider a CBC television reporter. Schneider wanted to ask Vander Zalm about comments attributed to him in a biography of the premier by Alan Twigg. Commenting on the Nazi occupation of his village in Holland, Vander Zalm had told Twigg, "Even when I refer to those times, I don't refer to them as dark times. Knowing they were. I'm still, you know, looking at what the brighter side of what it was and saying, 'Ya, but during those times we did have order.' And things were principled."

Schneider's private chat with Vander Zalm somehow became a media scrum. Everyone was intrigued by the conversation. To reporters who weren't initially aware of what Schneider was talking about, it sounded like the reporter was suggesting that Vander Zalm was endorsing the Nazis.

About an hour after the scrum, Vander Zalm bounded into the media campaign bus looking for Schneider.

"Where is he? What the hell is he trying to do? He's trying to destroy me with that. I can't believe it," said Vander Zalm.

Aides travelling with the premier had never seen him so upset. Even Schneider felt bad about the incident, and few media outlets ended up touching the story.

As the campaign closed, Vander Zalm was put under RCMP protection.

The Socred party had received an anonymous tip that Vander Zalm's life would be in danger if he showed up for a speech at the Hotel Vancouver. The RCMP took the threat seriously. Vander Zalm was running a gauntlet of angry woodworkers at nearly every campaign stop.

Officials sneaked Vander Zalm into the hotel through a back door, while a crowd of angry demonstrators waited outside another entrance. The hotel lobby was crawling with undercover police officers.

Vander Zalm wasn't happy about all the security. Because of the threat, an earlier plan for him to have driven to the hotel in a Model T with the Socred candidate from downtown Vancouver, Bob Gardner, had been nixed. Unfortunately, nobody had told Gardner about the threat; after the speech he somehow got Vander Zalm alone and the two walked out of the hotel and into the waiting open-air Model T. They drove through downtown Vancouver to Vander Zalm's next campaign stop. The premier made it there without incident.

On election day morning, a thick grey fog had enveloped the premier's Fantasy Garden home. He and Lillian got up early to vote at the polling station just doors away from the Gardens. The station was jammed with reporters and cameramen. The premier pulled out his wallet to provide the necessary identification. He didn't have any.

"How embarrassing," he said. His headband-bedecked wife scurried to their car to scrounge up some credentials.

Later that day, Vander Zalm put on his favourite dark blue mohair suit, navy socks, and maroon paisley tie; Lillian helped straighten a red rose in his lapel. She put on a white silk blouse, brown skirt, and white-and-gold headband. They gathered up their family and headed off to the top-floor suite at the Hotel Vancouver.

The couple sat on a pastel-coloured couch, before two television sets. Reporters and television cameras were everywhere.

The polls closed at 8:00 p.m. At 8:17, BCTV declared a Social Credit majority.

When all the votes were counted and results certified, the Socreds had forty-seven seats, the NDP twenty-two.

Vander Zalm and Lillian embraced for the cameras, their lips pressed together for an eternity. Then Vander Zalm was hugged and kissed by his children. Vander Zalm stared intently at the television set as NDP leader Bob Skelly appeared in Port Alberni to give his concession speech.

And then Vander Zalm turned to reporters and offered an insight into what his administration would be like.

"My office," he said, "is going to play a stronger role in the governing of the province." No one imagined at the time that he intended single-handed rule, with as little involvement of his cabinet colleagues as possible.

He took the elevator to the hotel's main ballroom, where only three years earlier the Socreds had held their annual convention while 60 000 people marched in the streets below to protest Bill Bennett's restraint program.

On the surface, the Socred victory appeared to be massive. Indeed, measured by the sheer number of seats, it was the biggest Socred majority in B.C. history. But was the victory as impressive as it was made out to be?

In terms of the popular vote, Vander Zalm's 49.3 per cent was even less than the 49.8 per cent that the "detestable" Bill Bennett had received in 1983. And Vander Zalm had been blessed with an extremely weak opponent, who didn't have nearly the populist appeal of his predecessor, Dave Barrett.

The Socreds had also made a mess of the election campaign. Vander Zalm had started with a 20-point lead which was whittled down to seven points by election day. Vandermania, a legitimate phenomenon during his first couple of months as premier and in the early stages of the campaign, had gradually worn off. As well, the Socreds' once-vaunted campaign machine was in disarray, because Vander Zalm had thought he wouldn't need it, that charm alone would win the voters.

The NDP only lost three very weary MLAs (Karen Sanford in Comox, Frank Howard in Skeena, and Don Lockstead in Mackenzie) and took three seats from Social Credit in Coquitlam, Prince George North, and the Kootenays. Were it not for the twelve new seats added from redistribution (eleven of which were added to Socred-held ridings), the results would have been much the same as the 1983 election, where the lead over the NDP was much slimmer.

Despite increasing concerns during the election campaign about his leadership qualities, Vander Zalm had managed to convince voters that he was a better choice than a "loser" like Bob Skelly. He also in large part owed his success to the media, which had made the sunny optimism of his slap-happy campaign *the* event to cover.

British Columbians had been in a relationship with a premier they didn't like. They had been vulnerable to an affair with charisma. Bill Vander Zalm had come along at just the right time.

The Fresh Start

At 8:30 a.m. on November 6, 1986, Bill Vander Zalm and his faithful companion Bill Kay left their offices and strolled over to the small Michigan Street Deli behind the legislature buildings. The air was crisp and the sun was shining in the capital. It was an exciting time for the new premier, and there was a bounce in his stride. In less than three hours, he would unveil his new cabinet and a bold new plan for government.

Symbols mattered much to Vander Zalm, and today's designated slogan was "Fresh Start." No more ties to the previous premier, Bill Bennett. A new man was in charge and things were going to be different.

The deli was almost deserted at this hour, the government office workers having finished their coffee and gone to work. Three people remained at a corner table; Vander Zalm gave them a friendly wave. They were reporters from the Vancouver *Sun*'s legislative bureau, talking about the upcoming swearing-in ceremony and speculating about the new cabinet.

Almost on a dare, one of the reporters, Keith Baldrey, approached Vander Zalm to see what the chances were of getting the new cabinet posts ahead of time on an embargo basis for the paper's mid-morning home edition.

Such a request would have seemed preposterous under Bill

Bennett, or indeed with most premiers. Cabinet appointments are strictly confidential until they are formally announced, and premiers are not supposed to leak such information—or any information, for that matter. But Vander Zalm nodded understandingly.

"Here, I'll give it to you right now," Vander Zalm said, whipping out a pen. He started to scrawl the names on a paper napkin.

Baldrey was taken aback. Other reporters from the nearby press gallery could suddenly walk in at any moment. The *Sun* was already resented for getting so many leaks from the government. Other reporters would be furious if they saw the paper getting this, the biggest leak of all. Baldrey suggested that maybe a public café was not the best place to exchange such information.

"You're right," said the amazingly agreeable premier. "Anyway, you'll want the whole package, not just the cabinet posts. It's a great program we've put together. Wait till you see it. You'll love it," he said between bites on a bran muffin.

With ninety minutes before his paper's deadline, Baldrey suggested waiting until they all got back to the legislature before obtaining the announcement.

"Okay, sure. I'll send Lillian over to the press gallery with the stuff," Vander Zalm said.

Baldrey blanched. The sight of Lillian Vander Zalm wandering the halls of the maze-like legislature, clutching sensitive documents and looking for the press gallery, was sure to attract attention among other reporters. He suggested using somebody else.

Vander Zalm agreed, much to Kay's annoyance. The premier's Man Friday didn't like it when reporters bugged his boss. Nevertheless, a short time later one of the premier's aides met Baldrey's colleague in the *Sun* bureau, Gary Mason, in a legislative corridor. Like two spies, they furtively passed the documents, and the *Sun* beat its deadline.

It was not the last time that an obliging Vander Zalm would go out of his way to accommodate the media, even if it meant breaking traditions or offending his colleagues.

Less than an hour later, at Government House, the official residence of the Lieutenant-Governor, dignitaries drank coffee in the luxurious setting while reporters camped out on the front steps to see which of the forty-seven Socred MLAs elected that October were to join the premier's inner circle. The *Sun* reporters kept to themselves, trying to pretend they were as much in the dark as everyone else.

The MLAs arrived one or two at a time, some with spouses. The veterans strode purposefully up the front steps. The rookies approached the venerable hilltop mansion gingerly, still unable to believe they belonged. Once inside, many of the new ministers enjoyed the limelight and waited excitedly for the swearing-in ceremony. No longer mere municipal politicians arguing for local road repair, now they would wield real power. Or so they thought.

Five new ministers–Peter Dueck, Lyall Hanson, Mel Couvelier, Stan Hagen, and John Savage–had never held political office at the provincial level before. The only three backbenchers who had supported Vander Zalm in the leadership race–Jack Davis, Bill Reid, and Rita Johnston–were rewarded with cabinet posts. Davis and Reid had languished under Bennett after being tainted by scandals. Johnston was part of the Surrey connection, having served with Vander Zalm during their days on Surrey municipal council. In fact, several of those promoted–Dueck, Hanson, Couvelier, and Johnston–had once been mayors or aldermen, just like their new premier.

And then there was Jack Kempf, the blustery, erratic, and unpredictable maverick from the north country. He, too, never got anywhere under Bennett until the last few months of his administration. He had been given the minor housing portfolio in the spring and then promoted by Vander Zalm in August to replace Jack Heinrich in the important forestry portfolio. Like the new premier, Kempf had been an outsider. In less than six months, however, he would find himself back on the outside, looking in.

Those nine ministers represented Vander Zalm's attempt to put his personal stamp on the cabinet. Rookies, mavericks, outsiders, and loyalists, they owed their good fortune to the new premier.

Some eyebrows were raised when Stephen Rogers trotted up the steps. After all, he had been openly critical of Vander Zalm during the leadership race, at one point saying he wouldn't serve under him in cabinet. But here he was, the new environment minister.

"It's a wonderful day, isn't it?" Grace McCarthy asked reporters on her way up the steps. Accustomed to her cheery, ultra-positive greetings, the reporters smiled right back and nodded in agreement. An old friend of Vander Zalm's, she had been rewarded with the economic development portfolio. She had lost her deputy premier title, but shrugged that off with her trademark smile. There was to be no deputy premier; Vander Zalm was not interested in sharing any part of the office.

Among the Bennett cabinet ministers Vander Zalm had dropped was Russ Fraser, whose suggestion that kids shouldn't expect to go to college if they couldn't afford it had caused a lot of grief for the Socreds during the election campaign.

Fraser showed up at Government House anyway and attended the fancy cabinet reception. Reporters badgered him to admit that his comment was the reason he was no longer a cabinet minister. Fraser wouldn't bite on anything except the free food.

Two names from Whistler were absent, to no one's surprise. Bud Smith, whose dramatic crossing to Vander Zalm after the third ballot had startled the convention, was left out in the cold. So was Kim Campbell, the icy young lawyer from Vancouver whose prophetic quote at the convention about charisma without substance would follow her for the next two years.

Despite their qualifications for holding cabinet posts (for example, both were lawyers, a profession not well represented in this bunch of Socreds), it was obvious they were not great friends of the new premier.

Both Campbell and Smith had been key aides to Bill Bennett. That alone was enough to guarantee that Vander Zalm would bar them from the inner circle. They both had the image of elitists, above the uncouth rabble of the party's "grassroots." Naturally, that didn't sit well with the champion of the non-elites, Bill Vander Zalm.

Bud Smith's crossing the floor at Whistler, which was interpreted at the time as an obvious bid to join the inner circle of the new premier, had backfired. However, despite their absence at Government House, Smith and Campbell would eventually come to command more influence and attention than most of their colleagues who were sworn into office that morning.

The actual swearing-in ceremony took place in the estate's ornate ballroom. The new cabinet stood in front of the assembled crowd as cameras whirred and clicked. One by one the ministers took the oath and signed the century-old parliament book that contained the signatures of virtually all B.C. ministers since Confederation. Lieutenant-Governor Robert Rogers, a stately figure with white hair and walrus mustache, was garbed in full ceremonial dress.

But there was more to come. In an unprecedented break with parliamentary tradition, Vander Zalm used the occasion to deliver a political speech about his government. It was an early indication of Vander Zalm's inability to understand the propriety of the premier's office.

Two nights before the ceremony, two aides from the premier's office had met with Bob Plecas, the deputy provincial secretary and the government's top protocol officer. The aides, David Poole and Bob Ransford, had told Plecas that the premier intended to give a political speech as part of the swearing-in ceremonies.

Plecas, the veteran bureaucrat, had been aghast. A political speech in the home of the Queen's representative broke protocol. It simply wasn't done, he had told the aides. Lieutenant-Governor Bob Rogers would never go for it.

"That's what we're doing, period," Ransford had said. "That's what the premier wants."

Plecas had said that he would have to phone Rogers. At the very least, the lieutenant-governor would perhaps want to leave the room during a partisan speech in his house.

In the end, however, Rogers had agreed to stay in the room.

There he and the others present heard Vander Zalm ardently promise an open government with as little secrecy and as much public input as possible. The premier's words sounded impressive in the hushed, grand ballroom:

"It's a great day. A super day. Because it's the day when together, we really begin our fresh start.

"Open government means a number of things. It means consulting with people and it means letting the light shine in on the decision-making process so the public understands what's being done." Those words would prove prophetic, but not in the way Vander Zalm had envisioned.

He announced a "work schedule" for his ministers. "While that may raise some eyebrows among old hands in government, it shows how committed we are to a fresh start and a new approach. I know there will be those who'll say it's maybe a bit radical, that it's never been done before. I don't buy that argument."

He laid out his plans to bring television to the legislature and to reduce the size of government. All in all, an unusual speech for such a nonpartisan occasion.

Back at the premier's office, the day-to-day routine was still unsettled. The office complex sits apart from the rest of the legislature, housed in its own stone annex and connected to the main building by an underground tunnel and overhead walkway. Although it is less than thirty yards away from the main building that houses the ministers and MLAs, the premier's office would gradually come to seem remote to many of them.

Vander Zalm occupies a large corner office on the second floor. If he swivels his desk chair around, he can look out over the legislature lawn to the city's picturesque inner harbour in the background. Off to the right and two blocks away is the ancient Empress Hotel, green ivy covering its facade. During the spring and summer months, huge numbers of tourists crowd into the area. From a side window, the premier can see the NDP leader's office about 150 yards away, in an annex on the other side of the main building. Like anyone who works in an office facing the harbour, he is forced to listen to the irritating wail of a street-corner bagpiper much of the day during the summer.

The premier's office complex is a maze of antechambers and side offices. His top aides occupy offices on the second floor, near the premier's. The cabinet room is directly overhead. A spiral staircase between the second and third floors was installed on Bill Bennett's orders. It is supposed to provide direct access to the cabinet room for the premier, but it also conveniently allows the premier to avoid nosy reporters waiting outside a cabinet meeting.

About ten or so secretaries try to keep the place running. The main floor is a bright, cheery area with large windows, wildlife paintings on the wall, and a dull blue, patterned carpet on the floor. There's a small kitchenette with a refrigerator in which Vander Zalm likes to keep leftover food. The reception area, where even cabinet ministers must cool their heels while waiting for an appointment, adjoins the premier's office, but there is no door between them. To get into Vander Zalm's office, one must make one's way through the maze past two gatekeepers—his personal secretary and his principal secretary.

One day, around the time of the November swearing-in ceremony, Bob Ransford gathered up a few letters and documents from his desk and made the short walk across the hall to Vander Zalm's office.

Ransford had just been appointed scheduling coordinator for the premier, and was therefore responsible for the seemingly impossible task of trying to govern Vander Zalm's time. Ransford carried with him a request from Glenn Babb, at that time the South African ambassador to Canada, for a private meeting with the premier. Since anything remotely linked to South Africa was potential political dynamite, Ransford had brought the letter almost as a lark; he was curious to see the new premier's reaction.

After running through the rest of the correspondence, Ransford said, "Oh yeah, Premier. The South African ambassador wants to meet you. I guess you don't want to do that one."

Vander Zalm's eyes lit up. "Sure. I'll do that," he said.

Surprised, Ransford offered the obvious objections, but there was almost a mischievous look in Vander Zalm's eyes. "No. Let's do it, let's do it. Phone them up and tell them we'll do it."

When news of the Babb visit leaked out, there was outrage from Vancouver's anti-apartheid organizations.

Babb, of course, was adept at creating maximum publicity for himself. He had once visited a Manitoba Indian reserve to see what he considered a Canadian version of apartheid, and his speaking engagements were routinely the target of protests and disruptions. Some thirty-five people demonstrated in front of the legislative buildings in Victoria while Vander Zalm and Babb held a twenty-five minute meeting. Across the water in Vancouver, about twenty people occupied the government's downtown cabinet offices.

A spokesman for the federal government tried to dismiss the affair as a routine protocol visit, a position weakened more than a little when Vander Zalm emerged from the meeting to announce that he wanted to sell South Africa millions of dollars' worth of wood for housing. He later said he wanted to sell pre-fabricated housing to the country to ease its housing shortage. He defended his right to meet with Babb in an ironic choice of phrase: "Let's not discriminate."

In late November Vander Zalm met with External Affairs Minister Joe Clark, who managed to explain to Vander Zalm why doing business with South Africa was not a good idea for B.C.; after that, Vander Zalm toned down his enthusiasm for easing South Africa's housing shortage.

Then along came a Socred cabinet minister to fire up the controversy again. Transportation Minister Cliff Michael distributed a column among his party colleagues that referred to Joe Clark as a "pompous ass" for his position on sanctions. The article, which appeared in Michael's home-town newspaper, also called Archbishop Desmond Tutu a "clown" and said apartheid was a "Sunday school picnic compared to the despots that Canada trades with and calls friends." Although he hadn't written it, Michael said he sympathized with the views expressed in the article.

The Babb affair lingered in the minds of some government strategists for several more months. Vander Zalm had long been considered right-wing on many topics, but issues like South Africa were "non winners." Six months later, in May 1987, George Gibault, a policy analyst in the premier's office, went so far as to send a confidential memo to David Poole, outlining some concerns.

Gilbault thought it would be a good idea to schedule meetings between Vander Zalm and the "Jewish and multicultural communities" in an effort to counter any suggestions that the premier was linked to some of the more right-wing, reactionary organizations.

Poole rejected Gibault's suggestion outright, saying that such meetings could backfire. He instructed Ransford to respond to the policy branch. Ransford's memo stated: "The premier has clearly not in any way identified himself with these reactionary antisemitic organizations and, therefore, would not want to draw attention to perceived relationships with them through any affirmative-action type efforts."

Along with any long-term electoral damage it may have caused, the Babb affair showed some signs of what life would be like under Vander Zalm: no consultation with his advisers, his cabinet, or his caucus before embarking on a path that was sure to upset many people, some of whom were in government. His was a gut-instinct approach based on personal opinion, and it landed him in trouble.

Said one MLA: "Most sensible people of the political centre understand the South Africa issue is a very difficult one. Many people are violently opposed to apartheid and are against sanctions. But we knew Vander Zalm's understanding of that issue could be measured in microns, yet here he was our leader, blathering on about it."

Even more upsetting to many Socred MLAs was the feeling that such incidents detracted from the government's accomplishments. It was a pattern the government found increasingly hard to break.

Another scandal popped into view a few months later, in February 1987, when Victoria *Times Colonist* reporter Les Leyne revealed that Stephen Rogers, the environment minister, owned shares in a mining company that could possibly benefit from new boundary changes to a provincial park on Vancouver Island.

The boundary changes had been recommended by a government-appointed committee set up by Rogers's predecessor, Austin Pelton. The fact that the new environment minister held shares in a mining company that in turn had a claim inside a provincial park was more than enough to get people shouting conflict of interest.

Part of Rogers's problem was his name. The Rogers family, one of B.C.'s founding industrial clans, had built the Rogers' B.C. Sugar business empire. Stephen Rogers, an MLA since 1975, was only one of many Rogerses left in B.C., but he had the highest profile. He also had a lot of money invested in a lot of companies.

The story broke on Wednesday, February 25. Vander Zalm was at the Kootenays town of Cranbrook, in the southeast corner of the province, for a cabinet meeting. Just before Vander Zalm delivered a luncheon speech to the local chamber of commerce, two press gallery reporters finally caught up with him.

Yes, he had read the story. No, he had not had a chance to talk to Rogers about it.

"If the reports are correct, it does appear there could be a problem. If there's an apparent conflict we have to address it. He would have to divest himself of the shares or the trust," Vander Zalm casually told the two reporters, and then hurried to his lunch.

In response to a single story in one newspaper, Vander Zalm had quickly taken action.

By now it was almost noon. The two reporters filed their story. The premier's reaction left Rogers stunned. He faced an ultimatum: get rid of the shares or possibly leave cabinet altogether.

Anyone who invests in the stock market in a province where the resource companies that drive the economy spend much of their time digging up or cutting up the environment would have a hard time heading B.C.'s sensitive environment ministry. As Rogers, who had also served as Bill Bennett's environment minister, said to reporters at the time, "I guess you have to be holier than thou to be minister of environment or come from another planet."

Selling the shares was not as easy as it sounded. They were owned by a family trust held by himself and two other family members. The quick-tempered Rogers blew up at reporters on a couple of occasions because the more he tried to explain how he couldn't divest himself of the shares, the more obvious it became that he was out of the environment portfolio.

Rogers had long harboured a grudge against the media for what he considered to be its penchant for "going after" him, and for seemingly ignoring other cabinet ministers with stock portfolios. He had been dumped from cabinet once before–by Bill Bennett, in May 1985–for neglecting to disclose that he owned some shares in a pulp company while holding the environment portfolio. He remained ultra-sensitive about any public suggestions that tied him to the Rogers family fortune.

At one point, he had phoned a Vancouver *Sun* reporter and chewed him out–in a conversation that consisted almost entirely of profanities–because the paper sometimes referred to him as "an heir to the B.C. Sugar fortune."

The tag threatened the security of his children, he argued, adding he was only "one" heir of many and that it was not fair to constantly single him out. The paper agreed to change the reference in the future, but when it appeared again by accident two years later, Rogers again blew up, claiming there was a conspiracy among editors to "get him." He was arrogant and quick-tempered, and his relationship with the media alternated between wary acceptance and utter contempt.

Vander Zalm went one step further, announcing that Rogers's complex financial holdings pretty well precluded his remaining environment minister: "I expect he probably has other shares in the trust which perhaps at some later date may also be the subject of somebody alleging a potential conflict so he's got to address the whole problem."

Adding to Rogers's dilemma were the government's new conflict-of-interest guidelines—which were merely guidelines, not legally enforceable or even legislated into existence. Basically, they allowed Vander Zalm to decide what constituted a conflict.

Just one month earlier, for example, the NDP had alleged that Rogers was in a conflict situation because he owned shares in forestry giant MacMillan Bloedel and its parent company, Noranda Mines. Rogers denied the allegation. Vander Zalm agreed with his minister.

But now Rogers, who had never for a moment believed or acknowledged he was in a conflict situation, found himself moved out of environment and into the intergovernmental affairs ministry.

"Poole and Vander Zalm panicked and said, 'You've got to go,' " Rogers remembers. "It was done very hurriedly. In those days they hadn't managed a crisis because they hadn't had one to manage. . . . He cannot say no to a microphone. Anyway, he made the decision right there and then, and remember he was still a very popular guy at this stage."

In Victoria, the premier gathered the reporters in his office to announce Rogers's new job. Surprisingly, Vander Zalm said he didn't think Rogers was in a conflict situation either. It was all the media's fault, Vander Zalm said, reading from a statement while sitting at his desk.

"I do not accept those allegations. Thorough checks have disclosed no evidence of any benefits to the minister as a result of decisions he has made. However, these allegations—unfounded as they are—have been given wide publicity in the media. As a result, there is now a public perception that there could be a conflict of interest and I have therefore accepted his resignation."

It was pointed out to the premier that he had contributed to the "perception" by quickly acknowledging that there was an "apparent" conflict and by giving Rogers an ultimatum. And why was the case different from the previous "perception" regarding the MacMillan Bloedel shares?

Vander Zalm shrugged those questions off and continued his criticism of the media. He chided the reporters present and suggested they be more responsible. At the back of the room, David Poole nodded his head in agreement. Rogers had committed a mortal sin in Vander Zalm's media-induced reasoning: he had garnered bad publicity for the government.

To the public, it seemed like just another Stephen Rogers conflict story. Vander Zalm's instant decision to fire him, based on an unsubstantiated news story, was never apparent. Instead he looked like a decisive leader who would brook no nonsense when it came to conflict of interest.

Rogers was not to be the only minister to taste scandal during Vander Zalm's first six months in power. In February, a secretary named Donna Hall approached the attorney-general's office. She was uncomfortable about some of the things she knew about her former boss, forests minister Jack Kempf.

The outspoken Kempf had always been a little unusual. An MLA from the north country riding of Omineca, he quickly earned the nickname "Wolfman Jack." His deep voice, bushy eyebrows, bombastic manner, and endearing malaproprisms made him one of the legislature's unforgettable characters.

So when Donna Hall blew the whistle on her ex-boss, not everyone was surprised. Kempf, it seemed, had failed to pay back more than $10 000 in travel advances he had received as minister or during his time as a parliamentary secretary.

Vander Zalm acted quickly. He met with Kempf the morning of March 6 and asked for his resignation, then had the locks on Kempf's office door changed. Reporters were called to a news conference that afternoon, just as everyone was packing up for the weekend.

Kempf was shocked that Vander Zalm would demand that he resign before the accusations had been checked out by the comptroller-general's office (whose investigation was to take about a week).

Over the next few days, Kempf tried to avoid the press, with good reason. On one occasion, while being chased down a legislative corridor, he suddenly turned around and faced the mob of braying reporters. With characteristic pomposity, he puffed out his chest, stared into the television cameras and said very seriously, "I am not innocent of anything!"

Shortly afterwards he told a television interviewer that "my wife and I have been trying to figure out what else there is that we're guilty of."

While the comptroller-general continued his investigation, a few more stories emerged.

Kempf had been investigated by the RCMP in 1983 for possible influence peddling. A letter he had written–on his MLA stationery–to potential Chinese log buyers had allegedly given them the impression that Kempf had some sort of authority over export permits for logs. The six-month investigation eventually cleared him.

Kempf had also hired a friend of the family to help write his newspaper column and his constituency newsletter and had paid her out of ministry funds.

And it was eventually revealed by the Vancouver *Sun* that Kempf had engaged in some bizarre clandestine diplomacy. At the height of the trade dispute between Canada and the U.S. over lumber tariffs, Kempf had secretly discussed B.C.'s position with Washington state lumbermen. Although he claimed that he hadn't compromised the province's position in any way, the news came as a shock to Vander Zalm and federal trade minister Pat Carney, who was outraged.

Kempf saw himself as the champion of the little guy, who in this case was the small logging operator. Consequently he had made enemies among the powerful forest companies. He later blamed them for his downfall. But it was really just the latest in a series of questionable actions that tripped up Jack Kempf. The comptroller-general said Kempf had acted improperly in failing to pay back the travel advances and did not meet standards of accountability in "certain significant financial matters."

The evidence, said Kempf, was "frivolous," but Vander Zalm kept him out of cabinet. Kempf, embarrassed, enraged, and unwilling to admit he had made any mistakes, stood in the legislature in late March and dramatically announced that he was quitting the Social

Credit caucus. He crossed the floor to sit as an independent, where he would be free to criticize the government's forestry policy at will. A few Socreds, basically glad to see a loose cannon gone, jokingly invited the NDP to ask him to join their caucus.

Political scandals are something of a tradition in B.C. The public almost expects them from time to time, and it became apparent that Vander Zalm's administration would not differ from previous governments in that regard. But two unexpected events played out over a period of weeks early that spring, though not scandals of any sort, once again provided ample evidence that things were going to be a little different under Vander Zalm.

In March, the premier, a devout Roman Catholic who had vowed to bring "Christian principles" to government, quietly decided to allow a Christian group to use a room in the legislature building for prayer meetings once a week, during the lunch hour. His office never announced it, of course, but word leaked out to reporters through the office of the sergeant-at-arms.

For Vander Zalm's political enemies, the story was too good to be true. Here was the premier of B.C. giving a legislature room rent-free to a fundamentalist Christian group while shutting out non-Christian groups wishing to engage in religious activities.

The designated "prayer room" was a nondescript, small third-floor space with a large table and several chairs. The first Wednesday meeting was uneventful. A few strongly religious Socred MLAs showed up—Nick Loenen (Vander Zalm's seatmate in Richmond), Terry Huberts from nearby Saanich, and Duane Crandall, a Seventh-Day Adventist from the Rocky Mountains—and only a handful of reporters bothered to take a peek.

About twenty people, gathered under the leadership of Ray Jansen of the fundamentalist group Prayer Canada, prayed for everyone from Margaret Thatcher and local cabinet ministers to the reporters present. Opposition critics, of course, said that the cabinet ministers needed all the help they could get.

For the first two weeks, a few reporters and some curious onlookers attended to check things out. If nothing else, it was at least an interesting place to eat lunch. Meanwhile, on the front lawn of the legislature, a young man named Lloyd Hart quietly pitched a tent, moved in, and began a hunger strike to protest the government's decision to lift its seven-year moratorium on uranium exploration.

Reporters were sceptical of Hart's starvation claims, especially when wine bottles and pizza boxes were occasionally found outside his tent. Hart maintained that the food and drink had been consumed by his supporters. The media mostly ignored Hart until he hit on the idea of liberating the prayer room.

Hart and a small knot of his supporters showed up at the prayer room one Wednesday in early April. And, as media reports gleefully put it at the time, "all hell broke loose."

Hart's group, dressed in green fatigues, ponchos, hand-woven dresses, and tie-dyed T-shirts, was like an invading army. They included environmentalists, Moslems, pagans, and even a self-described Sufi (a member of an Islamic sect whose goal is communion with God through contemplation and ecstasy). And they were not without tactics: they showed up early and got all the chairs. Jansen came to the meeting a bit late to find his bewildered followers standing outside the door, unsure whether to enter or not. Reporters salivated at the impending confrontation.

"You've got some warfare on your hands inside there, Ray," one man said darkly. "They're not praying to Jesus. They're praying to someone else in there."

Jansen began by trying to interrupt one man praying for an end to "the disruption of the food chain." He was shouted down.

A brief silent prayer ensued, but it was punctuated by a woman wailing in a corner. A young couple groped and kissed each other in the name of the Lord.

Jansen tried again. "I'd like to open this prayer meeting," he started.

"It's already open, sir," a voice interjected.

A few of Hart's people chanted mantras, which didn't go over well with Jansen's group. Shouting matches ensued.

"This is supposed to be a peaceful meeting," one person yelled.

"It is not! It's supposed to be a prayer meeting!" screamed another.

One of Jansen's people, a guitar-carrying man named Fred Freitag, shouted: "Tolerance is ignorance!" Everyone mulled that over briefly.

"Peace is not always tranquillity, sometimes it can be more excit-ing," a woman shouted back.

"I heard something about Buddha here, and I didn't like it," Freitag replied.

"Buddha and Jesus were friends!" screamed another woman.

"Who says?" said another.

It all proved too much for the woman arguing with Freitag. She threw up her hands and said: "Why doesn't everyone just drop their egos and start loving one another?"

Her request was ignored.

A man watching the meeting from a hallway said, between bites on his baloney sandwich, "It's sure not like Sunday school."

No, it sure wasn't. Jansen stormed out to look for security guards, who refused to get involved, although they joined the growing crowd of fascinated onlookers. By this time, word had spread through the building, and some office workers also wandered by to take in the action.

Jansen went back inside, laid his head on the table, and silently prayed. Around him, Hart's people chanted and sang.

That night, television viewers were treated to lengthy and bizarre footage, which eventually embarrassed the government into closing down the prayer room.

But that didn't stop Hart. The front lawn was still available for uranium protests. More supporters showed up and pitched tents.

Hundreds of tourists visited the legislature daily during the summer, and hundreds more walked by the buildings. The setting was remarkably beautiful–bright flowers, acres of finely trimmed grass, grand old buildings, and the nearby harbour. But suddenly several large tents had begun to grow right in the middle of the postcard.

No matter which window of his office he looked out of, Vander Zalm couldn't help but see Hart's tent on the lawn. At one point, accompanied by David Poole, he quietly walked over to Hart's tent and had a little chat with the protest leader. But it was no use. Vander Zalm, who deliberately did not tell the media about his visit, was mainly worried about the flowers and the tourists; the right to protest did not concern him.

Then, one day in April, acting on orders from the premier's

office, the troops moved in. Staff from the sergeant-at-arms' office waded into the tent city and not so gently hoisted the protesters out of the tents. Then they tore down the tents and loaded all the protesters' belongings onto a flatbed truck.

It was great television. The sergeant-at-arms' staff, mainly retired military men, were past fifty years of age and spent most of their days making sure that tour groups didn't stray out of bounds and reporters observed the dress code.

Now they suddenly found themselves in a whole new ball game. Sometimes it took three of them to lift a single protester. And when they finished with one, another would slip between their legs and wriggle back inside a tent.

They finally figured out that the best way to deal with the situation was to dismantle the tents while the protesters were still inside, then cart the equipment away piece by piece.

The NDP supported the protesters' goal of blocking uranium exploration, and a few party MLAs were on the lawn, viewing the mayhem. Party leader Bob Skelly, almost apoplectic with rage, screamed at the guards to stop.

In the legislature, the NDP claimed that the Socreds lacked the authority to police the front lawn. Tent responsibilities, said the NDP, lay with the speaker's office. The Socreds mocked the Opposition for agitating for the "right to tent."

Repeated incidents culminated in what was supposed to be the final showdown. Hart's group vowed to erect a huge tent city covering the entire lawn. The weary guards, uncomfortable with all the media attention, braced themselves.

Instead of large canvas tents, however, Hart's supporters erected tiny paper ones all over the lawn–an anti-climax, to say the least. The guards employed a weapon they perhaps should have thought of at the beginning: they turned on all the sprinklers.

The tiny tent city quickly turned soggy. The protesters went home dejected, the guards went back to boring hours standing in the legislature's corridors, the reporters went back to covering politics, and Hart, in a last act of defiance, squatted in the middle of an official legislative display commemorating the Queen. The guards, who brook no nonsense when it comes to disrespect for royalty, had had enough of him by this time and literally threw him out through a side door. Hart screamed "police brutality," but the media ignored him.

Protests and heated demonstrations were nothing new in B.C., but this was like a month-long circus. People speaking in tongues and living in tents in the house of government were giant steps into the theatrical.

For Vander Zalm, trying to establish himself as a political leader with serious plans for government, the scandals and sideshows only contributed to the growing sense that this perhaps was a directionless government, easily able to veer out of control at any moment.

Indeed, if the public had been able to peer inside the operations of government at that time, they would have been less than reassured. Hidden from public view was a chaotic and disorganized administration that was undergoing fundamental changes under the new premier's direction.

Everything from the mail to the bureaucracy was in disarray. It would be quite a while before things improved.

Each day, a mail avalanche fell on the premier's office. Bill Bennett had received a few letters, but nothing compared to the 4000 pieces of mail a month that went through Bill Vander Zalm's office.

There was no system to deal with the new load. Aside from opening and sorting the mail, it all had to be logged onto a computer. The idea was to keep track of who was writing to the premier and what the correspondence was about. As well, the premier's office did not want to embarrass itself by sending out two replies to one letter, especially if those replies were not consistent.

"People would take mail to Fantasy Gardens or mail it there directly, and the letter would be about problems they were having or something they wanted done or even invitations for the premier to some event," remembered a former office aide.

"So what the premier would do is go home on the weekends and open all the mail and he'd take his dictaphone. . . . He'd bring all the stuff back in a cardboard box on Monday and there'd be a bunch of tapes and all the letters."

Adding to the confusion was the fact that little of the correspondence was actually recorded on the computers. Instead, Dorothy Sage, Vander Zalm's personal secretary, would type all of the premier's letters herself and then get Vander Zalm to sign them.

Off the letters would go, sometimes without the correspondence people ever being informed. "It was ending up that Dorothy would type up one letter and these people would not only write to Fantasy Gardens but also to Victoria," the former office aide remembered. "They'd send two letters, maybe sometimes even copies. We'd respond from Victoria with one letter and Dorothy would be responding to the same letter in a totally different way based on what the premier had dictated into his dictaphone."

Dorothy Sage was one of Vander Zalm's most faithful servants. She had been his secretary for a time when he served in cabinet under Bill Bennett, and then had moved into the premier's office. But no matter how hard she tried, she simply could not handle the entire correspondence load herself.

The carpeted floor around her desk would sometimes be littered with letters. There was no system to match Vander Zalm's taped response with the proper letter. Sage would have to try to match them all up as well as perform her other duties.

"It was ridiculous. Some of these letters went through four drafts. It was a colossal waste of time. It was all done on typewriter and it took hours. And then the premier would insist on editing the letter and it would go back for another revision," one office worker recalled.

Vander Zalm admits correspondence was a big problem. "I used to get every letter on my desk. Everything that came in, like hundreds of pieces of mail. And I found that even if I worked around the clock I couldn't get to it all. It was impossible."

Things got so bad that the correspondence headaches would consume a large part of weekly staff meetings in the premier's office. Instead of discussing policy or strategy, top government officials sat around talking about problems with the mail.

Vander Zalm became a one-man ombudsman's office, promising almost everyone he talked to that he would meet with them to look at their particular problem. He assigned staff to follow up on problems explained to him by people who visited him at Fantasy Gardens or called him on radio talk shows.

Compounding the disarray was Vander Zalm's chronic lateness and his stubborn refusal to play by the rules when it came to scheduling engagements. He constantly made commitments to attend openings or speak at luncheons. His staff was often the last to know about such promises, and sometimes found themselves having to break the news to disappointed supporters.

"People saw me on the street or wherever and they would be inviting me places and I'd say, 'Okay, sure,' " Vander Zalm recalls. "I found it difficult to turn people down."

Says Ransford: "He would want to go to everything or nothing. And then you'd suggest things to him and he'd put you through this whole thing of justifying it. It was a bit of a game with him, I think. He did not understand how local political things worked. He couldn't understand why when you went to an event, why he and Lillian couldn't just go. Like, why do we have to work up all this paperwork? He didn't understand that there are all kinds of work that goes into these kinds of things. He thought they just happened."

Vander Zalm complained to his staff about the many constituency associations that demanded his time around the province. Once there, of course, he turned on the charm and dazzled the crowd of Social Credit supporters. But he kept insisting on meeting what he called "real people." He never really explained to his staff what he meant by that, but he evidently felt those people did not exist in Victoria. So he tried to convince his staff to schedule a minimum of engagements in the capital. He once sent Ransford a letter he received at Fantasy Gardens, a request by a Surrey dance company for his attendance at a function. "Good opportunity to meet Real People," Vander Zalm had scrawled on it.

Meanwhile Lillian Vander Zalm would sometimes independently book an engagement for herself and her husband, not knowing or caring that the date was already filled on the premier's calendar.

And Dorothy Sage would also personally book people while Vander Zalm was in Victoria, ushering them in to see the premier.

Despite the organizational problems, Vander Zalm occasionally complained that too many people were responsible for scheduling.

Ransford eventually left that position to become David Poole's executive assistant.

But answering the mail and attending ribbon-cuttings were not the only things Vander Zalm had problems with in his office.

Just after the election, Vander Zalm became obsessed with government spending. He was convinced that large amounts of money were being wasted, and he was suspicious of some firms long associated with the Bennett government. He asked the comptroller-general's office to supply a computer printout of all the contracts the government had issued in the first month after the election. A two-foot-high stack of paper came back.

The review confirmed some of Vander Zalm's suspicions, at least in his own mind. "This is crazy," he said to his staff at one point. "Why are we spending so much money?"

He set up a system that required all government contracts over $5000 to be approved by the premier's office. Three top-level aides were responsible for the time-consuming task. They would put questionable expenditures on Poole's desk, where they would often sit, ignored or forgotten. Poole simply did not have the time to go through them all, despite Vander Zalm's wishes.

The government ministries, however, needed that authorization before they could spend the money on contracts, and they would complain loudly if they didn't get it. Finally, after four hectic months, Vander Zalm abandoned the system. Contracts could once again be handed out without his approval, unless they were for more than $100 000.

Vander Zalm recalls: "It created a lot of work and it probably slowed things down some. We saved a lot of money. I think over the first few months we saved over a million dollars in contracts that weren't necessary." But while the government may have abandoned some contracts, total contract spending actually increased during Vander Zalm's first years in office.

Vander Zalm's obsession with detail led him to read every line of all the cabinet orders he was required to sign. "Once, we were to drive to the airport together and I went into his office to pick him up," Grace McCarthy recalled.

"He was sitting at his desk, reading this big stack of orders. He actually read every one of them, trying to catch something that wasn't right. I told him he didn't have to actually read them all since his ministers had already done that. But he insisted."

Looking back, Vander Zalm agreed that he was almost fanatical about small details like the fine print on orders-in-council. The approach was part self-educational, part distrust of bureaucrats. "If I was to do it over again, I would do it exactly the same way. Unless you read them all initially, you don't know what all these orders are," he recalls.

Publicly, Vander Zalm was a man of action, a hands-on premier who made decisions fast and who cut through bureaucratic red tape. But he was quite a different man inside his office. While his government drifted along in a disorganized state, Vander Zalm spent much of his time–and the time of senior officials and aides–looking after small details. Far from not being able to see the forest for the trees, Vander Zalm had a hard time seeing the trees for the leaves.

The structural changes in government and the changing role of the premier's office set the stage for the crises that would occur over the next two years. Despite Vander Zalm's oft-stated vow to decentralize the decision-making process, the exact opposite began to occur. By January 1987, the premier's personal staff totalled forty-six people at a cost of about $1.5 million. By comparison, Bill Bennett budgeted for only thirteen people in his office.

Of course, Bennett used other government appointees as well, seconding them from various ministries when he needed them. But Vander Zalm kept his staff working for him at all times.

Vander Zalm's staff was organized into branches dealing with policy, politics, and administration, but all branches reported to David Poole, whose gradual accumulation of power made everyone except the premier uneasy.

Poole's responsibilities included giving the premier political advice, overseeing policy development, managing the bureaucracy, and dealing with the Social Credit Party–a massive workload for a former college administrator who had less political experience than most of the people he was boss to.

Bennett had divided those responsibilities among two or three officials. Since some tasks (dealing with the caucus, firing bureaucrats, making tough political decisions) were more sensitive than others, Bennett thought it better to distribute them over several people's shoulders.

But Vander Zalm wanted to work with just one person. Such an approach minimized Vander Zalm's contact with other individuals in government. He told Poole to follow one maxim at all times: "Get things done." Results, not methods, counted.

To "get things done" meant exerting some control over the bureaucracy, Vander Zalm and Poole reasoned. So Poole took control of the deputy ministers, the most powerful bureaucrats in government.

Deputy ministers usually possess considerable political and administrative skills. Their bosses may come and go, but deputy ministers generally stick around until a new political party takes over government—and even then, a few survive.

In early April, Vander Zalm did something no premier had done in nearly twenty years. He shuffled nearly all the deputies. Not only that, he re-assigned the deputies without letting the ministers pick the ones they wanted.

As well, a new wrinkle was introduced: from then on, deputies were to report to none other than David Poole every Monday morning. They would provide updates on ministry initiatives and discuss future government policy. They were also there to get instructions from Poole.

Vander Zalm had invested almost total power and trust in an unelected official—a move that was precisely the opposite of a key promise he had made during the leadership and election campaigns. As a minister under Bill Bennett, Vander Zalm had come to despise political aides like Norman Spector and Patrick Kinsella. He distrusted them and thought they wielded too much influence.

It's true that the "fresh start" shuffle was long overdue: some deputies had served in their minstries for more than a decade. As well, some capable and talented bureaucrats deserved promotion from the lower ranks. For example, Frank Rhodes, who would eventually become Vander Zalm's deputy after David Poole left, was languishing in the attorney-general's ministry as an assistant deputy.

But some ministers, particularly the new ones and McCarthy, were uneasy about the shuffle.

Says Grace McCarthy: "The new ministers were very concerned because, you see, they didn't know their portfolio at all and they had deputies that knew them like the back of their hand. And therefore, to then change two or three or four months into the administration was upsetting to them."

McCarthy had long sought a deputy shuffle but questioned Vander Zalm's timing. She also disliked not being able to choose her own deputy and was especially upset at the new meetings between Poole and the deputies.

"It has been a time-honoured tradition in government that you choose your own deputy. You don't choose them above and beyond your premier's wishes. Back in the days that Bill [Bennett] was there, I wouldn't think of hiring a new deputy without going to him first. But this was a whole new way of doing things."

It certainly was. It planted the seeds of the ultimate break between those two old friends, McCarthy and Vander Zalm, and it was also one more grab for power by the premier's office and its chief denizen, David Poole.

"[The deputies] were told very clearly that they were to report directly to the premier through David Poole," McCarthy said. "There you found a whole new strength to the arm of David Poole."

Although the deputies were ostensibly reporting to the premier through Poole, in reality they had little contact with Vander Zalm himself, aside from a few private dinners the premier would throw for them. Instead, Poole gave them the orders.

"You must remember one thing always," Poole told the deputies at one of their first meetings. "You work with your ministers, but you work for the premier."

Naturally, the new structure created friction between ministers and their deputies. The trust between some of them began to collapse. Suddenly, deputies were informing their ministers how certain programs were going to be conducted and why. Because of their constant meetings with Poole, the deputies were usually one step ahead of the ministers when it came to knowledge of upcoming programs and policies.

Deputies sometimes found themselves having to cancel meetings with their ministers because they had to attend the sessions with

Poole. To miss one without an excuse–and a mere meeting with a minister was not necessarily an acceptable excuse–meant that a deputy risked Poole's considerable wrath. And Poole also made it quite clear that people considered to be "on-side" would find it easier to get their way.

Being "on-side" meant supporting the premier and Poole over any individual minister.

"There was a saying among the deputies about that time. You had to be 'on the train.' And we used to say, 'the train's left the station and you better be on it.' You had to be on that train with Poole," one deputy recalls.

Poole's arrogant, cavalier manner didn't help. Ministers waiting outside his office for an appointment were sometimes summoned inside by Poole with a snap of his fingers. But not all the bad blood was Poole's fault. Some ministers–notably McCarthy–and deputies didn't like having their cozy nests disturbed by two people they considered to be inexperienced and uninformed.

The new system had been devised by Poole after he talked with some senior bureaucrats from other provinces during a first ministers' conference in Vancouver in November 1986. He had quickly seen that such a system could aid in following Vander Zalm's top order to him: "Get things done."

By controlling the deputies, Poole knew he could cut through red tape and even bypass cabinet to implement whatever Vander Zalm wanted. Any premier is largely inaccessible, even to his own cabinet. There is only so much time in a day to meet with people. Vander Zalm was no exception. Poole, therefore, became the link between cabinet and the premier's office and provided decisions and opinions for individual ministers.

Some ministers, like Lyall Hanson, Brian Smith, and Stephen Rogers, didn't mind the new system because they knew they could get a quick answer from Poole without having to wait to see the premier. But others, like McCarthy, hated it. She had enjoyed access to Bill Bennett and she expected the same with Vander Zalm. Resentment slowly grew. Poole became aware of it, but he did nothing to stop it.

Meanwhile, even Vander Zalm's relations with his own office staff were cool. For all his public charm and slap-on-the-back friendliness, Vander Zalm was not a warm man to those around him. Although he wasn't one to lose his temper, he was not outgoing.

His manner was in direct contrast to that of his predecessor. Although to the public Bennett appeared unemotional and aloof, within his own office he was friendly and almost jovial at times. He commanded the fierce respect and loyalty of his staff, who arranged for a rose garden on the legislature lawn to be named for him when he left office.

"Bennett used to come in and he'd go and talk to the secretaries and get to know them. In the morning, he'd come and take his cup of coffee and go and sit down at one of the secretaries' desks and ask how they were doing," a former premier's office worker recalled.

"But Vander Zalm never came out of his office to talk to the secretaries. He'd come in that back door and walk straight into his office. He'd come out, and maybe talk to Dorothy, at her office or near David's office, but he wouldn't come out of that little area there. He never went upstairs, never, ever walked around the office. He didn't even know who was in those offices upstairs, because he never went up there, or down in the basement."

Vander Zalm could also be cold even to top aides like Ransford, Kay, and Bill Bachop, his press secretary. "He didn't like staff around, period. It got better near the end [of 1988]. Near the end it wasn't so bad," Ransford recalled.

Vander Zalm also didn't like seeing his staff–except Poole– anywhere but at their desks in Victoria. If one of them should happen to show up in the Vancouver cabinet offices where Vander Zalm's other office is, the premier would suspect they were simply "goofing off," according to Ransford.

But in those first few months following the election, Vander Zalm still enjoyed a warm relationship with the institution he perhaps valued the most–the media.

Vander Zalm would frankly tell reporters that he expected them to "do their part" and tell the province all about the smiling new premier and his innovative ideas.

He knew he could get on television or on the front page almost every day simply by making himself available. Reporters thought nothing of sending notes into cabinet meetings, asking the premier to spare a few minutes. He usually obliged. He knew how important the noon radio newscast was to radio reporters, how long television reporters needed to put together a story for that night's newscast, and when the Vancouver *Sun*'s two morning deadlines were. Whenever possible, he tried to accommodate all of them.

During the first year or so of his administration, Vander Zalm rarely turned down reporters' requests for "scrums," those large, impromptu news conferences that are reminiscent of the rugby huddles from which they get their name. Many politicians avoid scrums or participate reluctantly. The setting does not favour the person being interviewed. The camera lights can be blinding, and the crush of bodies means the temperature gets hot very quickly. With reporters and cameramen jostling each other for position, shoving matches sometimes break out, and occasionally a microphone hits the subject in the face.

The questions come fast and furious from the reporters, who listen carefully for the subject to pause for breath so they can jump in with their own question. One question might be on education funding, the next on health care, the next on the environment, then back to education again.

With microphones and cameras jammed in one's face, ready to catch a slip of the tongue, the right answer or at least a good "non-answer" is essential. Losing one's temper looks very bad on television.

Yet Vander Zalm would patiently stand amid the crowd of reporters while television cameramen set up their gear. He would carefully smooth his hair, flash his smile, politely ask when the reporters would like to begin, and rarely walk away until all the questions had been exhausted.

Reporters' arms would get tired from holding microphones in the air for twenty minutes or so. Television cameramen sometimes ran out of film. If, for some reason, a scrum only lasted a few minutes, Vander Zalm would pretend to complain. "What, is that it? What's wrong with you guys today?"

Once, just after the election, he held a lengthy scrum with reporters outside the Vancouver cabinet offices and answered questions on a number of topics, from the IWA dispute to the lumber tariff dispute to the upcoming cabinet shuffle. Reporters left the scrum dazed, trying to determine which of the premier's many pronouncements was the "lead." Radio reporters spent all morning cutting up tape. Vander Zalm created twelve separate stories—on everything from a forest industry strike to an upcoming cabinet shuffle—that day from the one scrum. Radio listeners were treated to different ones almost every hour throughout the day.

Covering the last few years of Bill Bennett's administration had not been easy for reporters. Relations between many of the MLAs were strained, and that tension spilled over into the press gallery. As well, Bennett ran a secretive government in which the news outflow was as tightly controlled as possible.

So when Vander Zalm rolled in, the change in the government's attitude was like a breath of fresh air for the press gallery. Vander Zalm chanted "open government" like a mantra, and that meant access for reporters. As had happened when he was a cabinet minister, he was often late for meetings as premier because he always stopped to chat with any reporter he met in the legislative corridor. Of course, much of the government was operating as secretively as ever. Getting details on government spending, for example, was always difficult. But that was almost forgotten in the constant, hectic encounters with the new premier.

The number of news stories out of Victoria increased, and so did the level of enthusiasm in the press gallery. One of the few downsides for reporters was the fact that much of their time was spent covering the utterances of one man, while other parts of government were ignored. Now it seemed that "scoops" could be obtained only if one reporter had a private interview with the premier.

The scrums with Vander Zalm were mandatory for reporters. To miss a "Vander scrum" was to miss a potential page-one story. Independent reporting sometimes suffered as a result. Sometimes the cabinet was the last to know about upcoming government policies. Ministers would occasionally be informed by reporters about a new program in their ministry. The reporter would have gotten the information from the premier, who had neglected to tell the minister.

Even Vander Zalm's staff was often caught off guard. Most

politicians insist on having one of their own assistants attend scrums and tape the proceedings so they can be protected against any misquotes. But since Vander Zalm didn't allow any of his staff to attend scrums, they would frequently be unaware of what he had said until they heard it on the radio newscasts.

Recalls Ransford: "We would never tape his stuff. I find it amazing that we didn't do that. I used to tell him that right at the beginning. He'd get pissed off if we went out there with a tape recorder. He just didn't like it. He'd go, 'Why do you have to tape this stuff? Why do I have to have you standing there? You're not a media guy.' So we wouldn't know what he was telling you guys in the scrum.

"So he'd come in in the morning and he'd go into his office and we'd turn the news on and hear something the premier said. And you'd say, 'Premier, did you say that?' 'Oh yeah, I told them that outside this morning, didn't you know?' So there was no preparedness.

"He would come in in the morning and tell you guys something. You guys would go and make a big news story about it. The minister wouldn't know about it, because we wouldn't know about it to tell the minister. And then you'd go and interview the minister and he'd be caught off guard and didn't know what to say. I would suggest easy ways of remedying that and it would never be accepted. I'd suggest a form and structure and he would say, 'Oh, we don't have to do that.'"

Vander Zalm's stubbornness sometimes had his aides beating their heads against the wall. But the premier's openness to the media was working in his favour. For all the internal problems, the public image was holding together. The simmering disputes between ministers and the premier's office took the form of occasional grumbles voiced privately. The media coverage would not begin to hurt the government for a few months yet, and the premier was still smiling his way through every day.

Publicly, the "fresh start" lingered. The Vander Zalm that had emerged behind the scenes–the man obsessed with small details, who could not grasp organizational basics like scheduling and correspondence, who made spur-of-the-moment decisions without consulting anyone, who didn't understand the propriety of his own office, and who consolidated as much power as possible in that office–would be revealed bit by bit over the next two years. The fresh start was beginning to wear thin only to those inside government.

All the King's Men

During the first two years of his mandate, Bill Vander Zalm was accompanied everywhere by two men who constantly hovered nearby, hanging on his every word and being protective. One was pudgy, short, and tired-looking; he became the second most powerful man in government. The other was loudly dressed, garrulous, and friendly; he became the last survivor of Vander Zalm's inner circle of friends and advisers.

The two men were David Poole and Bill Kay, respectively. Poole was Vander Zalm's principal secretary, top political adviser, time manager, policy analyst, confidant, and deputy premier. Kay was the premier's driver, bodyguard, valet, sounding board, and man Friday.

There was also a third friend, one who was rarely seen in public with Vander Zalm: a large, hot-tempererd millionaire businessman who had come up the hard way. Peter Toigo was a restaurateur, hotel owner, and dog-food manufacturer whose association with Vander Zalm would plunge the two of them into a long, steadily worsening controversy that would include an RCMP investigation—that turned up nothing—of their involvement with each other.

The three men had two things in common. Each was relatively new to the game of politics and each had only known Vander Zalm a short time. Unlike most political leaders, Vander Zalm did not choose old cronies or associates to be his advisers.

Other figures fluttered about the edges of Vander Zalm's inner circle, which was a bizarre coterie of friends and advisers whose common denominator seemed to be inexperience and a lifetime spent on the outside trying to get in. There were few business establishment types and no political insiders. There were no Social Credit party veterans, no women, and no cabinet ministers. In many ways, these misfits and amateurs were like Vander Zalm himself—unsophisticated, slightly eccentric, and out of the mainstream. Some liked Vander Zalm's right-wing views; others saw a chance to further their own ambition through him.

Less than one year after coming to Victoria as an executive assistant to a cabinet minister, David Poole had become Vander Zalm's top political adviser and principal secretary.

Before then, Poole had been a relatively unknown career administrator and a sometime backroom political hack. He had always been a manager and organizer instead of an on-field player. In school, he preferred managing teams and clubs to actually playing in them.

Poole, the second of four children, was born in Toronto on February 26, 1944. Three years later, his family moved to the small manufacturing town of Brantford, Ontario, home town of hockey superstar Wayne Gretzky.

His staid, conservative father was an accountant for a local manufacturer. He instilled ambition in his children. Poole's older brother, Douglas, is a Harvard graduate working in Switzerland as a commodities broker. His younger brother, Richard, is a Toronto lawyer whose wife, Dianne, was elected to the Ontario legislature as a Liberal. Poole's only sister, Margaret, is a teacher in Vancouver.

His parents sent Poole away to Ridley College, a private boys' school in St. Catharines, Ontario. The school still employed the rigid old boys' system in which seniors used junior students as personal servants, and caning was practised. Poole was the quarter-master of the cadet corps, where he managed supplies and honed his administrative skills.

Poole says he was shy and retiring before he entered Ridley. Its tough disciplinary attitudes and insistence on participation in sports and theatre brought him out of his shell.

After graduating from Ridley, Poole went to Saskatchewan, where he studied theology for more than a year. He considered becoming an Anglican priest, but eventually decided it wasn't his calling. After earning a bachelor's degree at Queen's University in Kingston, Ontario, he spent twenty years in the community college system in five provinces and became an able administrator, his specialty being "competency-based education," which matches college curriculum to skills graduates need in the working world.

Bill Cruden, president of St. Lawrence College, where Poole once chaired the academic division, told a Vancouver *Sun* interviewer that Poole was "clearly a person on the go. There are some people you expect to move onward and upward, and he was obviously one." Bob Gervais, principal of Northern Institute of Technology in Prince Albert, Saskatchewan called the hard-working Poole "task-oriented and a good people person. He'd meet and greet people, that's probably his forte."

Poole had two hobbies: politics and gourmet cooking. At one point, he toyed with the idea of opening a restaurant on Vancouver Island. While in Ontario, he successfully ran for school trustee–the only elected office he has ever held–and worked on some of Conservative MP Flora MacDonald's early campaigns.

By 1980 he was working at the Pacific Vocational Institute in Burnaby, a large Vancouver suburb. There, he met Elwood Veitch, the institute's chief bursar. Veitch asked Poole to manage his 1983 Socred MLA campaign, and Poole said yes. Veitch was elected, and nearly three years later, when he was elevated to the cabinet and needed a ministerial assistant, he phoned Poole.

Back in 1983, Vander Zalm happened to be in Victoria one day and saw Veitch and Poole eating lunch together in a nearby hotel.

"I was introduced to David Poole by Elwood. Right away, he seemed to me to be a man in a hurry. I liked that," Vander Zalm recalls.

The two men did not see each other again for almost three years. During the leadership race Poole, ironically enough, supported Grace McCarthy–who eventually would become his mortal enemy–

but despite backing a losing candidate he was able to move upward. The party needed a new executive director, and Poole fit the bill in many ways: he had no ties to the Bill Bennett administration and he got along well with Grace McCarthy, who wielded considerable power over such decisions. He got the job in August 1986.

When he started having more contact with Vander Zalm, the two men got along well. Poole felt comfortable telling Vander Zalm when he was wrong; Vander Zalm knew he could count on Poole for loyalty. Trust soon grew between them.

"The chemistry worked from the very first day," Poole recalls. "I don't know what it was, really. We just seemed to hit it off. He wasn't like that with too many people. Politicians don't trust too many people."

Vander Zalm actually trusted very few people. He did not have many close friends and tended to rely tremendously on people who treated him with utmost loyalty and respect. Although Vander Zalm barely knew him, Poole was one of those people.

During the election campaign, Poole was appointed co-campaign manager. Jerry Lampert, Vander Zalm's first principal secretary and an old associate of Bennett's, actually ran the campaign itself. Poole's job was to stay close to Vander Zalm on the campaign bus as they toured the province. It was during that hectic twenty-eight day campaign that a bond developed between the two men.

Immediately after the election campaign, Vander Zalm appointed Poole his principal secretary. Vander Zalm disliked having too many advisers. In fact, he wanted just one man he could rely on rather than having both a principal secretary and a deputy minister. The problem was that the principal secretary was a strictly political appointment, while the deputy premier was supposed to be a "nonpolitical" person to oversee the bureaucracy on a nonpartisan level.

A principal secretary dishes out political advice, deals with politics, the party, appointments, polling, and caucus relations, and exercises damage control. His job is to carry out the boss's wishes and protect him and his party above all else. But a deputy minister deals with policy and the bureaucracy. He cannot be concerned only with doing the premier's bidding; procedures and regulations largely govern how he does his job.

Few government administrations mix the two jobs; the result can be chaotic and explosive. Vander Zalm, who had little idea how the premier's office was supposed to operate in the first place, made things worse by choosing an inexperienced person to do both jobs. It would turn out to be possibly the worst move Vander Zalm made as premier.

The new structure led to charges that Poole had politicized the civil service, particularly given that Poole saw his job as implementing his boss's wishes. The motto Vander Zalm and Poole operated by was "get things done." Vander Zalm wanted no bureaucratic delays jeopardizing his plans, and Poole saw to it that none occurred.

Poole was the gatekeeper to Vander Zalm's office. All policy information and reports crossed his desk. Only he decided when a person or a report should go to Vander Zalm for consideration.

Poole's personality did not allow him to do things slowly. Consultation and studies were a waste of time. As Vander Zalm says, he was a man "in a hurry."

He was a workaholic, the type of person who is poor at delegating authority or tasks; who is so full of energy–and themselves– that they believe they have to do everything. Poole's hard-driving work habits were admired–he sometimes arrived at the office before 6:00 a.m. and did not leave until after 10:00 p.m.; frequently, his car was the only one parked outside the premier's office complex, the others having long left for home–but they also contributed to the chaotic nature of the premier's office. Only Poole, because he was the only one allowed to hold extended meetings with Vander Zalm, knew what was going on. Still, his reputation for hard work forestalled some of the sharper criticisms of his operating style.

Says former cabinet minister Stephen Rogers: "I actually had a lot of time for David Poole. But he didn't play his cards right."

One deputy said Poole had improved communication between the premier's office and senior bureaucrats, but that Poole didn't realize his limitations.

"I think that David Poole, had he had some prior background, could have been exceptionally useful to the government," remembers Grace McCarthy, his most vocal critic. "What he didn't have was the balance. But he did have an ability to work. And he wasn't afraid of hard work. His problem was that he didn't know what the parameters of his job were. He went beyond his job."

McCarthy feels that Poole's ambition got in the way. "He almost wanted to become premier, and when he gave the premier backing and so on, he did it through his own biases and not allowing the premier to make his own mind up. That influence was very great on the premier."

Poole remembers, "There were times when I had to say you can't do it this way, and [Vander Zalm] would listen. You don't really tell and advise. You work together. We had disagreements, but we worked together."

However, Poole maintains that his only role was to serve, not to lead. "People would say, oh, there's Poole telling [Vander Zalm] what to do again. Well, that just wasn't the case. We didn't sit around talking like that. We just wanted to get the job done. I don't think you can accuse me of running my own agenda. I was just doing what the premier wanted."

It is a comment that speaks volumes about David Poole: "Just doing what the premier wanted." Concern for the larger picture—the province, the party, the future—often took a back seat to the premier's whims. But any advice to a premier that overlooked those larger concerns would ultimately be bad advice.

Poole and Vander Zalm gradually become more isolated from the rest of the caucus and government. The two men closeted themselves for hours inside Vander Zalm's office for long "philosphical" discussions, and at night Vander Zalm frequently phoned his top aide at home to continue their conversations.

Cabinet ministers were taken aback by Poole's enormous power. He usually sat in on meetings between ministers and the premier. Vander Zalm would frequently stop the meeting and ask Poole for his opinion. Poole rarely left cabinet meetings, unlike his predecessors, who exited when certain political considerations were discussed. He also sometimes chaired meetings, and on at least one occasion, Poole actually *started* a cabinet meeting when Vander Zalm was late.

Poole's image as a haughty, ego-driven power lord was partly a function of his dealings with the media. His predecessors in the position had usually refused to allow themselves to be quoted by name by reporters, and would instead occasionally provide information on a strictly background, off-the-record basis. Poole, however, saw nothing wrong with being quoted on any number of topics.

His prominence did little to ease the egos of cabinet ministers who resented an unelected official being the government's chief spokesman. It also flew in the face of one of Vander Zalm's major campaign themes: to take power away from the "backroom boys" and put it back in the hands of elected people.

"You could almost see that this was the highest point of his life and that he was just revelling in the importance of it all," remembers Stephen Rogers.

Once, Poole wanted Vander Zalm, who was on a plane headed for Vancouver, to come back to Victoria. Two other aides suggested waiting until Vander Zalm had landed, but Poole picked up the phone, saying, "If I can't divert a plane in this province, who can?"

But there was another side to Poole, one of the public rarely saw. He was usually accommodating to reporters, even when his contact with them landed him in trouble with the cabinet. He did, however, occasionally lose his temper trying to extricate himself from various messes he had landed in. He genuinely disliked having to say "no comment," and he viewed most interviews as the chance to get his point of view across. They were also good for his ego. His sense of humour and his gift for playful banter rarely left him. And he was well liked by his staff for his calm, rational approach to thorny problems.

"He doesn't think in Machiavellian ways. He had a good gut sense and doesn't worry about the political consequences when it comes time to make a decision," says his executive assistant, Bob Ransford.

Poole's favourite saying was, "I'm not trying to play games with you." One of his nicknames was "Top Gun," after a hit movie about young macho fighter-plane jocks. He revelled in the name, which he acquired after a business magazine ran a cover story on him with that as the title. He even had a "Top Gun" baseball hat made up. He had other nicknames, too, including "Napoleon," a reference to his autocratic style and his lack of height. He had a distinct, staccato speaking style, which fit his manner of operation: always in a hurry.

Bright and a quick learner, he was able to grasp concepts and ideas in a flash and translate them into action. But he was not able to work with people who, theoretically at least, were supposed to have more power than he had. And in his haste to implement Vander Zalm's plans, he ran headlong into a basic truth about governments: they move very slowly. As well, certain processes are followed. Poole, on the other hand, frequently ignored such processes.

"We knew the resentment would build. I did some stupid things. But the rule was to get on with it, get it done. But yes, there were some politically stupid things done," he recalls. "Some things were not handled well from a human relations point of view."

Vander Zalm himself told the authors, "When it came to the political side of things, he had some problems. . . . If there was something needed doing, he was a gung-ho guy, he'll move things along. But it was also what did him in, in the end."

Bill Kay recalls, "Nobody worked harder than David Poole, and he was very smart. You could ask him any question and he knew the answer, real quick. Without him, a lot of things would never have got done. For example, the privatization program would never have got through so quickly were it not for Poole. He just made that thing go. But politically, he made a lot of mistakes. There's no question about that."

Poole served his master too well. In his feverish quest to ensure that his boss's every wish was granted, he occasionally anticipated how Vander Zalm felt about some things. He sometimes made the wrong move, once with horrendous results: pressuring a liquor branch official into putting a polling company owned by one of Vander Zalm's former associates onto the government's authorized list of such companies who were allowed to conduct neighbourhood referendums on local pub proposals. It was an appalling example of political pressure, all in the name of "getting things done." And his refusal to back down from confrontations with ministers such as McCarthy did not serve anyone in the government well.

But it was not all Poole's fault. After all, it was Vander Zalm who had hired him, and it was Vander Zalm who was unable to provide any guidelines to his top aide; both were so inexperienced when it came to running a government that they never realized how bad some of their mistakes were.

Poole's third nickname was "Rasputin," and he proved almost as hard to get rid of as the Russian monk. Eventually, however, his personality and style drove him out of government and the province. Unable to get a job in B.C., he fled to Ontario to work for Peter Toigo.

He has few regrets but is slightly bitter. "You know, we got a lot of things done. And we tried to have fun, too. We didn't take it all too seriously until near the end when things got pretty bad around there. We tried to keep our sense of humour. The thing that got to me was when I couldn't walk into a restaurant without someone yelling at me. That became just a bit too much," he told the authors.

As for Vander Zalm, he is reluctant to blame Poole. Indeed, the problems stem from Vander Zalm's very style, his insistence on centralizing power in his own office. As late as May 1989, Vander Zalm and Poole still chatted frequently—but by long-distance telephone, not sequestered in Vander Zalm's office.

The only other aide who enjoyed as much contact with Vander Zalm as did Poole was a burly ex-Navy brat named Bill Kay. Brusque, raw-edged, and unsophisticated, Kay was Vander Zalm's chauffeur, bodyguard, confidant, and occasional policy analyst. There are distinct differences between the two men: where Vander Zalm is smooth, charismatic, and charming, Kay is rough, raw, and coarse. But they also share certain traits: both are men of simple tastes, both are distrustful of "experts," and neither is very sophisticated.

Kay was Vander Zalm's shadow, and the two of them were quickly dubbed "the odd couple." If the premier walked from his office to a corner deli, Kay went with him. Vander Zalm never went back to his hotel at night alone; Kay always accompanied him. A recurring joke was that Kay was the only person in the premier's office who was qualified to do his job—he had a driver's licence.

Kay is a fastidious but eccentric dresser. His loud ties and louder shirts bring to mind Yogi Berra dressed as Don Cherry. He wears starched high collars and a wealth of jewellery. Sometimes he looks like an extra from a cheap gangster movie.

His voice is a gravelly rasp that suggests one too many drinks the night before. (In fact, he rarely touches alcohol.)

Kay lives in the hotel suite next door to Vander Zalm's. When the Premier is in Victoria, Kay calls on him shortly after 7:30 a.m. and helps pick out his suit of clothes. Vander Zalm is unable to put his own cufflinks on; Kay does that for him. The two men breakfast together, munching on bran flakes and discussing the day's news.

In Victoria, where they usually reside three or four days a week, Kay drives Vander Zalm to work each morning, steering the white Ford the three blocks to the legislature. Occasionally the two men walk.

In Vancouver, Kay is always the driver, picking Vander Zalm up at the downtown cabinet offices or at Fantasy Gardens and ferrying him around town. They fly over to Victoria on the government air shuttle together, and Kay drives him in from the airport. The two men constantly squabble while driving. "He's the world's worst back seat driver," Kay says.

Kay occupies an office just around the corner from Vander Zalm's, right next to that of the premier's personal secretary. On his walls are autographed pictures of astronauts, Bill and Lillian Vander Zalm, members of the premier's office staff, and Navy admirals and their ships.

Kay has spent most of his adult life serving people. Born in Chippewa, Ontario, in 1938, he joined the Canadian Navy when he was seventeen and soon became an officer's steward. For the next twenty-one years, Kay waited on officers.

Fed up with armed forces life, he struck out on his own. His marriage had ended in divorce in 1975 with no children. He landed in Calgary, where he took over a tennis club and then a golf club. "I didn't like all those wishy-washy tennis players. All they wanted to do was drink lemon tea and eat salads," he recalls.

In 1985, he moved to Vancouver. "For a while, I worked at an outfit that computerized homes. You phone something and it would turn on the jacuzzi, that sort of thing." That job lasted just six months.

Things were not going well. Kay was lonely and depressed. He had few friends in Vancouver. Job prospects looked bleak. Then Bill Bennett quit.

"Things weren't going all too well with me at the time and I was pretty down. I didn't know anybody. So I thought the leadership race wouldn't be a bad place to meet people and get involved again," he recalls.

He wasn't even sure what the Social Credit Party was—"I thought it was just one of those off-the-wall B.C. things where everyone brought their own tea or something"—but he phoned the party's office anyway. He was living in Richmond, which happened to be the location of Vander Zalm's campaign headquarters. The party office gave him the number of Fantasy Gardens.

"Who answered my call but Lillian Vander Zalm. I said I needed some information and she said why don't you talk to me. Well, that was great. I needed some of this positive stuff. I couldn't believe how exuberant she was, and I was at a real low ebb at that time," Kay remembers.

He showed up at party headquarters. "I did real joe jobs for a while, made boxes, took out the garbage, and made coffee."

One day early in the campaign, Vander Zalm needed to be picked up at the Vancouver airport. Could Kay go? "I went out there and Lillian saw me. 'Hi guy! How are you? Isn't this great?' Vander Zalm wasn't too interested in me, though," Kay recalls.

In fact, Kay was treated with downright suspicion in the early days. "They used to watch me in the office, see what I was xeroxing, that sort of thing. They were always eyeing me. One time, Lillian asked me, 'Bill Kay, are you a good guy?' She was always sizing me up back then."

Kay gradually started driving Vander Zalm to more places. Vander Zalm got a kick out of someone actually chauffeuring him around town and picking him up at the airport. No one had ever done that for him before. "Hey, look! It's Bill Kay! Hi, Bill Kay!" Vander Zalm would say when Kay arrived at the airport.

Soon Kay was spending more time with Vander Zalm than anyone else on the campaign. As someone with absolutely no experience, Kay fit right in. One day, he drove Vander Zalm to the airport. Campaign manager Charlie Giordano was supposed to accompany the candidate up north for a small tour of some ridings. At the last minute, Giordano couldn't make it, so Vander Zalm decided to go alone. Kay said that wasn't possible. "You're going to be the premier. You can't go alone," he told Vander Zalm.

Kay reached into his bag and pulled out a tie. "He was very impressed by the fact that I put a tie on," Kay remembers. Vander Zalm was also pleased to find that Kay had packed his pipe with tobacco for him. "He was really impressed. He looked at me and said, 'No one's done that for me before.' "

The two men flew off to Kitimat, and the sidekick act was born. By the time they reached Whistler for the leadership convention, Kay was part of Vander Zalm's inside circle. It helped that Lillian was, by now, a firm Kay supporter. She was grateful for the way he looked after her husband. Kay even ironed the premier's shirts.

During the election campaign, Kay was again Vander Zalm's special assistant and occasional driver. He was quick to make a name for himself. Early on, the campaign rolled into an Interior town and visited a prehistoric-style rock village. It looked like something out of a Flintstones cartoon. "Gee, I half expect Barney and Betty Rubble to show up here," said one of the organizers. Kay frowned and checked a piece of paper. "No, no, I don't think so. They're not on the guest list."

Kay, however, was nearly bounced from his position for driving Vander Zalm to a destination not on the official itinerary. David Poole and Jerry Lampert, the two campaign managers, thought he had too much influence over the premier. But he survived any attempt to remove him; by now Vander Zalm was his staunchest ally.

"I made it clear to them and everyone else: I worked for one man only, Bill Vander Zalm. I didn't work for the Party, I didn't work for anything else, just the premier," Kay says.

After the election, he moved to Victoria and the premier's office. He was the only person on the leadership campaign team, aside from the three MLAs, who made the transition. His official title was "special assistant to the premier." It was not immediately clear what his responsibilities would be. But he knew he would be serving Vander Zalm and no one else.

"I was used to pandering to people. I was used to being an aide. I knew how to participate in things and how to always be aware of the formalities," Kay says.

Kay's responsibilities shifted over time. For a year, he spent most of his time looking after many of the problems average citizens contact the premier's office about. At Vander Zalm's monthly "meet the premier" town hall meetings across the province, Kay would occasionally play host and then collect all the names and phone numbers of people who wanted the premier to look into their problem.

A similiar procedure was followed with Vander Zalm's monthly radio programs; the caller would be put onto Kay who gathered the necessary details. But Kay grew to dislike dealing with so many people and trying to find solutons to their problems. Much of the time, he was bored.

Kay distrusts and in general dislikes politicians and bureaucrats. He considers some of them nothing more than opportunistic, ambitious people who would desert their principles at the drop of a hat. As time wore on and as the government's crises worsened, Kay would become more convinced than ever of that. He got tired of being glad-handed by backbenchers and office seekers who were eager to cozy up to the premier's assistant in a bid to further their own careers. As Vander Zalm's one-time allies broke with him during the course of his first two years as premier, Kay's attitude toward them grew bitter.

But Kay emerged with his reputation still intact, partly because he deliberately distanced himself from policy decisions. "I learned in the Navy that sometimes it's a lot better if you don't know something."

His pleasant personality also helped salvage his reputation. Cheerful, friendly, and outgoing, Kay would often bring flowers for the premier's office secretaries, who doted on him. People often made fun of his unsophisticated manner and his lack of political acumen, but Kay let any criticisms slide off his back.

Kay also loved to banter with reporters and play his role as the premier's designated protector to the hilt. He would sometimes crawl out on the window-ledge of his second-floor office and threaten to jump if the crowd of reporters below did not leave.

Once, while entering a Social Credit convention alone instead of with the premier, Kay was besieged by reporters, demanding to know the whereabouts of Vander Zalm. Kay hunched up his shoulders, put his briefcase to his ear and whispered into it: "Mr. Premier, are you all right in there?"

He was devoutly loyal, but knew he could be out the door at any moment. "Kay used to always tell me: 'Remember, we're all expendable,' " remembers Bob Ransford.

Kay has tremendous respect for Vander Zalm, but admits that the premier often tries his patience. "I always tell him he has to behave more like a premier, to be more formal. He finally started taking my advice after a couple of years or so," Kay says. "He can be frustrating to work for."

One measure of the two men's close relationship was Kay's renewed interest in religion in 1987.

"I had been a Catholic but not baptized. I started escorting him to church and started learning more about it. I used to drive him to Saturday mass at 5:00 p.m.," Kay recalls. "I got involved in it and he encouraged me. He stood for me to be my sponsor in 1987, for me to be confirmed in the church."

However, "[Vander Zalm] treated Kay like shit sometimes," a former aide recalls, adding that the premier would make plans to have dinner with Kay and then not show up, or ask him to come to church one Sunday and then leave without him. Indeed, Kay worked long hours and many weekends and was always on call, for a salary just over $40 000 a year.

"I guess the premier would make it up from time to time, be really nice and everything. He'd say, 'It's just you and me Bill, we work together.' But there were times. . . ," the aide said.

Vander Zalm simply calls Kay his "Mr. Everything." When Kay was toying with the idea of leaving his office in the spring of 1989, Vander Zalm couldn't bear the thought. He would send him photographs, with inscriptions like "There'll be many more good times."

Kay makes it clear Bill Vander Zalm was the best thing that ever happened to him. "It's a long way from where I've been, let me tell you."

The third man in Bill Vander Zalm's inner circle was a large, rotund millionaire businessman who grew up in the mill town of Powell River and eventually settled in Delta, a community on the mouth of the Fraser River.

He was Peter Toigo, a backwoods entrepreneur. Before his friendship with Vander Zalm became public, he was not well known outside his own businesses, although he liked to think he was. He would come to regret having any public profile at all.

Toigo is a strong family man and is close to his sons, who are in real estate themselves. He moved both his mother and his mother-in-law to Ladner to be nearer their families. He doesn't smoke or drink, but, as his appearance indicates, he does like to eat.

Even as a young man, Toigo made it clear he was a man on the go. He worked in his father's general store in Powell River, cutting up meat in the back while thinking of ways to cut more lucrative deals.

He made his first business deal in 1949, when he was just seventeen: he bought a dairy farm for $30 000.

He soon closed the dairy and subdivided the land for housing. He then moved into apartment construction and other developments, all the while working in his father's store, still cutting meat.

After realizing that Powell River was not B.C.'s centre of business activity, Toigo relocated to the Lower Mainland in the mid-1950s. Instead of setting up shop in downtown Vancouver, however, he settled in Ladner, a farming community on the mouth of the Fraser River, and jumped into the real estate game.

Toigo arrived just as the area around Vancouver was starting to take off. The suburbs were burgeoning in the late 1950s and '60s and had developed a reputation for cutthroat development practices and cozy relations between municipal politicians and land developers.

In 1966, he gained controlling interest of a public company that sold mortgages. By 1969, he had moved into buying hotels. He went in on a deal with Vancouver investors Lawrence Shatsky and Louis Simkin to build a motel in downtown Vancouver. The other two partners eventually withdrew, leaving Toigo with Shato Holdings, the company that acts as corporate parent to most of his business interests.

But Peter Toigo's business world looked as if it would come crashing down around him in 1977, when he was the subject of bankruptcy suits, pursued for debts up to $50 000 by a development company and the Royal Bank of Canada.

One of Toigo's former associates, Walter Link, a retired Surrey businessman, told the Vancouver *Sun* that Toigo had come to him "tired and desperate."

"A muffler on his green Cadillac was dragging on the ground and he couldn't afford to fill up his gas tank. He was very depressed. He told me I was his last chance," Link said.

Link put him in touch with two mortgage brokers for the Winnipeg Mortgage Exchange, which was trying to develop Surrey land. The two brokers, Dwight DeMille and Bob Stevens, owned Thompson Valley Mortgages, the B.C. agent for Winnipeg Mortgage. In mid-1978, Toigo became a director of two companies with close ties to Thompson Valley. The companies were trying to develop land, much of it Surrey land formerly owned by Link.

By 1979 these developments had run into financial difficulty, and the Manitoba government appointed a receiver-manager to take over Winnipeg Mortgage.

But just before that, Toigo had negotiated an agreement that released him and DeMille and Stevens from a number of financial liabilities associated with the company. As well, the deal stipulated that one of his companies–as a major creditor–would get sole control of the Surrey land. Toigo eventually got the rezoning he sought for that land and developed it.

At that time, some Surrey land deals were the target of an RCMP investigation. Walter Link, the man Toigo had come to for help, was sentenced in November 1979 to three years in prison for conspiring with former Surrey mayor Ed McKitka–an old nemesis of Vander Zalm's–on a land deal and on charges of fraud and possession of stolen property.

Toigo's name surfaced once in some of the evidence against McKitka. An RCMP wiretap disclosed that he was in Link's office when disposal of stolen jewellery from a robbery was discussed by others. He testified about that incident as a Crown witness in the trial of one of the principals of that robbery.

Meanwhile, Toigo continued to make money. He had developed

much of the Surrey land into a shopping centre and residential subdivisions. When the real estate boom collapsed in the early 1980s, Toigo moved into the restaurant business.

His chief target was the White Spot chain of thirty B.C. restaurants, along with Kentucky Fried Chicken.

B.C. White Spot is a hallowed name in B.C. restaurant history. The chain was founded by colourful entrepreneur Nat Bailey, who gave his name to Vancouver's pretty baseball stadium. White Spot's most famous product was its hamburgers with "secret Triple-O" sauce. The deal included a catering service, which provides food to, among other places, Pacific Press, the company that publishes the Vancouver *Sun* and *Province* newspapers.

After hearing that General Foods, then the chain's owner, was interested in selling it, Toigo negotiated a heavily leveraged $38-million buyout in 1983. Initial financing came mainly from the Continental Bank, which put up $25 million, and General Foods, which gave $9.25 million in credit. As well, long-term financing came from an Ontario-based investment arm of a group of public-service and other pension funds.

The actual purchase of the White Spot chain didn't get Toigo much media coverage, but his company's constant fight against his employees' attempts to organize themselves into a union did. The chain went through a bitter ten-week strike in late 1988 that saw Toigo's company engage in some questionable tactics. It closed two outlets and threatened to close more if the strike was not settled quickly, it pressured the employees to decertify their union, and it deliberately published misleading and incorrect information in newspaper advertisements.

The provincial government's labour relations council blasted Toigo's company for its actions, although it did not blame Toigo personally. The company was found guilty of unfair labour practices and was ordered to publish newspaper advertisements stating that it had deliberately misled its employees. (It wasn't the first time. Two years earlier, the labour board had ruled that the company had "coerced and intimidated" some of its union employees.)

But Toigo's biggest move of all was his attempted purchase of the assets of B.C. Enterprise Corp., the Crown corporation responsible for selling off chunks of government land around the province. The most valuable piece of land was the former site of Expo 86, which sat on some choice downtown Vancouver waterfront real estate. Despite Vander Zalm's best efforts to help his friend's purchase attempt succeed, the deal fell through. And it was that deal that thrust Toigo into the limelight for the first time in his life.

Tony Hepburn, a prominent Vancouver stock analyst, said at the time: "When I first heard about him in connection with the Expo lands deal. I thought, 'Who the hell is Peter Toigo?' "

There was a reason why Toigo was referred to by the business and media community as the "mystery man." He is intensely private. He refused all requests for interviews for this book, and even had his lawyer send two letters to the authors threatening possible legal action.

"Our client would prefer that you neither name nor refer to him in your book on Premier William Vander Zalm. . . . In the event that you defame Mr. Toigo in any manner in your book an action will be brought by him immediately for an injunction restraining you from further printing, publishing, and distributing your book as well as for damages," said a February 8, 1989, letter from Toigo's lawyer, Sherman Hood.

In another letter, dated one day later, Hood said: "Mr. Toigo is no longer prepared to remain seemingly indifferent as regards libelous allegations made with respect to him in relation to the sale of the Expo lands and whatever investigation was conducted by the RCMP."

But past interviews reveal that Vander Zalm and Toigo consider each other "close" friends. Toigo has described himself as a "sounding board" for Vander Zalm.

The two men got to know each other during the development of Vander Zalm's Fantasy Garden World. Vander Zalm once considered retaining only the garden part for himself and selling off the shopping complex that surrounds the gardens. Toigo was interested, but changed his mind. Eventually, one of his companies would operate a restaurant in the complex and one of Vander Zalm's daughters would rent a house from one of Toigo's sons, right across the street from Fantasy Gardens.

The two men stayed in touch. Their children became friends; their sons went to Vancouver Canucks hockey games together. The families invited each other over for dinner. Vander Zalm and Toigo were alike in many ways. They were strong family men and both were right-wingers, outsiders, and wary of the downtown business establishment and the labour movement. They were not born into wealth—their parents had come to Canada seeking their fortune—and both had made their money in the land development business. More important, the two men consoled and reinforced each other. They were each other's cheerleaders.

When Bill Bennett quit, Toigo was one of the first people to contact Vander Zalm. Originally, Toigo advised Vander Zalm to look after his business and remain out of politics. Soon he would advise Vander Zalm to run; Toigo would look after the finances of the campaign.

Toigo was brand-new to politics. He arrived at the Whistler convention a professed rookie who didn't have a clue about political machinations or strategy. Given Vander Zalm's amateurish campaign, he fit right in.

Despite his habit of avoiding publicity, Toigo still liked to name-drop around anyone other than reporters, according to former associates. He keeps an autographed picture of Ronald Reagan on his wall (he had been introduced to Reagan by Nevada Senator Paul Laxalt). He has even described Grace McCarthy as his good friend. McCarthy maintains that she hardly knew Toigo, even during the tense days when he tried to buy the Expo lands, which she was in charge of selling.

After the leadership race, Toigo became a major fundraiser for the Social Credit Party, but his lack of ties with the province's boardrooms reduced his effectiveness in that role. Toigo may have lacked close relationships with the Howe Street crowd, but with Bill Vander Zalm as premier he could claim a close friend inside government.

In June 1987, for example, Vander Zalm appointed him to the newly created "premier's economic advisory council," a twenty-three person body composed of elite businessmen from B.C. and from various countries. Its job was to bring more business to B.C. The idea for the council had been discussed by Toigo and Vander Zalm before the election; it was an early indication of the relationship Toigo had with the new premier.

Toigo was also interested in getting gambling legalized in B.C. He favoured bringing full-fledged casino-style gambling to the province, preferably in destination resorts and perhaps even on the Expo site, where one of his restaurants was located.

Vander Zalm tried to convince his caucus to accept the idea of destination gambling, but he was unsuccessful, much to Toigo's disappointment. One cabinet minister recalls: "I always figured [Vander Zalm] gave in on gambling so he could win on abortion."

Soon after Vander Zalm became premier, Toigo started phoning him regularly. More often than not, his calls were put through to the premier's desk. He liked to offer his advice on a number of subjects. Vander Zalm rarely refused one of his calls.

"If he phoned, he got through right away. There were times when he wouldn't phone for a couple of weeks, then there were times he would phone six times a day," remembers a former premier's office worker. Few people enjoyed that kind of access.

For Christmas in 1987, Toigo sent Kay and Poole leather desk sets with their names engraved on them.

Despite their friendship, Vander Zalm admitted that he didn't like facing Toigo's fiery temper, which was also meted out to others in government. According to a September 1988 report on the Knight Street Pub affair by ombudsman Stephen Owen, Toigo once threatened to have a liquor branch manager fired if he did not give preliminary approval to a pub application that involved land once owned by Toigo.

"You will be sorry. You have turned me down once too often," the report quoted Toigo as saying to the manager.

According to the report, Toigo also phoned Poole and told him his friend Charlie Giordano—also the co-campaign manager for Vander Zalm's leadership campaign—needed work. Poole then phoned a liquor licensing branch and gave instructions to put Giordano's polling company on the list of government-approved companies that could poll residents on whether they wanted a neighbourhood pub in their area.

When, through Owen's report, all this information became public in the late summer of 1988, it confirmed many people's suspicions about Toigo's way of doing business and the effect of his close relationship with Vander Zalm.

Bob Ransford remembers: "No, not everyone had the access that Peter Toigo had, but I don't think the premier viewed it that way. He viewed him as a friend, a guy who happened to have a good idea. He didn't view it as Toigo wanting half in."

Toigo, however, always the name-dropper, liked to boast of his friendship with Vander Zalm, telling all who would listen that he had the ear of the premier. It was a long way up for a kid from Powell River.

Vander Zalm was occasionally told of the things Toigo was saying, and he would back off a bit. Even Lillian was concerned. But the relationship between Vander Zalm and Toigo continued.

"Toigo was a very strong personality, and I think the premier was rolled over by strong personalities. I don't think he could stand up to them," Ransford recalls.

When he talked to the premier's office staff, Toigo liked to say "we" as if he were part of the government team. It turned more than a few of them off.

"He has a very, very opinionated, strong personality," Ransford remembers. "I didn't trust him at all. I just didn't like the way he operated."

Gradually, the cabinet and caucus became aware of Toigo's friendship with Vander Zalm. "The impression I always had was that Poole looked after [Vander Zalm] during the week and Toigo got him on the weekends," remembers one cabinet minister.

After the botched Expo lands affair, Toigo threatened to flee B.C. He was extremely bitter toward the media. He felt betrayed, and threatened to pull his business out of the province. He started spending more time at his property in Palm Springs.

When he could not get through to Vander Zalm at the drop of a hat any more, Toigo started phoning David Poole at the office and at home. Eventually, however, he gave up on the premier's office and drifted away from Vander Zalm.

The two men rarely spoke for several months after the fall of 1988, according to Vander Zalm, who said Toigo, with his "Italian temper," had chewed him out several times.

But questions about the two men's relationship lingered. Toigo has long maintained that he has never discussed with Vander Zalm anything that even borders on violating cabinet confidentiality, and he heatedly denies exerting any influence on the premier.

In July 1988, in one of the few interviews he has granted, Toigo told Mark Hume of the Vancouver *Sun*: "I've never been an adviser to the premier. And I can assure you he has never discussed anything of confidence to that office with me. We may discuss things, or he may say things that might be happening but he has never, ever talked to me about cabinet."

However, Vander Zalm's continuing efforts to go to bat for Toigo during the BCEC process of selling the Expo lands were extraordinary; at every turn the BCEC board found itself having to deal with Peter Toigo simply because the premier–or David Poole–insisted they do so.

In the end, Vander Zalm was as ill-used by Toigo as he was by Poole. It was the first flirtation with power for both Toigo and Poole and they tripped up.

Before the 1986 election, during the leadership race, Vander Zalm surrounded himself with a group of friends and advisers who could only be described as odd. Not much was known about them, and they had varying degrees of influence on Vander Zalm. Remarkably, none of them would have much contact with Vander Zalm after they had helped him win the leadership race. The new premier showed little loyalty to them.

One of the most visible figures on the leadership campaign was Bill Goldie (later Goldy), a business consultant who dabbled in numerology (which inspired the name change). A dead ringer for Colonel Sanders of fried chicken fame, Goldy, who also had a penchant for white suits, looked like a dignified Southern gentleman just off a cotton plantation.

Goldy was a business consultant who had met Vander Zalm when the two men were active in the B.C. Chamber of Commerce. Vander Zalm liked Goldy's confident style, but still felt uneasy around him. Inevitably, the two men had a falling-out. Goldy did not receive the plum job he thought he deserved after the campaign and left on strained terms.

Goldy's counterpart on the campaign was Charlie Giordano, a college journalism instructor. Giordano, president of the fractious Delta constituency of the Social Credit Party, had worked on many Vander Zalm campaigns, dating back to his days as Surrey mayor. He did not get along with Goldy, and the two men's bickering created heachaches for Vander Zalm.

Then there was Allan Robertson, a mysterious self-described "thinker" whose ideas fascinated Vander Zalm. Unknown to the public, Robertson once penned a speech he wanted Vander Zalm to give at his first premier's conference in August 1986, shortly after winning the leadership. The speech was an "international banking conspiracy" diatribe that blamed the banks and the monetary system for many of the world's economic ills (a theory, by the way, that formed the basis of classic Social Credit doctrine). One of Vander Zalm's aides blanched when he saw it and tore it up before Vander Zalm headed to the meeting.

Robertson says he only wanted to make sure Vander Zalm had some "ammunition" when he was dealing with politicians and bureaucrats at the meetings. Robertson also told the authors he explained the "world banking system and the international monetary fund" at length to Vander Zalm, whom he described as keenly interested in his ideas.

"He always seemed to value my opinion on things," Robertson says. But Robertson's involvement with Vander Zalm trailed off after the 1986 election. The two men have talked only a couple of times since then. Still, Vander Zalm told the authors he has "a lot of time for Allan Robertson," whom he describes as "a very intelligent man."

Vander Zalm also enjoyed listening to the theories of one Jud Cyllorn, a "disciple" of Robertson and also a self-described racist of sorts. Like his mentor, Cyllorn is a numerologist and also considers himself a "philosopher and thinker." He is conservative in both philosophy and dress (short hair, dark pants, white shirts with the top button always done up).

In the early 1980s Robertson and Cyllorn became active in an attempt to revive the moribund provincial Conservative Party. Dr. William McArthur, a former president of the combined provincial and federal Conservative parties in B.C., told the Vancouver

Sun that Cyllorn's views were "extremely right-wing. They were far to the right of most of the people I associated with in the Conservative Party."

Cyllorn has written several unpublished works, including a presentation called "White Men's Ways," in which he declares he is the "most sophisticated racist in the market place." He described himself to Vancouver *Sun* reporter William Boei as "not a genetic racist, but a trust racist," saying he discriminates "on your ability to handle trust."

Cyllorn hates bilingualism, citing historical "high cultures" such as Persian, Greek, and Roman, as proof that only one language could and should survive in a culture. He also blames the governments of former prime ministers Lester Pearson and Pierre Trudeau for plotting to "confiscate the wealth of the middle class."

During the leadership, Cyllorn sat in on some strategy meetings and helped plan slogans and choose campaign colours. He was distant from people like Goldy and Giordano, but, together with Robertson, Cyllorn was able to remain in Vander Zalm's inner circle.

Like Robertson, Cyllorn dropped out of Vander Zalm's sight after the 1986 election. But he re-emerged in the spring of 1988, when he was given a contract to "prepare a strategic outline identifying key issues that the province should address with respect to its role in world financial markets [and] the ramifications of recent events such as the 1987 stock market crash."

The contract was never signed, and David Poole cancelled it after it became public. Vander Zalm and Poole tried to downplay Cyllorn's influence, saying only that he had some "interesting" ideas and was going to be hired merely as a consultant, nothing more. However, unknown to the public at the time, Vander Zalm and Poole had dined with Cyllorn at Victoria's posh Union Club just before the contract became public knowledge. There, they had discussed some of Cyllorn's ideas, including his economic theories. Cyllorn stayed out of the news for almost another year, until he spoke at a public forum on immigration in Vancouver in the spring of 1989. There, Cyllorn cited the need for restrictions on non-Caucasian immigration. The sentiments were similar to ones he has expressed at other meetings, including some held in Edmonton in 1979.

How did people like Cyllorn and Robertson gain access to the ear of the premier of B.C.? For one thing, Vander Zalm often simply cannot say no to people.

"I think these people have their views on some things and some of the things that they have to offer might be quite valid. It's not for me to say that it is or isn't," Vander Zalm told the authors.

"I'm fairly accessible to people, and when you're accessible to people some of the people that might have been ignored elsewhere, I'm willing to give a chance. You know, I don't know any crazy people. I don't label people that way. I say they may be different from what I am or from what other people are but the world wasn't made up of people that were all the same, thank heaven. I don't like to call them weird."

But Vander Zalm does have a penchant for attracting unusual followers. Says Ransford: "He attracted nuts. He was a populist. He would sit there and listen to their advice, because he felt that he couldn't piss anybody off. You'd say, 'Premier, why did you encourage him?' 'I didn't encourage him.' 'Yes you did, you told him that was a good idea and that he should come back and talk to you.' 'Oh, I wouldn't meet with him again.' But he could not see that, that he operated that way."

Ottawa the Bad

Darkness had fallen on a rustic lodge at Meech Lake, Quebec. Inside, Prime Minister Brian Mulroney and Canada's ten provincial premiers still haggled about making Quebec a full partner in Confederation.

No one believed Mulroney had much chance of getting an agreement. But on April 30, 1987, inside an oak-panelled meeting room at the government lodge north of Ottawa, something phenomenal was taking place. One by one, provincial premiers were saying yes to an agreement that met Quebec's special demands for becoming signatories to the Canadian Constitution–which Réné Lévesque had refused to sign in 1982.

Eventually, only one premier stood in the way of an historic breakthrough–British Columbia's Bill Vander Zalm.

During a coffee break wisely called by Mulroney when discussions had stalled, Vander Zalm said to David Poole, "I really do not like this deal. I am not comfortable at this meeting."

Vander Zalm distrusted the accord's unanimity clause, which stated that all ten provinces and Ottawa must unanimously agree to future constitutional changes, such as Senate reform. Vander Zalm believed that a reformed Senate was an important first step in ensuring greater equality in Confederation. And, he thought,

Senate reform would never happen if it required the consent of all ten provinces.

Not long into the meeting, Vander Zalm lost an important ally. Alberta Premier Don Getty, the strongest proponent of Senate reform, threw his support behind the accord after getting a constitutionally entrenched promise from his fellow premiers to discuss Senate reform in the next round of constitutional talks.

Vander Zalm recalls the mounting pressure on him: "I was in the awkward position of being the lone man out," Vander Zalm recalls. "Relations with Ottawa would have been terribly damaged (if Vander Zalm hadn't supported the accord). And I also probably would have been criticized across the country."

He remembers Mulroney urging him to get on-side for the good of the country. "He would say, 'You're a Canadian by choice and you want this country to stand united.' There was flag waving and all that stuff. The pressures were enormous."

For the members of the national media who were trying to predict the chances of success at Meech Lake, Vander Zalm was clearly a wild card. All anyone had heard of his thoughts on Quebec were two celebrated remarks he had made during his days as a Socred minister.

Once, while singing a song at a Socred fundraiser, he had referred to René Lévesque as a "frog." And in 1982 he had said it wouldn't break his heart if Quebec separated from Canada because then he would no longer have to read French on cornflakes boxes.

But Vander Zalm remembers that, as he listened to Quebec Premier Robert Bourassa extol the accord at Meech Lake, he concluded that Quebeckers were more interested in preserving their culture and language than they were in making sure a "Coke can in B.C. had both English and French, or whether we in government were able to speak both languages, or whether we would keep Hansard in English and French."

It was then, Vander Zalm recalls, that he realized Quebec really was a distinct society with a distinct culture and language. And he thought that if English Canada recognized Quebec as distinct, then Quebec might ultimately recognize English Canada as distinct as well.

"Then maybe we could have things in English," Vander Zalm

says today, "without the requirement of people in government, for example, to have to have both languages." Or cornflakes boxes with French on them.

Vander Zalm was, of course, also worried about his relationship with Mulroney. Being the only stumbling block to what would undoubtedly be one of Mulroney's greatest achievements wouldn't help B.C.'s efforts to get a greater share of the federal spending pie. Conversely, being the last piece in the puzzle might bring B.C. new wealth.

With the eyes of his fellow premiers and the prime minister squarely on him, Vander Zalm had to decide whether to stick to his guns or to capitulate because he didn't want to be ostracized by his fellow premiers. He chose the latter route.

It was a remarkable decision for the self-styled man of principle, who liked to quote former B.C. premier W.A.C. Bennett's line: "If you don't stand for something, you'll fall for anything."

On Meech Lake he was prepared to surrender his beliefs: less than a year later he would bring his party to the brink of chaos on the abortion issue because he wouldn't go against his principles.

An exhausted-looking Vander Zalm returned to the B.C. legislature, where he claimed that the accord would even improve the Senate.

"British Columbia and all the provinces have been offered new rights, powers, and responsibilities in the areas of immigration, appointments to the Supreme Court, federal spending, and a range of changes and amendments that will result in the Senate and other national institutions becoming truly representative of the nature of Canada," a proud Vander Zalm said.

In fact, Vander Zalm had been forced to compromise on Senate reform, an issue that had always been atop B.C.'s priority list for constitutional changes. Even though he believed Meech Lake might make reform impossible, Vander Zalm signed anyway. Such is nation building.

When the premiers met a few weeks later in Ottawa to hammer out a final text, Quebec's Bourassa was despondent because he was afraid that an agreement might not be reached. "Don't worry, we'll do it tonight," Vander Zalm consoled Bourassa. Vander Zalm had already committed himself to the accord, so his role had become peacemaker rather than troublemaker.

Vander Zalm waited for his reward for supporting Meech Lake. And waited and waited. Far from improving, B.C.'s relations with Ottawa got worse. Vander Zalm was losing his patience.

For instance, B.C. dairy farmers were restricted by federal marketing agencies to exporting only 3 per cent of all the cheese manufactured in Canada in order to protect cheese factories in Ontario and Quebec; B.C. dairies were thus forced to pour thousands of gallons of industrial milk down the sewer. During his leadership campaign and the subsequent provincial election, Vander Zalm had wondered aloud at one campaign stop after another why it is that B.C. has 11 per cent of Canada's population yet is restricted by Ottawa to producing 3 per cent of the country's cheese.

(British Columbia would threaten to pull out of several agricultural marketing boards but would later renege on that threat).

Vander Zalm's frustration was also born out of personal experience. Before becoming premier he had an interest in an eight-acre greenhouse growing lettuce hydroponically. The company expanded successfully into the U.S., but when it tried to establish operations in Ontario and Quebec discriminatory freight rates made expansion there impossible. The rate from Vancouver to Toronto was far higher than the rate from Los Angeles to Toronto.

The province was only getting 5 per cent of Ottawa's business, yet B.C. represented 11 per cent of the country's population. Meanwhile, Ontario had 35 per cent of the country's population and received 53 per cent of government contracts.

Vander Zalm's frustration with Ottawa was nothing new for British Columbia premiers. Since the nineteenth century, the battles of successive B.C. premiers with Ottawa had earned the province the reputation as the "spoiled child of Confederation." In the twentieth century, B.C.'s three greatest premiers, Richard McBride, Duff Pattullo, and W.A.C. Bennett, were at war with Ottawa through much of their terms.

Bill Bennett had begun by trying a conciliatory approach with Ottawa. It didn't work, and by the end of his term Bennett had become the country's harshest critic of federal spending policies.

In picking up the crusade for a better deal. Vander Zalm was following a grand tradition of B.C. politics. It was likely to be a popular stand. On this issue, Vander Zalm's instincts were bang-on. But if there was any doubt, polling commissioned by the Socreds in the fall of 1987 confirmed that British Columbians didn't like Ottawa.

Half the B.C. public, according to Decima Research's survey, thought the federal government had been treating British Columbia worse than other regions in the country. And 46 per cent of British Columbians thought the provincial government was being too soft on Ottawa and not pressing B.C.'s demands hard enough.

Vander Zalm took up his complaints personally with Mulroney prior to the November 1986 First Ministers' Conference in Vancouver. Mulroney at the time was still smarting from the furor he had created by awarding the CF-18 contract to a Quebec firm, ignoring a Manitoba company with a lower bid. Vander Zalm was the only western premier besides Manitoba's Howard Pawley to speak out against the CF-18 decision.

What Vander Zalm wanted from Mulroney was the $450-million contract to build the federal Polar 8 icebreaker. Versatile Pacific Shipyards of Vancouver was widely believed to have come in with a lower tender than a rival Quebec firm, but the CF-18 fiasco showed Westerners that low bids meant nothing.

And indeed, Mulroney refused to give Vander Zalm a commitment.

But the Polar 8 was just the tip of the iceberg. Shortly after Vander Zalm had taken power, federal–provincial relations officials prepared a preliminary five-page goodie list for Vander Zalm to take to Ottawa.

B.C. wanted $400 million over five years to fund a high-energy physics operation–known as the Kaon Factory–at the University of British Columbia; a share of the Canadian space plan; $100 million more for research and development; the contract to build CF-18 drop tanks; and part of the proposed contract to build Armed Forces submarines.

In early 1987, Vander Zalm began to complain publicly, which infuriated the B.C. Tory caucus. Gerry St. Germain, then national caucus chairman, was on the phone to his former assistant Bob Ransford, who was now working in Vander Zalm's office, demanding to know what the hell was going on. St. Germain was particularly incensed that the Socreds had attacked the Tories in a fundraising letter meant for B.C.'s business leaders.

In an effort to mollify Vander Zalm, Mulroney agreed that March to set up a joint ministerial committee which included B.C. political heavyweight Pat Carney and deputy prime minister Don Mazankowski. B.C.'s representatives included Grace McCarthy, Stephen Rogers, and Mel Couvelier. The tactic worked long enough to get Vander Zalm's signature on the Meech Lake accord, but soon the committee was failing to live up to Vander Zalm's expectations.

In October 1987, just prior to the first ministers' conference in Toronto, David Poole phoned Mulroney's chief of staff, Derek Birney, with a stern warning: unless B.C. got immediate action from the feds on three issues, Vander Zalm was going to use the conference to attack Mulroney's indifference to the West.

One issue was the Kaon Factory, the pet project of B.C.'s scientific community. Poole told Birney B.C. wanted a public statement from Ottawa that the federal government was committed in principle—contingent on foreign financial participation. (The B.C. government couldn't convince foreign investors to put their money in Kaon, when Ottawa wasn't even backing it; Ottawa was reluctant to get involved because there was so little foreign participation.)

The second issue was a Pacific Accord. B.C. wanted the same kind of $1-billion deal reached with the Maritimes in the Atlantic Accord, but federal negotiators argued that B.C. wasn't as needy as the east coast. And B.C. wanted no mention of native issues in any Pacific Accord; Ottawa wanted a provision to divert revenues otherwise destined for the province to the settlement of any native land claims.

The third issue was immigration. Vander Zalm desperately wanted an immigration agreement with Ottawa that would enhance B.C.'s ability to attract the kinds of people the government wanted: entrepreneurs and investors, B.C. syndicates set up to attract entrepreneurial investors had been complaining loudly to the B.C. government that the rules had to be changed. One of the syndicates complaining the loudest was Tang Peacock, a firm of which Vander Zalm's close friend Peter Toigo was a director.

Birney agreed to inform the prime minister, but there was no action from Ottawa on the three key issues. By 1988, Vander Zalm was fed up. It was time for a louder attack.

In March, Lieutenant-Governor Bob Rogers took the floor in the B.C. legislature to open the new session by reading the speech from the throne. About mid-way through the usual long list of government accomplishments, the speech took a definite turn.

"British Columbia's financial contribution to Canada far outstrips what the federal government returns to our region," Rogers said. Journalists listening thought they were in for a few good shots at the feds. But Vander Zalm had much more in mind.

The throne speech said that despite all of the efforts by B.C. to help Ottawa, the province's share of federal resources and spending remained disproportionately low.

"The result has been a deepening feeling of alienation in our Pacific Region. For too long, British Columbia has been out of sight and out of mind of successive federal governments. For too long, the federal vision failed to see beyond central Canada."

People in the public galleries were now exchanging incredulous looks. Usually the throne speech is a platitudinous recitation of accomplishments and promises. People were appalled that this bitter attack on the federal government had been forced upon the Queen's representative, the lieutenant-governor, who is appointed by Ottawa. It was further evidence that Vander Zalm and Poole were ignorant of parliamentary traditions.

Vander Zalm wasn't finished.

The government said Ottawa's vision of western Canada was prairie grain and Alberta energy; the federal–provincial council of ministers was accomplishing little; Prince Edward Island appeared to be getting a federally funded fixed link while B.C. was still awaiting funding for a natural gas pipeline; B.C. had surrendered sovereignty and valuable land to establish South Moresby and still awaited federal compensation; Ottawa still refused to help fund the Kaon Factory.

And then the warning came.

"My government intends to remedy this situation. Action will be taken to enhance British Columbia's stature and increase its share of the benefits of Confederation. . . . We will monitor and evaluate British Columbia's standing within the federal system."

"My government will examine and evaluate areas of federal jurisdiction with British Columbia."

Monitor and evaluate? Evaluate areas of federal jurisdiction? No one had a clue what Vander Zalm was talking about, but it had the eerie ring of separatism.

Afterwards Vander Zalm assured everyone that he wasn't talking separatism. He just wanted to amass hard evidence with which to confront Ottawa. As Vander Zalm spoke, a group of federal-provincial officials in his office were quietly working on a project dubbed "Fair Share."

The brainchild of Vander Zalm and David Poole, Fair Share was the code name for getting a "fairer"–that is, greater–share of federal money. In April 1988, officials completed a massive study of B.C.'s treatment within Canada. The confidential report, entitled *The Economics of Canadian Confederation: A British Columbia Perspective*, concluded that federal nation-building has been more costly to British Columbians than to the citizens in other parts of Canada. The trade and transportation policies alone cost provincial businesses and residents several billion dollars in the post-war period.

"Federal spending in areas that depend upon the discretion of federal bureaucrats and politicians–areas that are vital to the long-term productive potential of the economy–has shown little response to the changing needs of British Columbia," the report said.

"For instance, federal expenditures on economic development programs remain 47 per cent below the national average, 31 per cent below in research and development and 58 per cent below in government procurement."

For B.C. to be in line with the national average, Ottawa needed to increase allocation of expenditures in B.C. by more than $1 billion.

What Vander Zalm needed next was a mechanism to drive the point home. Born was the Confederation Equity Act, which established an ominous-sounding Advisory Council on Confederation, to "review for the premier on an on-going basis the current situation of the province within Canada."

And how was the Advisory Council on Confederation going to keep track of how B.C. was doing? By something called the Confederation Equity Index, designed to measure federal expenditures in B.C. against the national average on a scale from 0 to 100.

The premier's office considered some potential council members: E. Davie Fulton, a former B.C. Supreme Court judge and federal justice minister; Gordon Gibson Jr., former head of B.C.'s Liberal Party; Bruce Hutchison, distinguished journalist and author; and Senator Jack Austin, a prominent Trudeau Liberal. But they were never contacted, and it is highly unlikely that any of them would have responded positively to Vander Zalm's overture.

Even advisers in the premier's own office didn't like the sound of the legislation. "Underneath it all was the feeling that the premier was a separatist," recalls Bob Ransford. "Poole would keep saying to me in subtle terms, 'You know what this is leading up to, don't you?'"

When Ransford confronted Poole directly with the question, "Does the premier want to separate?" Poole would mischievously reply, "Oh, you'd be surprised how far he'd go."

Ransford and another side, Bill Bachop, half jokingly discussed exposing Vander Zalm's plans for the Confederation council and stop any separatist plans in their tracks. But they didn't.

Ransford was on the phone almost daily to his former boss in Ottawa, Gerry St. Germain. Ransford warned St. Germain that Vander Zalm was serious about the Fair Share project and that he might take the province to the brink of secession. But St. Germain never believed that Vander Zalm, despite his loony reputation, would take matters that far.

As it turns out, Ransford and Bachop's fears were well founded. Vander Zalm and Poole discussed having a small, secret group, independent of the Advisory Council, examine the implications of secession. But those plans never went beyond the discussion stage and eventually were forgotten, at least partly because the premier's office in the spring of 1988 became increasingly preoccupied with other things—namely the ceaseless string of scandals and controversies involving Vander Zalm and Poole.

Poole also had the finance ministry examine the implications of establishing B.C.'s own taxation system, separate from the federal government's. Quebec had its own, and at different times earlier

B.C. finance ministers had threatened to set up an independent tax system as well.

Relations with Ottawa slowly began to improve, and the legislation establishing the Advisory Council on Confederation was never introduced in the legislature.

As it turned out, part of B.C.'s problem in securing Ottawa money had to do with the province's fuzzy policy on providing assistance to business. The confusion extended to the substance of the policy itself (does the B.C. government prefer grants, loans, loan guarantees?) and to which B.C. ministry was responsible for articulating the policy (premier's office, economic development, finance?).

Peter Heap, then director of federal-provincial government relations, wrote to Poole complaining that neither Heap's department nor B.C. House in Ottawa could tell its contacts where the government stood.

"This is particularly awkward for the Ottawa operation which has to try to keep on-side groups such as the B.C. Conservative caucus, and to explain B.C. actions in specific instances (e.g., project funding approvals) to increasingly skeptical federal officials," Heap wrote to Poole in a confidential memo on February 8, 1988. "Continuing uncertainty about this issue, which in many ways is central to federal-provincial cooperation, will have an adverse impact on the "fair-share" arguments which the province may shortly be making in a public way. It will lessen our credibility when we complain about the behaviour of the federal government, while at the same time the perception is widespread that we are giving mixed signals on . . . economic assistance to business."

B.C. eventually clarified its position, and the motto of the policy could best be put as follows: "Subsidies if necessary but not necessarily subsidies."

Throughout the spring and early summer of 1988, relations between B.C. and Ottawa continued to improve. The federal government announced in June that it would contribute $28 million to assist B.C.'s Okanagan grape growers who were going to lose their businesses to free trade. And in July, St. Germain announced a $16-million commitment by Ottawa toward a proposed commuter rail service between Mission in the Fraser Valley, and down-town Vancouver.

B.C. also got a solid commitment from Mulroney to help fund a proposed natural gas pipeline from the B.C. mainland to Vancouver Island. The pipeline had become a joke in B.C. because it had been promised so many times by the Socreds in election campaigns dating back to the 1960s. It had also become something of a symbol of Ottawa's indifference to B.C.

In June, the two governments were also able to boast the first native self-government agreement in Canada. The Sechelt Indian band of B.C.'s central coast won municipal status under the provincial government, local autonomy, tax-collecting powers, and freedom from the constraints of the Indian Act.

While the agreement was denounced by native Indians else-where in Canada, it stood as an example of the way both B.C. and Ottawa hoped other native groups would go in their quest for self-government.

The same month the native self-government agreement was reached, B.C. became the seventh province to ratify the Meech Lake accord. At the same time, Vander Zalm gave loud support to Mulroney's free trade agreement.

It is uncertain whether Ottawa's decision to move on some of B.C.'s demands had more to do with Vander Zalm's strident anti-Ottawa speeches or with the impending federal election.

In any event, by the summer of 1988 relations had improved significantly–except for the agreement to establish a park in South Moresby.

By July 1988, one year after Mulroney and Vander Zalm had agreed to create a national park reserve at the southern end of the Queen Charlottes, a final deal had still not been reached.

Described as the "jewel in the Crown," the South Moresby Island site in the Salmon River watershed is a haven for black bears and eagles that feed on salmon in nearby streams.

The battle to preserve the area from logging had become an international environmental cause célèbre. Mulroney and his en vironment minister, Tom MacMillan, saw a chance to cash in on Canadians' concern for the future of the site.

As well, the B.C. federal Tory caucus was also pushing hard for the park. Even the traditionally nonpartisan House Speaker, John Fraser, got involved, personally phoning the premier's office and lobbying David Poole's aide Bob Ransford.

The problem was that creating a park meant putting hundreds of loggers out of work. And for Vander Zalm to sign the deal, someone—namely Ottawa—was going to have to pay a very hefty price. Besides, Vander Zalm resented what he saw as central Canada's interference in B.C.'s affairs. He was particularly irked by strident editorials in Toronto's *Globe and Mail* calling on Vander Zalm to come to his senses and capitulate to world-wide calls for a park on Moresby.

B.C.'s forests minister Dave Parker was irritated by all the criticism focused on the provincial government for not quickly ratifying the park deal. Parker called the earlier Mulroney-Vander Zalm memorandum of understanding "shortsighted" and a "shame." The fact that Parker had been forests minister at the time the memorandum was signed illustrated the size of the rift in the B.C. cabinet.

Parker referred to the deal as a "land grab" brought about "by less informed people—I call it a *Globe and Mail* constituency."

The core dispute was over compensation for the logging companies which would have to forfeit their timber rights. B.C. didn't want to contribute to any compensation arrangements, since it was Ottawa that so badly wanted the park.

On July 11, after more than a year of haggling, a final $126-million agreement was reached which provided for 147 000 hectares of Crown land to be designated a federal park reserve by September 30.

Of the total, B.C. agreed to contribute $20 million: $12 million to establish a harbour at Sandspit, where most of the soon-to-be unemployed loggers lived, and $8 million toward compensation to the logging companies.

In total, MacMillan Bloedel and Western Forest Products, which was losing timber rights to 40 per cent of the region, would receive $30 million in compensation.

Ottawa agreed to pay $32 million for the cost of operating the park and $50 million to diversify the local economy in the Moresby area.

The deal was closed in time for the federal election, but it did little to help Tory fortunes; the NDP took most of the province's seats. Relations between the two governments remained cordial throughout 1988, but there would soon be new storm clouds on the horizon.

In the spring of 1989, the federal government announced it was delaying by one year commencement of construction on the Polar 8 icebreaker. The news came following Michael Wilson's cost-cutting budget, although Ottawa insisted the project was going to go ahead after "glitches" were worked out.

However, the shipbuilding industry worried about the CF-18 scenario being repeated in the West, with Polar 8 going to a Quebec company. That possibility seemed remote, but it would be all that it would take to awaken the separatist spirit in Bill Vander Zalm.

A young Bill Vander Zalm (top row, third from right) poses for a class picture while attending school in the Fraser Valley. Although he arrived in Canada unable to speak English, he eventually became one of the most popular kids in the school—especially with the girls.

The politician as gardener: a contented Vander Zalm sniffs deeply from a flower. There are few things he enjoys more—or knows more about—than caring for a garden.

Vander Zalm on the stump during his unsuccessful bid for the Vancouver mayoralty in 1984. He lost badly to incumbent Mike Harcourt, who later became the leader of the New Democratic Party.

Vander Zalm announcing his candidacy in Social Credit leadership race. Socred MLA's Rita Johnstone (centre) and Bill Reid (right) look on.

Grinning into camera during
leadership race.

Bill Bennett holding Vander Zalm's arm high after final ballot at Whistler.

The greaser and the bobby soxer: always willing to put on a show, the Vander Zalms wow the Socred Party faithful at its annual convention in October 1987 by dancing with a hula hoop at '50s theme party.

A beaming Vander Zalm shakes the hand of a happy Prime Minister Brian Mulroney after the two of them signed the deal creating South Moresby National Park in July 1987. The pact ultimately fell apart and would have to be renegotiated a year later—an indication of the fragile relationship between British Columbia and Ottawa.

Appearing thoroughly charmed by his dining companion, Queen Elizabeth II, Vander Zalm later said this dinner during her visit to Vancouver in October 1987 was one of the highlights of his term.

The premier doing what he likes best: being a movie star. Seen here during filming at Fantasy Gardens of the semi-autobiographical "Sinterklaas" movie.

Copyright Vancouver Sun. Mark Van Manen photo.

At signing of agreement with Concord Pacific to develop Expo land site are from left: BCEC president, Kevin Murphy, BCEC chairman, Peter Brown, Grace McCarthy, and Concord Pacific representative George Magnus.

Copyright Vancouver Sun. Dan Scott photo.

Like errant schoolboys sitting outside the principal's office, Vander Zalm's three key aides nervously watch their boss at a news conference. From left: David Poole, Bob Ransford, and Bill Kay.

Copyright Vancouver Sun. John Yanyshyn photo.

David Poole and Vander Zalm walking down steps behind premier's office building.

Brian Smith embraces Grace McCarthy moments after her resignation from cabinet.

Peter Toigo.

Two kings and a queen. The Vander Zalms are all smiles after purchasing a poster of Elvis Presley at a Vancouver flea market sale in December 1988.

Lillian Vander Zalm adjusting headband in front of Fantasy Gardens.

Lillian and Bill Vander Zalm with cow given to her on her fiftieth birthday by Delta municipal council.

CHAPTER 7

One Long Condom Ad

On Wednesday, May 27, 1987, Bill Vander Zalm's government faced its first major crisis. The powerful B.C. labour movement announced a one-day general strike in protest against Bill 19, Vander Zalm's provocative labour legislation. The premier held an emergency 6:00 p.m. cabinet meeting.

The unscheduled cabinet session would mean scratching a planned softball game between Socred politicians and members of the legislative press gallery. Reporters would now have to cover the cabinet meeting.

Vander Zalm was leaving the legislative chamber when a reporter jokingly admonished him for wrecking the much-hyped encounter between the Socred politicians and the media. Vander Zalm looked shocked.

He turned around and dashed up the two flights of stairs to the press gallery, where he found Vancouver *Sun* reporter Tom Barrett alone, quietly plunking away on a story.

"Tom, Tom, is it true you are going to have to cancel the ball game?" a breathless Vander Zalm asked Barrett.

"Well, it looks like it," the congenial Barrett replied, slightly startled by Vander Zalm's presence.

"Oh, no, I didn't realize that. I feel awful," said Vander Zalm. "Well, I'll see what I can do. I'll see what time we can get this thing over with. What time is the game again?"

Vander Zalm left promising to wrap the meeting up in time to play the game. Barrett shook his head in disbelief. In his effort to please the press, Vander Zalm seemed to have forgotten that the province was on the verge of grinding to a halt. By year's end, such solicitous acts toward the media would be unthinkable.

A month earlier, on April 27, Ken Georgetti, head of the 250 000-member B.C. Federation of Labour, and a group of British Columbia's top labour leaders had met with Vander Zalm in the cabinet chamber to try to talk the premier out of Bill 19, which gave the government unprecedented powers to end strikes.

Georgetti, a dark-haired, mustachioed former steelworker from the working-class town of Trail, was a new moderate leader on the B.C. labour scene. He knew that the province and the labour movement were still recovering from the bitter 1983 labour war against the government over its restraint program.

In 1983, marching under the banner of Solidarity, community groups and labour unions had joined together in protest. But talk of turning organized labour's escalating strikes into a massive general strike had been halted suddenly by the Kelowna Accord, an agreement negotiated between woodworkers chief Jack Munro and Bill Bennett. The government forfeited virtually nothing under the agreement, which left many in the labour movement angry and demoralized.

Following the 1983 fight, the recession caused a steady decline in union membership. In the construction field, the proliferation of nonunion contractors, whose workers did the job equally well for less money, forced labour leaders to accept wage rollbacks. By 1987, the union movement, while still enormously powerful, was much less radical than it had been four years earlier.

A bitter general strike was the last thing Georgetti or most British Columbians wanted to see. But the thirty-five-year-old Georgetti had come to warn Vander Zalm that Bill 19 was setting the province on the same confrontational course that the restraint program had in 1983.

The two sides convened shortly after 9:00 a.m. Representing the government were Vander Zalm; Poole; labour minister Lyall

Hanson; Hanson's deputy, Frank Rhodes; and another labour ministry official. Representing labour were Georgetti; his first lieutenant, Cliff Andstein; a federation lawyer; and a couple of other union leaders.

Vander Zalm had expected that the meeting might last two hours. Nine hours later, it was finally finished.

The two sides went through the bill clause by clause, with the labour leaders outlining their objections. Vander Zalm was calm and attentive, although he did appear irritated when Georgetti continued to use Lillian and Fantasy Gardens to illustrate his points: "Premier, let's pretend there was a boycott of Fantasy Gardens and Lillian wanted to. . . ."

It became clear to the labour leaders that many provisions in the bill were a direct result of complaints by friends of Vander Zalm and Socred supporters. The premier talked about a man he knew in Coquitlam who couldn't hire his son because of union hiring-hall practices. The bill attempted to change those rules.

The labour leaders were struck by the anecdotal nature of Vander Zalm's defence of the bill. When the premier was defending his decision to outlaw secondary boycotts in collective agreements, he said, "Say somebody from Ontario comes out and starts a gardening business and the workers go on strike. Woodward's should have the right to handle roses from that gardening business."

There were broad smirks on the faces of the labour leaders at Vander Zalm's choice of a gardening anecdote. But here was a clue to the source of many aspects of the bill: his own frustrations as a small businessman.

During a short break, the government team left the labour leaders in the cabinet chambers. Georgetti and his crew decided to make themselves comfortable, plunking their shoes up on the cabinet table. The cabinet door opened and a startled Elwood Veitch, the provincial secretary, walked in unaware that the regular meeting of cabinet had been cancelled and that the premier was meeting with the labour leaders.

"The expression on his face was unbelievable," remembers Cliff Andstein. "He thought we'd taken over the government."

Bill 19 was also born out of Vander Zalm's frustration at being unable to solve the forestry industry strike in the middle of the 1986 general election. Vander Zalm had badly wanted to grand-stand a settlement in the middle of the campaign; his failure had provided him with the sourest moment of the election.

As much as Vander Zalm wanted to legislate the woodworkers back to work, he couldn't. The legislature had been dissolved when he called the election; he was powerless.

Vander Zalm therefore put together a sweeping package of labour reforms that would give cabinet the power to impose a settlement in a labour dispute even when the legislature wasn't in session. (Of course, the only time the legislature is not in session and not available to be called back on short notice is during an election campaign.) Under the reforms, he could get workers back on the job just by signing a cabinet order. (This section of the bill has never been proclaimed and likely won't be until the government needs to use the powers in it.)

The job of putting the legislation together fell to Bob Plecas, who, next to Poole, was the most powerful and feared bureaucrat in Victoria. Tough, shrewd, and aggressive, Plecas had been a key architect of the 1983 Socred restraint legislation, which had cut the civil service by 25 per cent, given the government the right to fire without cause (which was eventually dropped), and abolished the Rentalsman, rent controls, and the Human Rights Commission.

Labour minister Lyall Hanson meanwhile carried out public hearings on labour code changes. The process was a sham. The legislation was pretty much drafted by the time the hearings were over and Hanson had put together a report.

Hanson nevertheless warned Vander Zalm that any law opposed by a majority of the people it affects will fail to achieve its objectives. That warning was not heeded.

Before Bill 19 was tabled on April 2, it was toned down considerably by cabinet. Vander Zalm's key concession was allowing closed shops. He had wanted to ban them, and such a provision had even made it into the draft legislation, but Vander Zalm grudgingly capitulated to arguments by his cabinet that the right to a closed shop was a basic union tenet and its removal might provoke labour into a prolonged confrontation.

Bill 19 already weakened union shops by giving employers very limited options of hiring nonunion workers; through assets sales and ownership transfers, unionized companies were now able to spin off nonunion firms; union members outside construction would not be allowed to refuse to work alongside nonunion workers; union members would not be able to refuse to handle "hot" goods from struck employers or nonunion employers; strike and lockout votes were banned until after "good faith" bargaining.

Vander Zalm also wanted strike and lockout votes to be held by secret ballot and the results tallied only after all balloting was complete. He thought a secret ballot would remove peer pressure on workers to vote for a strike. (A year later members of Vander Zalm's own party would demand a secret ballot—on his leadership, citing this part of Bill 19 as a precedent.)

Bill 19 also established an Industrial Relations Council, headed by Ed Peck, who was given broad powers to intervene in disputes.

The bill was denounced by the NDP as "union-busting." Georgetti called it a "flagrant insult" to the trade union movement. The head of the Business Council of B.C., Jim Matkin, saw the bill as fatally flawed because the extraordinary powers of Ed Peck and the government to resolve disputes removed the incentive to compromise during collective bargaining.

Even Graham Leslie, who was deputy minister of labour when the bill was drafted, denounced it after leaving government, saying that it was an attempt to de-unionize the province and would only lead to more confrontation.

The bill was also seen as one small businessman's vengeance for all the woes unions had ever caused small businessmen everywhere. As the former head of the B.C. Chamber of Commerce, Vander Zalm had heard all the complaints.

Bill 19 was accompanied by Bill 20, which gave B.C. teachers full collective bargaining rights, including the long-sought right to strike. The bill gave teachers in each school district the opportunity to vote on whether they wanted to be union or nonunion. The government gambled that several districts would elect to be nonunion, thereby weakening the power of the B.C. Teachers Federation. But none did.

Bill 20 was provocative, but it was Bill 19 that was plunging the province toward a mass walkout by labour.

Vander Zalm and his government defended Bill 19 throughout the spring, unmoved by the power of organized labour. At a press gallery dinner that spring, Vander Zalm got up on the stage in front of the entire NDP caucus and led everyone in a chorus of the union chant "Solidarity Forever." The New Democrats were not amused.

Shirley Carr, head of the Canadian Labour Congress, said that as a Dutch native, Vander Zalm had no right "bringing his right-wing fascist ideas into this democratic country."

The ever-moderate Georgetti denounced Carr's statements. He felt they would only incite union members, and that was exactly what Vander Zalm wanted: the government knew that if labour did stage a general strike to protest Bill 19 the public would object and the government would win support for an unpopular piece of legislation.

The B.C. Federation of Labour put together a three-part strategy to fight the bill. Part one featured an even-tempered Georgetti blaming the new law for any future labour turmoil. Part two involved rotating province-wide rallies; part three, a boycott of the IRC.

However, the government's refusal to withdraw the bill eventually led the B.C. Federation of Labour to announce a one-day walkout on June 1, a Monday, which gave workers a long weekend.

"We knew it was a risk," recalls Georgetti. "We knew that we would probably lose public support because of the inconvenience a massive walkout can cause people. But we figured it was worth the risk. We had to send the government a strong message."

Hence the May 27 cabinet meeting and the softball game that was in jeopardy. Cabinet decided that Vander Zalm should protest the "illegal" walkout in a letter to Georgetti, and the next day it was agreed that Brian Smith should prepare a writ to be filed in the Supreme Court of B.C. seeking a restraining order against any further walkouts by the union movement.

On Monday, June 1, 250 000 union members across the province refused to report to work, the majority walking picket lines that went up around the province.

Brian Smith instructed his counsel to file the Supreme Court writ. Smith, an ultra-conservative when it comes to law and order, said the writ was based on allegations of "conspiracy and intimidation. . . .

"The union leaders are trying to move the making of our laws out of the legislature and into the streets . . . the federation and its supporters are using their power in an attempt to coerce the constitutional authority of the government and of the legislature of this province."

The writ said the union leaders were advocating strikes as a means of "resisting legislative change, showing Her Majesty has been misled or mistaken in her measures, pointing out errors in the government of the province. . . ."

Strong language. Opposition MLAs and journalists investigating its origin soon discovered that the wording was lifted from a section of the Criminal Code of Canada dealing with sedition—the revolutionary overthrow of government.

The government became an instant laughingstock across the country. The sedition writ, as it became known, was a tremendous overreaction to a peaceful day of protest. As David Poole would later say, Smith "used a sledgehammer to kill a fly."

Vander Zalm immediately distanced himself from Smith's decision, saying he didn't even know what sedition meant. Vander Zalm also confirmed that neither he nor the cabinet had seen the wording of the injunction before it was issued.

The B.C. Federation of Labour was ecstatic. Georgetti remembers: "We couldn't believe it. Instead of losing us some support, which we expected, the writ gained us support."

Ten days after the writ was filed, the Supreme Court threw it out.

Debate over Bill 19 continued to rage. Georgetti and Poole began meeting secretly at out-of-the-way spots in Vancouver and Victoria, including Poole's home, to see if an agreement could be reached to cool tensions. By late July, a tentative deal had been worked out. The labour movement would not boycott the Industrial Relations Council if the government would delay proclaiming the section of the bill which gave the IRC its powers to intervene in labour disputes.

The government prepared an eight-page press statement that was to be released when the deal was announced. However, the tentative pact fell apart over wording in the release, which Georgetti and his sidekick, Cliff Andstein, felt made it sound like the B.C. Federation of Labour was tacitly supporting Bill 19.

Labour said the release had to be changed. Poole said no. The deal was called off.

Despite the fact that Bill 19 provoked the longest debate ever held in the B.C. legislature over a single piece of legislation, there was a new spirit of cooperation between the Socreds and the NDP Opposition. Vander Zalm wanted to end the decades-long acrimony which had given the legislature its nickname, "The Zoo."

Instead of indulging in bitter personal attacks, cabinet ministers and the premier would give an Opposition critic advance notice of news conferences or ministerial statements so that he or she could prepare a response. An all-party committee managed the legislature's finances and services to members. Vander Zalm personally silenced, with a quick motion of his hand, any Socred politician who heckled the Opposition.

With thirteen rookies among the NDP's twenty-two members and twenty-five among the Socred's forty-five member caucus, it was the perfect time to establish a new code of behaviour which mirrored the amiable nature of the leaders, Vander Zalm and the NDP's Mike Harcourt.

Harcourt had succeeded Bob Skelly in April 1987, following the latter's humiliating 1986 election loss. Skelly had announced his resignation in November, but until Harcourt took over, Skelly brought new meaning to the term "lame duck leader." He was regularly absent from the house and even missed the budget speech. When he did show up, he rarely spoke, still filled with bitterness over his election loss and the efforts his caucus had made to dump him before the election was called.

Harcourt, the immensely popular Vancouver mayor, was bland, boring, utterly non-threatening, and a remarkably successful politician. As Opposition leader, his first priority was not knocking the stuffing out of Vander Zalm's policies but introducing himself to British Columbians. Outside Vancouver, Harcourt didn't have much of a profile. He vowed to visit as many communities in the province as he could before the next election. As for his opponent, Bill Vander Zalm, Harcourt decided to let him destroy his credibility all by himself.

For example, before the legislative session began, Vander Zalm had made a trip back to the Netherlands to star in a made-for-TV film, *Sinterklass Fantasy*. Vander Zalm was to narrate the story of a successful Canadian gardener turned politician who returns to his native Holland on a magical rainbow and reminisces about Christmas. The film ends with a spectacular Christmas gathering at Fantasy Gardens.

It was all very bizarre, but the premier was happy to mug for the cameras in various Dutch towns, reciting his lines with Lillian. Vander Zalm even told a travelling reporter that he yearned to be a movie star and that being premier was his "dumb" job. The comment, though made in jest, did not go over well with the premier's staff back in Victoria, who were deluged with an increasing amount of work as a result of their boss the movie star's decision to centralize decision-making in his office.

And then there was the issue of hungry kids.

A survey by the Vancouver *Sun* in early April revealed that hundreds of children were going to school in the downtrodden east end of Vancouver without breakfast or lunch. Vander Zalm responded that hungry school kids were not the government's responsibility, then later exacerbated the resulting outrage when he suggested that kids were going to school hungry because their parents were "sleeping in" rather than getting up and feeding their children.

Vander Zalm's dubious generalization infuriated parents stuck on welfare or in low-paying jobs. People remembered Vander Zalm's days as human resources minister, when he was portrayed as a heartless oppressor of the poor, a characterization made famous in a cartoon showing Vander Zalm pulling the wings off a fly. (He successfully sued over the cartoon, but the judgment was overturned at the appeal level.)

Next up? AIDS.

Later in April, Vander Zalm got involved with an AIDS video that was to be introduced in Vancouver schools. The eighteen-minute,

New York-produced video, entitled, *Sex, Drugs and AIDS*, featured interviews with AIDS victims and explicit discussions on how the virus is spread.

As a gesture of his open government, Vander Zalm invited reporters to David Poole's office to watch the film. Vander Zalm sat expressionless in a leather chair in the middle of Poole's office, his hands folded over his face, as reporters surrounding him jotted down notes. Television cameras focused on the premier as the actors talked about anal sex and condoms. When the film was over, reporters crowded around Vander Zalm for his reaction.

"The part that troubled me most is the subtle message throughout the whole of it, starting from the very beginning, where it says 'I want to have sex, but I don't want to die.' " Vander Zalm then went on to describe the film as the "longest condom ad I've ever seen."

His insistence on imposing his opinion on every issue was eroding his popularity with cabinet, party members, and the electorate. A May poll by the *Sun* showed that Vander Zalm had fallen eleven points in seven months. But as Vander Zalm was a non-believer in the polls, the results had little impact on his behaviour.

The premier's love for a microphone began to irritate his cabinet colleagues, who were turning on their radios in the morning to hear whatever policy announcement Vander Zalm had made the night before.

The first week of July was typical. On his Sunday radio show he told a caller that patients should be charged a fee for visits to the doctor and promised to lobby his provincial counterparts for user fees. Asked about Vander Zalm's statement, health minister Peter Dueck the next day flatly contradicted his boss's enthusiasm for user fees: "That's a dead issue."

Just two days later, press gallery reporters were summoned to David Poole's office in the premier's block for a bizarre speaker-phone press conference with Vander Zalm, who was in Vancouver. "Hi, this is your premier calling," said the voice over the phone. Vander Zalm said he had struck a deal with Prime Minister Mulroney to establish a park on South Moresby in the Queen Charlotte Islands. B.C.'s parks minister Bruce Strachan wasn't even included in the triumphant announcement.

The telephone news conference disintegrated when Vander Zalm dropped the phone, creating a loud crash at the reporters' end. "Are you all right, Premier? Are you all right?" a reporter cried out mockingly.

After seemingly dusting himself off, Vander Zalm responded, "Yeah, yeah, I'm all right, I'm all right."

There would be other clashes with ministers. Vander Zalm and Mel Couvelier contradicted each other over a controversial real estate tax–Vander Zalm suggested the tax could be changed, Couvelier said no.

Meanwhile, deputy ministers were instructed to report directly to Poole and not to their ministers. When there were complaints about the decision to shuffle deputies without informing the ministers affected, Vander Zalm said: "We're not concerned about what a minister likes. What is more important is the overall functioning and effectiveness of government."

The cabinet wasn't pleased, and caucus was getting testy as well, a fact that David Poole's executive assistant Bob Ransford warned of in a spring memorandum.

"We often forget that the back-benchers are the people on the front lines and they have the least effective defence system (i.e. no bureaucracy to pad them against the public)," wrote Ransford.

Poole's young aide suggested that caucus members would be under intense fire over Bills 19 and 20, and it was important to keep Vander Zalm in touch with his troops. The premier should offer small groups of backbenchers informal chats about the direction of government; his office should prepare regular briefing material for caucus, containing anticipated public questions and suggested answers–Ransford presented these and more ideas that Poole wrote back were "excellent." Unfortunately, the excellent ideas were soon forgotten as tensions in caucus continued to build.

Ransford had some poor ideas, too. One was to hold a three-day caucus meeting at Vander Zalm's Fantasy Garden World. Naturally, Vander Zalm was enthusiastic. The gathering was to open on Friday, June 19, with a reception in the premier's castle, followed by some free time for dinner in the theme park's European Village, after which Lillian would serve dessert. The next day, a breakfast meeting was scheduled at Vander Zalm's friend Peter Toigo's nearby hotel. As well, all accommodation arrangements were made at Toigo's hotel.

The NDP, of course, accused the Social Credit Party, which was financing all costs associated with the meeting, of conflict of interest for pouring money into Vander Zalm's business. Vancouver–Point Grey Socred Kim Campbell fired off an angry letter to Vander Zalm denouncing the Gardens decision.

Although Vander Zalm, typically, couldn't understand all the fuss over the meeting, he agreed to change its location when he learned that labour was planning to picket the Gardens during the retreat. Vander Zalm didn't want anything cutting into business. (Later that year, however, Vander Zalm held a Socred fundraiser at the Gardens, provoking more conflict-of-interest allegations.)

In July, the first session of the thirty-fourth B.C. Parliament adjourned after eighty-four days. Vander Zalm, never afraid of hyperbole, called it "the greatest session ever held in the history of the legislature."

For Vander Zalm, the session had been a blend of charisma and chaos. Among his more outrageous comments was his response to a question regarding what the federal government should do about a freighter full of refugees that had landed in Nova Scotia: Vander Zalm suggested the freighter be sold and the money used to send the Asian immigrants back to "wherever it is they came from."

When he was a cabinet minister, such comments won Vander Zalm support because they reflected the feelings of many British Columbians. But coming from the premier, British Columbians found the same comments ignorant and racist.

Vander Zalm's propensity for the outrageous may have been one of the reasons he reneged on one of his prominent campaign promises–televising the legislature.

Officially, Vander Zalm claimed that the estimated $5-million cost was too much. But his real problem was that TV would give the NDP a platform they hadn't had before. The Socreds also worried that the new-found spirit of cooperation would be lost as politicians grandstanded for the cameras, as had happened in every legislature where television was introduced. And some advisers in the premier's office thought television would probably hurt Vander

Zalm more than it would help him, because when he gave speeches he often got so worked up that he looked out of control, wildly animated, his hands waving and his voice screeching. It was not the image Vander Zalm's aides wanted beamed into the voters' homes.

In August, Vander Zalm and his cabinet met in the tiny Vancouver Island seaside resort of Cowichan Bay.

News reached the retreat that Delta MLA and former speaker of the B.C. legislature Walter Davidson had been fined $1500 and placed on three months' probation following his conviction for counselling to commit a forgery. Davidson had asked a printing company to alter an invoice so that he could write off the costs of his 1986 election brochures as a legitimate business expense.

The government had waited until after sentencing to make any comment on Davidson's future as an MLA. If Davidson had received an absolute discharge, there would have been no question about whether he would be able to retain his seat. But, given the fine and probation, reporters and Davidson's Delta constituency executive wanted to know his status.

Attorney-General Brian Smith emerged from a cabinet session onto a sun-drenched patio at the hotel where the Socreds were meeting. His opinion: Davidson's seat was "technically vacant" pending the outcome of the appeal which Davidson was planning.

But shortly after Smith offered his opinion, Vander Zalm came out and offered his: he had no plans to kick Davidson out of the Socred caucus.

Smith stood firm, pointing out that the Constitution Act of B.C. states that any MLA who is found guilty of an "infamous crime" must automatically forfeit his seat and a by-election must be called within six months.

Smith said it was the opinion of his department that an indictable offence qualified as an "infamous crime."

Smith was privately furious that Vander Zalm would be so quick to publicly contradict his attorney-general's legal opinion. This first serious rift between the two men would widen irreparably within a year.

Davidson would eventually lose his appeal, but there was

sympathy for his plight within the Vander Zalm camp. Davidson had close ties to the premier's friend Peter Toigo; as well, Charlie Giordano, the premier's buddy and former campaign manager, was Davidson's Delta constituency president.

Thus, a secret arrangement was made between Davidson, David Poole, and Peter Webster, Vander Zalm's choice as head of the Social Credit Fund, to pay part of Davidson's legal fees, which were estimated at $20 000 to $30 000. (The Fund is the legal entity set up to collect party donations, which are then turned over to the Social Credit Party for use in operating its headquarters and running elections.)

Webster was opposed to using party donations to pay Davidson's legal expenses, particularly at a time when donations were down because of the government's and Vander Zalm's slumping popularity. But as in the case of Lillian's travel costs, Webster reluctantly bowed to the decision which was made in the premier's office.

It was not uncommon for Bill Vander Zalm to return to his Victoria office following a weekend at Fantasy Gardens, his head filled with "great" ideas that had come to him after reading an article or talking to someone. After one such weekend that fall, Vander Zalm arrived at the legislature shortly after 9:00 a.m. and was walking to his corner office when he passed Poole's office. The regular weekly meeting of key members of the premier's office staff was under way. Vander Zalm stuck his head in to offer his latest brainstorm.

He had talked to a friend who had told him crops were dying on the vines in the Okanagan because there weren't enough pickers. Vander Zalm said that in his native Holland, school children would get a couple of weeks off every year and would be bussed into the countryside to pick fruit.

"Why don't we do that here?" Vander Zalm asked.

Alan Filmer, a career bureaucrat who was reluctantly seconded to Vander Zalm's office as director of policy and legislation, thought it was a joke. But when he realized Vander Zalm wasn't kidding, he listed several reasons why the premier's idea was insane. Teachers would be up in arms; parents and bus drivers would be upset; the school year would have to be extended.

"And what would happen if one of those kids fell out of an apple tree and broke their arm? The liability cost to the province would be more than the entire value of the crop," said Filmer, who in a year's time would be only to happy to take an appointment to the bench.

Typical bureaucratic response, Vander Zalm thought. The bureaucrats were great at thinking up reasons why things couldn't be done, Vander Zalm would often say, but not so great at thinking up ways to make things happen.

(His orchard idea was eventually passed on to the education ministry, where it died a quiet death.)

But not all of Vander Zalm's ideas met a similar fate.

In 1986, Vander Zalm met in Los Angeles with Grammy-award-winning record producer David Foster, a native of Victoria who was now based in the U.S. entertainment capital.

Foster told Vander Zalm about a symphony soundtrack he was writing and was planning to record with the London Philharmonic. It would be great, the two thought, to use the music in a video featuring B.C. scenery, the Vancouver Symphony Orchestra, and market it as a tourism promotion package.

After follow-up meetings between Foster and David Poole, the government agreed to enter into a joint venture with Foster. The government would pay Foster $500 000 toward production. The video would be marketed internationally and the government would get its investment back first from whatever profits were made. Three payments would be made; the final one after the government had seen rough cuts of the video and was satisfied. The whole deal was arranged verbally and was followed up with a crude written contract.

David Poole phoned officials in Elwood Veitch's provincial secretary ministry to arrange financing for the project out of lottery funds. Poole was told there was no mechanism to fund such a project out of lottery funds. The bureaucrat was told to find a way.

Veitch then called Poole, his former executive assistant, to complain. Poole simply told Veitch the premier wanted it done. And so it was done.

Over the course of the next year, Foster worked on the video, and on September 17, 1987, Ransford was dispatched to Foster's Malibu home for a screening. Once the home of comedian Tommy Chong, the house was hidden in a wooded area and had a large swimming pool set in rockery in the back yard. When Ransford arrived, hockey star Wayne Gretzky was sunning himself beside the pool.

They went to a recording studio in Hollywood to view the video. The rough cut wasn't at all what Ransford was expecting. The cinematography was excellent, and combined with special effects and the symphonic score it sounded and looked great. But Ransford thought that someone watching the video would never know it was about British Columbia unless they read the credits at the end, and therefore it wasn't anything the government could use for tourism.

He was also concerned that there were too many spinoffs for Foster's commercial benefit. The video promoted an album which generated no benefits for the province.

Despite his reservations, Ransford handed over a cheque for $150 000, representing the government's final payment to Foster. When Ransford returned to Victoria he immediately phoned lawyers in the attorney-general's department to express his reservations about the video and seek advice about what the government could do about the contract. Ransford thought Foster had failed to live up to the terms of his agreement with the government.

The government lawyers told Ransford he should not have handed over the cheque if he was unsatisfied with the product. They suggested that the premier's office write Foster a letter demanding that he live up to the terms of the agreement.

In the meantime, Foster had been approached by the Social Credit Party about performing at a gala fundraiser in Vancouver. Foster agreed and also helped line up some friends such as Dionne Warwick to perform.

When Ransford approached Poole with the letter, Poole refused to sign it; he was worried that Foster would get angry and refuse to perform at the fundraiser.

The letter was eventually sent, but Poole phoned Foster first, telling him the letter was on its way but not to worry about it when it arrived. Poole was simply carrying out the instructions of the attorney-general's department.

The Foster video was eventually produced, but by the spring of 1989 the government had recouped only one-fifth of its $500 000 cost. When the new team of advisers around Vander Zalm found out about the video they were shocked that such a loose arrangement had been made with so much taxpayers' money. It was one video the government wouldn't be rushing out to talk about. Foster and Vander Zalm, however, remained good friends.

On September 24, 1987, Vander Zalm was scheduled to deliver a speech to the Union of B.C. Municipalities in Vancouver. His aides had been discreetly notifying political reporters that the luncheon address was important: the premier would lay out his "blueprint for the province."

Some 1000 mayors, aldermen, officials, businessmen, consultants, and journalists eventually listened to Vander Zalm's plan to "decentralize" government into eight regions of the province. Cabinet ministers were to be appointed as "Ministers of State" for the eight regions.

Moving the operations of government out of Vancouver and Victoria and into the regions had been a dream of Vander Zalm's since his days as a municipal affairs minister under Bill Bennett. He was concerned that the Lower Mainland was becoming overcrowded and its quality of life was being threatened. Now, as premier, he had the clout to realize his dream.

Vander Zalm's speech contained few details, but David Poole had information he was willing to share with reporters on a background basis (i.e., the information could be used but not attributed to Poole). He said that 1100 provincial civil servants could lose their jobs and at least another 10 000 workers could be affected.

In Victoria, where most of the government's operations are based, civil servants immediately began panicking about their futures. The head of the B.C. Government Employees Union, John Shields, said that the news was like declaring war on the bureaucracy. The loans department in Victoria's major bank branches were put on alert to make sure they didn't loan money to a civil servant who could soon be out of a job.

The day following the premier's speech, legislative reporters in

Victoria were invited down to Poole's office in the premier's wing for a background session. Again, reporters were told they could use the information but not attribute it to Poole.

Poole explained how each of the eight regions would become an individual fiefdom, controlling its own regional health, education, and social service systems, and with certain powers of taxation that would be administered by a regional elected council. Poole said the plan could be the precursor to a type of super-county or "house" system.

"It's like setting up the United States of British Columbia," Poole said.

The United States of British Columbia? Reporters exchanged incredulous glances. Poole would repeat the catchy phrase twice more to eliminate any possibility that it was a slip of the tongue. (Poole was later asked why cabinet ministers and not MLAs would oversee the eight new regions. In a comment that would not endear him to the premier's colleagues on the Socred backbenches, Poole said the role of MLAs was "overrated.")

Poole also explained how parts of government would be moved from Victoria. If workers wouldn't leave, they would be fired with appropriate pension and severance arrangements.

The next day, a Victoria newspaper ignored Poole's request for anonymity and mentioned Vander Zalm's principal secretary by name, attributing to him the soon-to-be famous line about the "United States of British Columbia."

It was a threshold for David Poole, the first public indication of his power and control. But his offhand remarks also showed his inexperience. Under the vague plans that had been made, movement from Victoria would happen over an extended period of time, maybe ten years. But by releasing the unreliable figures, he had distracted attention from the overall plan and instead focused attention on the misery the program would heap on thousands of civil servants, still recovering from the drastic reduction in their numbers during the restraint of 1983 and 1984.

Vander Zalm was privately upset with Poole for the disastrous backgrounder, but not angry enough to fire him. At this point, Vander Zalm was already too dependent on Poole to even consider letting him go. The incident once again displayed to the Socred old guard the amateurish nature of Vander Zalm's administration.

(Once out of government, Poole would say that the background briefing was one of his worst mistakes.)

The following week, the Socred caucus met in the Kootenay community of Nelson.

The caucus members were upset that they hadn't been briefed on Vander Zalm's decentralization plans. Inevitably, such a sweeping reorganization touched off speculation about who would benefit and who would be hurt; the government's own MLAs had no information to help them answer the flood of queries from constituents because there were no details.

After trying to explain decentralization to his caucus, he returned to Victoria to try again with reporters, who were given a copy of a news release so bewildering that it had most of the press laughing.

"Each economic diversification development group will . . . develop a full inventory of each region's manpower, infrastructure, facilities and natural resources and identify and make recommendations on what additional facilities and resources are needed to maximize each region's existing resource base."

The one thing that did seem clear was that the plan was a bureaucratic nightmare, with a whole new layer of "economic diversification groups," "resource teams," and "service development groups." Nobody knew for sure what the government was talking about.

Meanwhile the plan was being denounced as anti-democratic, with "Ministers of State" usurping the role of elected representatives. Others worried that decentralization would promote unhealthy competition among the eight regions, with all of them vying for the same government programs and agencies to be moved into their regions.

In October, Vander Zalm and his cabinet met at a resort at Lac Le Jeune, in B.C.'s Cariboo region. Vander Zalm arrived late, so David Poole began the meeting without his boss, explaining decentralization to the ministers. When Vander Zalm arrived, he and Poole had a nasty fight in front of the cabinet over the pace of the program.

Poole believed the government wasn't moving fast enough with the plans, such as they were. Vander Zalm won the dispute, much to Poole's dismay.

In late October, the cabinet authorized $8 million in special warrants to fund the decentralization program. The NDP charged that the special warrants–technically meant to be used only if the money were urgently required–violated parliamentary democracy. Even Vander Zalm had to admit that maybe cabinet had been rushed into authorizing funds for a program that wasn't fully developed.

(By the spring of 1989, Vander Zalm's decentralization plans had been quietly dismantled. All that remained were the titles and committees and a cabinet bloated by the addition of five regional ministers of state for eight regions.)

In contrast to the botched decentralization program, Vander Zalm used the October Socred convention to unveil the plans for a program that was much better organized: the most sweeping privatization ever attempted in British Columbia.

Propelled by the privatization successes of his hero, Britain's Margaret Thatcher, Vander Zalm announced that $3 billion worth of Crown agencies and programs were up for sale.

"Success comes from daring to begin, and we've only just begun," Vander Zalm told cheering Socred supporters at the convention.

Natural gas, rail, and research divisions of the Crown utility B.C. Hydro and the B.C. Systems Corp., the government's computer arm, would be put up for grabs, as well as eleven smaller government outfits and programs from sign shops to nurseries to branches of the Queen's Printer. Vander Zalm said that 7200 employees would be affected but that he expected minimal layoffs. Money earned from the sales would be used to reduce the government's $5-billion accumulated deficit.

Privatization, combined with the vague decentralization scheme, would allow Vander Zalm to realize his dream of reducing the bureaucracy, which, as a small businessman, he hated. And the money generated would permit addressing the other major problem he saw in government, the deficit. If Vander Zalm could reduce the size of government and get B.C.'s fiscal house in order, he would have achieved two major goals as premier.

But the beleaguered B.C. Government Employees Union, its numbers already ravaged by the years of Socred restraint, saw Vander Zalm's privatization program as a direct assault on its membership–which of course it was. Over the next six months, the union would launch an ideological war against privatization in a desperate attempt to preserve its membership.

The war spilled onto the floor of the B.C. legislature, which resumed sitting in November. House Speaker John Reynolds granted the NDP's request for an emergency debate on the government's selloff plans. It was the B.C. legislature's first emergency debate in ten years.

It was also the first to be broadcast live by radio. This prompted especially feisty speeches from the six politicians–three New Democrats and three Socreds–chosen to speak during the one-hour war of words. During Vander Zalm's wild harangue, listeners could hardly make out what he was saying sometimes because of the din prompted by his performance.

The ambulance drivers certainly heard him, though. During his speech, Vander Zalm told an anecdote about an employee of Lillian's at Fantasy Gardens. The premier said that the woman had phoned the ambulance service to attend to her daughter's choking two-week-old son. When no ambulance had arrived in fifteen minutes, the woman phoned again, Vander Zalm said, and was told to complain to "the government."

Vander Zalm's point was that government employees wouldn't be so impudent if they were working in the private sector, where they could be more easily fired for such remarks.

However, a review of the incident by the health ministry totally cleared the dispatcher in question of any wrongdoing. In his eagerness to use someone else's personal tragedy to bolster his point of view, Vander Zalm had not checked the facts.

Not just the ambulance drivers were upset.

A late November 1987 poll commissioned by the *Sun* showed that 56 per cent of British Columbians were unhappy with Vander Zalm's performance, so upset that if an election were held the Socreds would lose to the NDP.

By that November, four cabinet ministers had resigned. Forests minister Jack Kempf had left because of spending irregularities in the operation of his ministry; environment minister Stephen Rogers over a conflict in his ownership of some mining stock (he was moved to intergovernmental relations), and advanced education minister Stan Hagen after it was revealed that his cement company had done business with the government (he was later reinstated).

The latest to resign was transportation minister Cliff Michael. Michael confessed to approaching a West Vancouver businessman after a cabinet committee meeting and offering to sell him some land. Michael had followed that up with a phone call, then sent the businessman a company brochure listing Michael as president.

Vander Zalm admitted to knowing three weeks before he fired Michael that his minister had approached the businessman, but claimed he took no action because he didn't know the extent of the indiscretion. However, he decided to fire Michael just minutes before the story was exposed by a television reporter, Eli Sopow.

(Ironically, Sopow would later get a job in the premier's office and become one of Vander Zalm's chief political and media advisers.)

By 1987's end, Vander Zalm's fresh start had soured. His governing style, so much an asset during the previous year's leadership and election races, was now a liability.

"Refreshing as it was to have a man so open and amateurish at the head of government," said the *Sun*'s Vaughn Palmer, "the style is less of an asset if one is trying to project an image of competence and consistency."

There was dwindling communication between the premier's office and the Socred politicians, growing resentment about David Poole's enormous power, and frustration over the lack of any communications strategy to sell the government's controversial programs. (The government's public relations arm had been disbanded by Vander Zalm because he felt it was a waste of money. This was a move he would come to regret.)

Vander Zalm also demonstrated his lack of the discretion his office demanded. His "gut instinct"—which he always boasted was more reliable than professional polling—also let him down as he increasingly found himself at odds with the majority of the public on issues such as feeding hungry schoolchildren. His total confidence in his own abilities and powers of persuasion had put him in charge of a one-man government.

Vander Zalm had established the pattern of governing that would almost destroy his administration in the year ahead. Yet, looking back on 1987, Vander Zalm still counted the year a success and boasted of his achievements.

He had forgotten the biblical admonition, "Pride goeth before a fall."

The Abortion Debacle

Hawaii's beauty made rainy British Columbia seem far away. Bill and Lillian Vander Zalm spent the first week of their holiday in late January 1988 lying on the bench, walking through the hills, and picking flowers. The couple had gone to Hawaii–a favourite escape for B.C. politicians–for a two-week getaway from political affairs back home.

Pressure drifted away–until the morning of January 28.

An early call awakened the premier in his luxurious suite at the Honolulu Hilton. David Poole had startling news from Ottawa: the Supreme Court of Canada had thrown out the country's abortion law.

The court decision to declare unconstitutional a law it considered "manifestly unfair" theoretically removed all barriers to women seeking abortions. The court had ruled five to two in favour of an appeal brought by abortion-rights crusader Dr. Henry Morgentaler on the grounds that the system of forcing women to have their abortions approved by a hospital therapeutic abortion committee was unconstitutional. The high court had said that the law was discriminatory because it was applied unequally and created delays that were dangerous to women.

Vander Zalm, shocked, his holiday ruined, rubbed the sleep from his eyes. It seemed possible his government would find itself paying for all abortions without restriction. He vowed not to let that happen.

Few issues affected Vander Zalm as deeply as abortion. Strictly political issues–budgets, labour laws, or even welfare spending– were one thing. Like any politician, he could bend a little here and there to expedite matters.

But, to Vander Zalm, abortion had little to do with politics and everything to do with religion. He was a devout Roman Catholic and considered the Church's view on the matter clear: abortion was a sin. On this issue, "compromise" was a dirty word to the premier.

Vander Zalm had never made any secret of the fact that he viewed abortions as morally wrong. Shortly after taking office in August 1986, he had ordered his health minister, Jim Nielsen, to investigate abortions in the province because he was sure women were using them as a means of birth control. Nielsen quietly took Vander Zalm aside and told him there was no evidence to back up such claims. Vander Zalm quickly dropped the subject and even told Kim Campbell, a pro-choice advocate in his caucus, that he had no more interest in touching the issue.

But at the October 1987 Social Credit convention, against David Poole's advice, Vander Zalm had ad-libbed a reference to abortion in his speech to the party faithful. It was the most emotional and aggressive part of his speech, and it raised more than a few eyebrows.

Most politicians avoided abortion as a no-win issue. The NDP didn't advertise that most of its caucus members were pro-choice. A considerable number of NDP supporters were anti-abortion, although still a minority in the party. And Socred supporters, particularly those in the Fraser Valley, were considered to be mostly anti-abortion. But since many of each party's supporters were women, getting everyone riled up about it might not do either party any good.

The January 28 Supreme Court decision paradoxically gave Vander Zalm a chance to impose his beliefs on the population. He had once promised to reduce the number of abortions; now he thought he had the opportunity.

Health Minister Peter Dueck, Poole, and Vander Zalm discussed the issue in a hastily arranged conference call that same day. Their government controlled one aspect of abortion–paying for the operation. There wasn't much time for legal consultation, and messing with the sacred institution of medicare was chancy, but Vander Zalm was determined to fund only "medically required" abortions that had been approved by a therapeutic abortion committee and that were performed in an accredited hospital–in other words, to keep the status quo.

Attorney-General Brian Smith was sceptical, but he helped draft the government's response. He still considered himself a team player and, as a minister, he saw it as his duty to assist the premier.

The next day, January 29, Smith and Dueck called a news conference in Victoria. Under the glaring television lights in the legislature's press theatre, Smith said the province had full legal authority to control its medicare payments. He would go all the way to the Supreme Court of Canada to defend this authority if he had to.

(Actually, Smith and his colleagues thought the federal government would soon bring in a new law that would make any further court action unnecessary. Smith was neither an ardent prochoicer nor a zealous anti-abortionist, and he eventually became uncomfortable with the government's position; but at first he was incensed at the Supreme Court's decision. Why should a high court use the Charter of Rights to subvert Parliament's laws? Smith felt the supremacy of Parliament was challenged, in a dangerous parallel to the too-powerful U.S. Supreme Court.)

Meanwhile, in Hawaii, Vander Zalm became dependent on the hotel's fax machine. His office sent him the summary of the court decision, memos from Poole and his ministers, and a large stack of news clippings.

Each day for the remaining week of his vacation, Vander Zalm gathered up the papers from the fax machine, grabbed his reading glasses, and headed to the beach to discuss events with Lillian, who was just as devout a Roman Catholic as he, and essentially his primary adviser.

Back in Canada, Conservative governments, such as Grant Devine's in Saskatchewan, still tried to put up some roadblocks to abortions, while liberal-minded administrations, such as David Peterson's in Ontario, simply accepted the ruling and did little or nothing. All eyes turned to Ottawa, but the Progressive Conservative caucus, as reluctant as all the regional governments to get involved in the abortion issue, couldn't agree on a policy.

Without the federal cavalry riding to the rescue, the B.C. government immediately ran into a problem. It had neglected to explain how abortion committees could keep functioning when the law governing them had been abolished. (Smith had been advised that any policy requiring the committees to keep operating with full powers over abortion would likely be struck down by a court challenge.)

Before the new law, supporters of both the pro-choice and anti-abortion camps jockeyed for control of the all-powerful hospital boards, who appointed doctors to the committees. If an anti-abortion majority won election to the board, they effectively ruled the committee and a woman had little chance of obtaining an abortion at that hospital.

In B.C., 51 of 133 accredited hospitals had abortion committees at the time of the Morgentaler ruling. More than 11 000 abortions had been performed in B.C. in 1987, giving the province one of the highest abortion rates in the country.

In light of the court ruling, pro-choice advocates began to map out their strategy. Almost immediately, they revived plans to open B.C.'s first free-standing abortion clinic. Anticipating that move, the government had already stated that it would not pay for any abortions performed outside an "accredited" hospital.

And, unknown to the public at the time, Brian Smith had quietly ordered a private investigation of a Vancouver pro-choice group in early 1987. The investigation, conducted by a reputable local law firm and the private investigators they had hired, included covert operations and the infiltration of the pro-choice group. Since the abortion law was still in place at the time, Smith considered an abortion clinic to be illegal and therefore felt any group planning to carry out what he considered to be an illegal act should be watched closely.

The investigation, however, turned into a farce. The undercover detectives "infiltrated" public meetings, taped private conversations, and obtained copies of financial records. One operative tried to take pictures of some sympathetic doctors, but that failed when he forgot to put film in his camera. The private detectives evidently were also unaware that police occasionally attended some of the meetings at the request of the pro-choice group. The investigation lasted seven months before fizzling out. It had uncovered nothing even remotely illegal.

(The details of this escapade did not become public until several months after the Morgantaler decision. The whole affair had been hatched by Smith, who said he had simply been trying to accommodate Vander Zalm's strong feelings on the subject: everything must be done to prevent an abortion clinic from opening in B.C.)

But talk of abortion clinics was premature and, for the moment, the least of Vander Zalm's worries. In his haste to block access to abortions, Vander Zalm had forgotten to consult with the province's doctors. In outraged response, the B.C. Medical Association, the doctors' official provincial organization, urged its members to refuse to cooperate with hospital abortion committees. The BCMA felt the government was trying to make doctors "scapegoats" by forcing them to make a political decision on a medical procedure.

The government was taken aback. Dueck hinted that he had "contingency plans" to deal with the situation. What no one knew was that Dueck and Vander Zalm had already discussed a new, tougher policy to be implemented if the first one could not be.

Smith's office had prepared a position paper outlining three options: allow an abortion to result from a decision made only by the woman and her doctor; require that two doctors approve an abortion; or cut off all funding for abortions except in emergencies.

The first option was rejected out of hand: Vander Zalm wanted a say. The second option, which gave two doctors authority, was strongly favoured by Smith as a compromise that could stand up in court.

Vander Zalm, Poole, and Dueck talked of adopting the third option. Smith nervously began to withdraw from the debate as he became more and more convinced that the government's attitude and policy was losing it public support.

The provincial cabinet had still not met to formally discuss the abortion issue. The only people involved in the discussions so far had been Vander Zalm, Poole, Dueck, and Smith. Most ministers were in the dark about the new policy.

On Saturday, February 6, nine days after the Morgentaler decision, Vander Zalm and Lillian talked things over on the flight home; the conversation was the shot of confidence the premier needed.

They arrived shortly before midnight and were greeted by two dozen cheering supporters praising his anti-abortion stand.

Vander Zalm had called a news conference at Vancouver International Airport. Tanned but visibly tired, decked out in a white sport coat and golf shirt, he walked into a boardroom on the fourth floor of the main terminal and said to the assembled reporters, "I will recommend to cabinet tomorrow that the government no longer pay for any abortions, save those in emergency situations."

Like most premiers, Vander Zalm never "recommended" anything to cabinet; if he wanted a policy implemented, it passed no matter how cabinet felt.

He continued to speak as reporters were given a two-page news release. Lillian stood off to the side, watching.

"I want to free taxpayers from abortions," he said. "Abortions diminish society's respect for human life."

On Sunday morning, most British Columbians learned of the new abortion policy. The morning tabloid, the *Province*, screamed the story from the front page. Radio broadcasts carried the story at the top of the hour all day.

Vander Zalm hosted his regular monthly open-line radio program that afternoon at CKNW's downtown studios on the old Expo site. He handled the phones with the ease and grace of an old radio pro.

One caller from the province's Interior was repeatedly cut off by Vander Zalm, who got into a loud argument with him. The man said that, as a taxpayer, he was willing to pay for abortions and said Vander Zalm had no right to arbitrarily cut off funding for them.

"Oh, obviously you'd pay for it. You're in support of it," bristled Vander Zalm. "And if an organization you would like to join would like to put on a fundraiser in order to provide monies [for abortions], go ahead and do it."

Another caller suggested that many women who request abortions would not be able to pay the full cost of them.

"It could be argued by some that people could be denied the opportunity," Vander Zalm replied. "The other argument is: should the taxpayers fund abortion on demand? And given that choice, we really had no choice but to take the course we did."

After the broadcast, Vander Zalm waded into a pack of waiting reporters, one of whom asked a seemingly innocuous question: would the policy of not paying for abortions apply also to rape and incest victims?

Vander Zalm seemed surprised at the question. He thought for a moment, and then said yes, it would apply to such cases. "There will be no exceptions," he said.

His reply to this question was buried in the day's avalanche of media coverage; yet it eventually triggered an emotional split in the Social Credit caucus and among party supporters. The Socreds, not aware of his responses, would later assume that rape and incest victims could still rely on government-funded abortions.

Overlooked in the hectic ten days following the Morgentaler decision were the confused and apprehensive Socred MLAs. They finally got their chance for some input in Powell River, a pulp-mill town 150 kilometres up the coast from Vancouver. The Social Credit caucus began arriving there in the evening of Sunday, February 7, for two days of meetings. While checking into a resort on the out-skirts of town, they queried reporters about the abortion policy. Once again the MLAs were asking the news media what was going on in government.

At the cabinet meeting that night, Vander Zalm and Dueck briefly explained the policy. Only two ministers spoke out against it: Stephen Rogers, who as a one-time health minister knew full well the politics of abortion, and Rita Johnstone, the municipal affairs minister and the only woman present at the meeting. (Grace McCarthy didn't arrive until the next day, Brian Smith was also absent. Neither liked the new policy.)

No other ministers spoke out, although some looked uneasy. The cabinet ministers were not used to taking sides against their boss, and they were well aware of his strong opinions on abortion.

Shortly after nine o'clock the next morning, the full caucus gathered in a large room off the main lobby in the lakeside resort. Just as the meeting started, Vancouver South MLA Russ Fraser asked Vander Zalm for an explanation of the abortion policy.

The presentation by Vander Zalm and Dueck lasted less than ten minutes. Vander Zalm explained that without his new policy, there would be no checks on access to abortions in the province. Government money could be used to fund abortions under any circumstances—"abortion on demand," as he called it. That simply was not going to be allowed to occur, he told his caucus. (He did not mention certain other issues that were involved, such as his version of morality versus that of others, or the propriety of cutting off funding for a legal medical procedure.)

Vander Zalm asked if there were any questions. A few MLAs expressed support for the new policy. No one else spoke. Over the next few weeks it would become clear that several of the MLAs had grave concerns about the policy. But they did not raise them on that day. For some of them, the enormity of the situation had yet to sink in. Others were simply scared to confront the premier on such a key issue.

Vander Zalm, when interviewed for this book, said: "We opened the meeting with that. Everybody had an opportunity to speak out on the issue. A few people did. A very few. And those that did speak out were largely on the supportive side. I guess I was impressed by the solidarity of the caucus, at the time."

In short, as he had misjudged the public's feeling about his abortion policy, Vander Zalm also misjudged the level of the caucus's opposition. "I didn't know how strongly they felt. I really hadn't had an opportunity to meet one on one, or to hear one on one the views of the caucus members," Vander Zalm recalls. "I could identify relatively easily those that I thought would be relatively supportive, in any event, of the stance we took. But I did not know how some of the others felt. I became aware of it later on."

And so the caucus moved on to other matters. Through two days of meetings, they never returned to discussing abortion, with the exception of one person: Bill Vander Zalm discussed the issue at length with reporters, but not with his caucus.

In that spring of 1988, Vander Zalm still enjoyed what he considered to be a warm relationship with the media. He had received a large share of negative press during the previous eighteen months, but he had shrugged most of it off. Much of the criticism concerned his style of governing, and Vander Zalm considered such talk to be inconsequential and not reflective of how the voters felt. And to a large extent he had been right.

Abortion changed everything. He had always been able to use the media as a tool, but it didn't work in Powell River.

"That's where I lost the media, no question. Up until then, things had been fairly positive. But I knew then I had lost the reporters. It was a real turning point," Vander Zalm recalled.

The reporters' scrums gradually became long arguments and bore little resemblance to interviews. Reporters trained to appear objective found themselves getting angry at Vander Zalm over his rigid anti-abortion stand.

"I can't remember any issues where reporters got more emotionally involved in what they were covering," remembers Margot Sinclair, a veteran political reporter for Broadcast News in Ottawa and Victoria.

The coverage was not slanted, though. News stories at the time simply detailed the mounting opposition to the government and accurately characterized Vander Zalm as holding fast to his position. No exceptions, no compromises, no change—that was the message from the premier.

After it became clear that the premier was not going to change his mind, the media's questions narrowed, for a time, to one aspect of the abortion policy: no exemptions for rape and incest.

The percentage of women seeking abortions whose pregnancies result from rape or incest is small, but statistics weren't the issue so much as the image of a mean-spirited government. What kind of leader would deny funding to such tragic victims?

"Where I got into bigger trouble, where I went beyond what I think many of my colleagues wanted to see, was when we started to talk about the issue of incest and rape, how we would deal with that," Vander Zalm recalls.

"That came as a bit of a, not a surprise entirely, but a twist we hadn't figured on when we first talked about what it was that we would do."

On the second night in Powell River, while enjoying a glass of white wine at a caucus reception hosted by a local business group, Vander Zalm engaged in yet another discussion with several reporters.

"What about a fourteen-year-old girl who is raped in a park and becomes pregnant? What if she has no money to pay for an abortion? Are you saying you won't provide funding for her?" he was asked.

"There can't be any exceptions," Vander Zalm maintained.

The questions persisted. David Poole hovered nearby, watching anxiously. A few local Socred supporters chided the three reporters, telling them to leave their premier alone. The same question about the fourteen-year-old girl was asked again, and this time Vander Zalm's reaction startled even the growing number of party supporters who had stopped to watch the discussion.

The premier put his hands over his ears and closed his eyes.

"Don't ask me those questions. I don't want to hear them," he said.

But the reporters kept after him.

"I don't like hearing that. I don't like those questions," Vander Zalm said again, backing away with his hands still over his ears. Poole rushed in to help. "I think you've had him enough times for today," he told the reporters. The room had grown much quieter and a few party supporters stared into their glasses, looking embarrassed. Vander Zalm and Poole left a short time later.

The next day, just before Vander Zalm left Powell River, two reporters were ushered into his hotel room. They told Poole they had discovered a new angle on the rape and incest question and wanted to talk to Vander Zalm about it.

Poole and the premier's press secretary, Bill Bachop, were wary yet curious. The reporters had found that another area of government funding–the criminal injury compensation program–could possibly pay for abortions caused by rape or incestuous acts. The reporters asked Vander Zalm for his opinion. It was an opportunity to put the rape and incest victim question behind him, but he wouldn't give in that easily.

"I would be disturbed if I found another arm or agency of government was using another piece of legislation to do what we wouldn't normally do. I expect, really, the adjudicators would keep that in mind," he responded.

Instead of paying for the abortion, the fund should pay for counselling for the victim, he said—a response that pretty well guaranteed he would stay on the hook.

After Powell River, Vander Zalm fled B.C. for the anonymity of Europe. For two weeks, he combined business with another holiday for himself and Lillian. They visited London, West Germany, and the Netherlands. There were no reporters along on the trip to remind him of the problems at home. Indeed, even his office didn't know where he was at times. Only David Poole could contact him, and even he could not find the premier on short notice.

After forcing his rigid policy on his caucus, Vander Zalm took off and left them to defend it. It was a task many of them found distasteful, to say the least. By now, the Socred MLAs were well aware of the furor created by the premier's stand.

When they arrived back in their ridings after Powell River, most of the MLAs found huge stacks of telephone messages. Their offices had been blitzed with phone calls on the abortion issue. The Socred riding office that received the most anti-government calls was backbencher Kim Campbell's. Her riding, Vancouver–Point Grey, was very liberal, populated by upper-income professionals with university educations.

Campbell herself was vehemently opposed to the policy. As a woman, she considered the policy offensive. As a politician, she saw it as an almost suicidal move for her party. As a lawyer, she thought the policy stood little chance of being upheld in court.

Although it wasn't much of a secret that she was pro-choice, Campbell refused to comment on the new policy until several days after the Powell River retreat. Finally, on February 11, emerging from a last-minute meeting with Dueck, an emotional Campbell ran right into a CBC television crew and spilled out the reasons for her opposition.

"It would be hypocritical to suggest I support the policy. My pro-choice views are well known," she said, adding that the calls to her office were running four to one against the government.

Tough, bright, and independent, Campbell was respected by her caucus colleagues. Her break from caucus solidarity made it easier for other backbenchers to follow suit. Over the next week, six more MLAs, including cabinet minister Grace McCarthy, publicly criticized the policy. Only Campbell said she was pro-choice. The rest said they backed the premier except for one aspect of the policy–funding for rape and incest victims. Some MLAs, notably Campbell's colleague-in-exile, Bud Smith, remained silent throughout the whole ordeal.

The spectacle of six MLAs publicly breaking with the government on such a key and emotional issue–no matter how small that break actually was–garnered tremendous media attention. Social Credit had a long history of maintaining caucus unity. Despite the party's coalition roots, Socreds seldom criticized their leader publicly. No MLAs had broke with Bill Bennett, even during the tough restraint years. The image now was of a government on the run from its own members.

Of course, public outrage was considerable. "Premier's abortion policy will result in deaths" read one headline from the Victoria *Times Colonist*.

The health ministry's own medical ethics committee was also appalled. Its members hadn't even been consulted by Dueck on the issue.

In Victoria, the premier's office was shell-shocked, especially with the premier incommunicado in Europe. "We had no idea it was going to get that bad, no idea at all," Bob Ransford remembers. "And it just got worse every day, day after day. And [Vander Zalm] looked at it as more of a challenge every single day. The tougher it got, the more worked up he got over it."

The Social Credit caucus, meanwhile, was also in a state of turmoil. "We were dealing with [caucus members] who simply didn't know how bad it was going to be," remembers Stephen Rogers. "I knew what the bomb was going to be like."

On the other hand, the caucus refused to deal formally with the abortion question. "To discuss the policy as if it was a serious problem came too close to questioning the leadership," one MLA remembers. "It just cut too close."

Challenging Vander Zalm would have been almost suicidal, both for the individual's political career and for the government itself, or so it seemed at the time. And some of the members swept to office in the 1986 election were as religious as Vander Zalm. Still, even the anti-abortionists in caucus were uneasy; they had seen the polls too.

But instead of confronting Vander Zalm, the government MLAs met in twos and threes, trying to take comfort from each other. "There was a singular lack of courage, on that and many other things," remembers one MLA. "A lot of people were afraid they'd become the objects of ire of the pro-life movement."

"Oh, those were truly bad times," remembers caucus chair Carol Gran. "There were so many rumours, and so much intrigue. I finally decided I didn't want to hear any more. The whole mess just took on a life of its own. It was a very, very difficult time for everyone."

Says Kim Campbell: "The abortion issue was tearing the party apart. Our party is not a pro-life party. We come together because we share certain views on the relationship between governments and the economy and the individual in society. We don't come together on the issue of abortion, which cuts across parties."

When Gran publicly criticized the policy on rape and incest victims, it was a stroke of bad luck for Vander Zalm. Suddenly, the caucus's official spokesperson was opposed to a policy and philosophy strongly held by the premier.

At Social Credit Party headquarters in Richmond, extra staff members were hired to answer the endless phone calls. Poole and other party officials, including party president Hope Wotherspoon, were bravely saying that most of the calls were strongly supportive of the government's abortion policy. In fact, the opposite was true.

Confidential party documents show that more than 1400 people had phoned between January 29, the day the B.C. government's first policy was announced, and March 11. Of those calls, 55 per cent were opposed to the policy.

Reading public opinion based on phone calls to an office is a risky proposition. But the government also had access to a more scientific method. The Social Credit Party had commissioned a private Decima Research province-wide poll in mid-February. The poll showed that the public was solidly against Vander Zalm's abortion stand, with more than 60 per cent saying they were pro-choice. And abortion had emerged as the most important issue in the minds of voters, eclipsing unemployment by a two-to-one margin. It would not be the last time the premier's office would conceal the depth of the public's opposition to government policy.

It was time for damage control. Vander Zalm phoned Poole from Europe, and the two men decided that rape and incest victims would indeed receive funding for abortions through the criminal injuries compensation program, with the government's full blessing. The move was intended to show that the premier was capable of compromise and compassion.

But many points the government scored from the announcement were lost by the way in which it was made. With Vander Zalm in Europe, it was Poole who called reporters to the premier's office on the afternoon of February 17, and there announced the change in policy.

The next day, Poole was hammered in the press. Who was he— an unelected official—to take on such airs and be the official spokesman? Some of the criticism came from cabinet ministers who privately attacked Poole in off-the-record conversations with reporters.

The incident reinforced Poole's image as power-hungry and arrogant. What no one knew at the time, however, was that Poole had been told by Vander Zalm to have a cabinet member make the announcement. But at the cabinet meeting that day no one, not even Dueck, wanted to touch the abortion issue. Even the anti-abortionists in the cabinet were deserting the premier. Poole informed Vander Zalm of the ministers' collective loss of resolve, and the premier ordered his top aide to step in front of the cameras instead.

Vander Zalm, after taking ill during his last days in Europe, returned to B.C. on Friday, February 26, and held another news conference at Vancouver International Airport. This time, Lillian stood out of sight, behind a curtain off to the side. She was bitter toward the news media for its treatment of her husband on an issue so close to her heart.

For forty minutes he made it clear that he was not going to back down. Then he left, accompanied by Poole. The two men knew they had a crisis on their hands, but they didn't know what to do. Ever the optimist, Vander Zalm was convinced he could weather the storm.

But, as the polls showed, the premier was completely out of touch with the public and also with a significant portion of his own caucus, some of whom were almost in open revolt against his leadership. Many MLAs began to worry that Vander Zalm was willing to destroy the government over the issue. They slowly realized that there was little anybody could do to stop him. The public outrage was already considerable; it couldn't get much worse. A significant number of MLAs opposed him, but that didn't seem to matter to the premier. All the arguments had been made.

Vander Zalm was genuinely mystified by the charge that he was imposing his own views on the populace. He thought that people should laud him for being a person who did not abandon his principles for political expediency.

He had provided an insight into his thinking on "moral issues" a year earlier, saying that his moral views would influence the type of sex education students would receive in B.C. schools: "My views will have an influence, no question about it. . . . I think people elect others to represent them basically on what they stand for, which includes, certainly, their moral values or the way they approach things. . . . Otherwise it wouldn't hurt to hire somebody from the Mafia or somebody who has no moral values," he said.

That weekend, Vander Zalm returned home to Fantasy Gardens. He knew he had to do something, but he was not sure what it should be. "Those were tough days," he remembers now. "I was getting hammered and I decided I wanted to make a statement in the legislature [which had just resumed sitting] about it."

On Friday evening, after the news conference, he couldn't sleep. Finally, he got up and went to his bedroom desk. There, he began to piece together his statement. All through the night, he worked on it. At one point, he broke down crying. Lillian got up to comfort him and encourage him. For two days, he laboured on what he considered one of the most important speeches of his career.

"For two nights I was up and working and getting up and writing things, and rewriting, and I was caught up in the emotion of all of this that was taking place," Vander Zalm recalls. "That whole weekend. . . . I just lived that. I slept it. I just lived it. I couldn't eat without making a note, or getting back to it."

He finished it on Sunday, and phoned Poole to read it to him. Poole became worried as he listened. The speech was emotional, defiant, and graphic. Poole convinced Vander Zalm to take out, or at least tone down, some of the more graphic parts where he described an actual abortion in his own words.

Vander Zalm reluctantly agreed. He wanted the statement to show just how strongly he felt about the issue, and he also wanted to let off a little steam.

On Monday, February 28, just after question period, Vander Zalm rose to make a ministerial statement. Both sides of the house listened eagerly. Although the Socreds knew Vander Zalm would speak on abortion, they had no idea what he would say this time.

He informed the legislature, accurately enough, that he would provide some "frank answers with no fancy political language."

He started by comparing the abortion issue to the Holocaust. "Remember when I'm accused by members opposite or others not here, of exaggerating, of overstating or using words too strong, that the same thing was first said about those who described the Holocaust," Vander Zalm said.

Then the graphic detail. "Abortion at a later stage can often only be done if the baby's body is cut up. This happens without so much as an anaesthetic being given to the baby. A process without an anaesthetic to remove the pain and suffering that's afflicted. No one here can imagine such suffering and no one ever lived to tell about it," he told the house.

He moved on to the subject of abortion clinics, where "people work for profit, big profit, performing abortions much advanced of what might be considered in a doctor's office or hospital. Abortions requiring dismemberment of a baby before removal without as much as a baby aspirin for the victim."

Vander Zalm referred to a young couple who he said discovered during pregnancy that their baby would have a severe birth defect that made survival an impossibility. The couple decided to have the child. It died shortly after birth.

What no one knew was that the young father was Vander Zalm's unofficially adopted son, Jos Van Hage, and the incident had been a trying and emotional one for the Vander Zalms.

Although the baby soon died, said Vander Zalm, "the couple stated openly that words could not describe the love for their son. It was almost supernatural and unforgettable, and the experience has affected their lives more positively than anything they have ever experienced before.

"Their love touched everyone. Lillian and I attended a funeral that filled the church with people, many of whom normally would never attend church or a funeral. The tears were of admiration, tears of respect and tears of love. Little Christian may have done more for the world and humanity during his three weeks on earth than many normal people could do in a lifetime. How sad things might have been if abortion had been the choice."

His lurid characterization of abortions minimized any emotional impact the story of little Christian might have had. Throughout the speech, many MLAs from both sides of the house stared open-mouthed at Vander Zalm. The NDP caucus briefly discussed walking out in protest and most of them eventually turned their chairs around so their backs were to Vander Zalm. Many Socreds appeared embarrassed, and looked down at their desks or busied themselves with paperwork.

But Vander Zalm continued, defiantly stating that he would not change his policy to accommodate what he considered to be the cold-blooded killings of little babies. When he finally finished, only a few Socreds bothered to thump their desks in approval. Shouts of "Shame! Shame!" came from the NDP.

Socred backbencher Russ Fraser termed the speech "offensive," and other government MLAs said the premier was far too graphic. By now, criticizing their own leader in public had become routine for some of them.

Vander Zalm spent the next week holed up in his office, meeting and talking only with Poole. He was becoming more isolated from his own party.

The caucus wished the issue would go away, but instead it dominated the legislature's question period day after day, with the

NDP endlessly arguing that Vander Zalm was imposing his moral views on the rest of the province.

Abortion had also caused problems for the NDP. Its caucus was also uncomfortable with the issue as well, and leader Harcourt didn't even like to talk to reporters about his caucus's views about it. After Vander Zalm's speech to the house, rookie NDP MLA Joan Smallwood called the premier a "coward" in the legislature. Since "coward" is considered unparliamentary language, Speaker John Reynolds asked her to withdraw the comment. Smallwood refused, and was expelled for the day.

At the NDP caucus meeting, the normally mild-mannered Harcourt tore into Smallwood and her small group of supporters within caucus, who had been warned against getting overemotional and risking expulsion.

Harcourt yelled at her for several minutes, nearly reducing her to tears. The rest of the NDP members were shocked. They had rarely seen Harcourt so angry. Smallwood's performance had robbed Harcourt of some much-needed news coverage that day.

Meanwhile, the Socred caucus's research department issued each MLA a thick blue binder containing a chronology of events surrounding the abortion policy, a collection of newspaper articles, a condensed version of the Supreme Court of Canada ruling, details of how other provincial governments were dealing with the problem, and a copy of the statement Vander Zalm had made upon his return home from Hawaii.

The binders also contained seven government abortion "strategies," including examples of soon-to-be-unveiled government advertising. The idea was to make Socred MLAs feel they were all part of the decision-making process, but blue binders couldn't make them less alienated from their leader.

Finally, after a month of bitter emotional debate, the B.C. Supreme Court stepped in. On March 7, Justice Allan MacEachern, responding to a suit by the B.C. Civil Liberties Association, threw out the government's regulations cutting off abortion funding. The government had overstepped its authority and gone beyond "common sense," the judge ruled.

Most Socred MLAs felt relief, and as luck would have it Vander Zalm was not even in the province. He was attending a free trade conference in Saskatoon, where he obligingly said he was upset and was considering an appeal. He was about to learn, however, that he had lost control of the issue so dear to his heart, at least temporarily.

Brian Smith wasn't particularly surprised by Justice MacEachern's ruling. Smith had always felt that high courts took public opinion into consideration, and public opinion was certainly against the government on this one.

Smith twice tried to contact Vander Zalm by phone with no success. By 3:00 p.m., a mob of reporters had gathered outside his Victoria office, and if he wanted to so much as go to the bathroom, he would have to run a gauntlet of cameras and questions.

Smith was convinced that large numbers of Socred women voters would desert the party over Vander Zalm's position. He had told Poole—whom he viewed as having a "calming" influence on Vander Zalm—that the premier was out of sync with the caucus. And several MLAs had privately approached him to complain about Vander Zalm's direction.

Smith was convinced that an appeal would be useless. He had always regarded the policy as legally suspect. And Justice MacEachern had made it clear in his judgment that the policy would fail under a Charter of Rights argument. Smith also knew that Vander Zalm would have an extremely hard time reversing any legal decision made by his attorney-general.

Finally, Smith got up out of his chair and walked outside his office to the waiting throng of reporters. No, he told them, there would be no appeal. And no, he said, he hadn't discussed the issue with Vander Zalm. The decision had been reached, premier or no premier, Poole or no Poole. Smith had always asserted the independence of the attorney-general's office; this was independence with a vengeance.

He told the reporters that he still planned to talk to Vander Zalm, however. "If he phones us first, would you like us to get him to phone you?" one reporter asked. Smith broke into a wide grin.

When Vander Zalm arrived back from Saskatoon the next day, he told reporters at the Victoria airport that he would accept his attorney-general's advice and wasn't in the least upset that Smith had gone public before consulting him.

After the news conference, however, Vander Zalm and Poole jumped into their waiting car and drove back to the legislature. Poole immediately grabbed the car phone and called Smith. He ordered him to be in the premier's office by the time they arrived.

During their meeting, Smith was able to convince Vander Zalm of the futility of trying to defend the government's policy in court. Smith also told him about the mob of reporters, and claimed there was no way he could have avoided issuing a statement. Vander Zalm accepted his explanation, albeit reluctantly. He knew he had lost a big battle.

"We had words," Vander Zalm recalls. "We didn't really argue too deeply, because the final analysis was that we probably could not have gone with an appeal in any event."

Vander Zalm made a few half-hearted attempts at keeping the issue alive, including suggesting to cabinet that they reword the regulation that had been thrown out by the court. But cabinet, the caucus, and the public had had enough. Vander Zalm finally accepted the fact that he had lost.

The court decision took abortion off the front pages for a while, and it seemed as though the Social Credit caucus might calm down.

But then, at the beginning of April, the fragile relationship between Vander Zalm and his caucus was rocked again. The *Sun*'s Gary Mason, granted a long-sought interview, was ushered into Vander Zalm's office one morning.

"I've only got ten minutes," Vander Zalm said as he stuffed tobacco into his pipe.

How disappointed was Vander Zalm over his failure to cut off abortion funding?

"I was mostly disappointed that my colleagues didn't have the moxie to really fight alongside," Vander Zalm nonchalantly replied.

When the interview was over, Mason rushed back to his office and played the tape for his colleagues in the *Sun*'s bureau. They couldn't believe it; why would Vander Zalm throw yet another firecracker into the Socred caucus?

Mason interviewed several Socred MLAs for their reactions. Kim Campbell was incredulous. Russ Fraser just shook his head. Carol Gran, the caucus chair, was the most upset of all: "I can't believe he would say something like that about his caucus colleagues."

Vander Zalm phoned Gran and denied having said "any such thing." Gran felt relieved.

Shortly before 7:00 p.m., one of the press gallery's phone lines lit up. It was Vander Zalm, demanding to talk to Mason.

"What's all this business about you telling MLAs that they were weak-kneed, didn't have guts or lacked moxie?" Vander Zalm asked. "I never said any such thing."

It would not be the last time Vander Zalm would deny having said something or done something, even when there was physical evidence to prove him wrong. Often, his first reaction was to deny whatever it was that had gotten him into trouble.

He asked that Mason come to his office and play him the tape. When Mason arrived there, he found Poole standing outside the door. Worried that Vander Zalm would still deny having made the quote even after he heard the tape, Mason asked the principal secretary to accompany him inside to act as a witness.

Mason put the tape on Vander Zalm's desk and played it. Within seconds, the incriminating words filled the room. For a second, there was silence. Then Poole said: "Yup, you said it."

Vander Zalm sat motionless and silent as the tape kept playing. Then he started fidgeting with the recorder, trying to shut it off. "I said it, you're right. But I think you're placing a different emphasis on it than I did," Vander Zalm said as Poole paced in the room, trying to think of ways to prevent the incident from inflicting too much damage.

"The paper's going to come out and there's going to be this screaming headline: 'Vander Zalm Criticizes Caucus Colleagues.' That's what it's going to say and I'm going to be in all sorts of trouble," said Vander Zalm.

"It's not what I need," he concluded, slipping his reading glasses on and dismissing Mason. "But you do what you have to do."

The next day, the *Sun* put the story on the front page. There was also another story about Vander Zalm's denial and his summoning of Mason to his office. Vander Zalm had succeeded in turning one front-page story making him look bad into two front-page stories making him look bad.

(Vander Zalm was upset, but he still didn't want to hurt his relationship with any reporter. Walking up the back stairs to his office the next day, he turned to Keith Baldrey, who had been interviewing him about the incident, and said, "Tell Gary I'm not mad at him, okay?")

The "moxie incident," as it came to be called, was another blow to Socred caucus morale. One day, Brian Smith walked down a legislative corridor toward a handful of reporters, pretending to pour salt in an open wound on his arm.

The government's other business went on, of course, and gradually the abortion crisis faded from view–but not from memory. The bitterness lingered among government caucus members and with the public. Two weeks after the court ruling, Vander Zalm finally conceded that there was really nothing he could do about funding abortions until a new federal law was adopted. Instead, he created a $20-million program designed to enhance traditional family values and alternatives to abortions, such as counselling and adoption.

"You know, if I look back and if I could be self-critical–if I look back and say how would I do it differently–I'm not saying that I might not do the same thing again," Vander Zalm says now. "I might not be as emotional about it as I was. Perhaps my own emotions became the thing a lot of people objected to. And I was very emotional about the issue. I still am."

Something Rotten
in Fantasyland

"**Y**ou *what?*" Grace Mc-
Carthy screamed over
the telephone at Kevin Murphy. Murphy, who was president of the
B.C. Enterprise Corp. (BCEC), a Crown corporation for which
McCarthy was responsible, had just told her that David Poole had
had McCarthy's staff set up a special meeting with Bill Vander
Zalm's friend Peter Toigo. Toigo was seeking information on which
to base an offer to buy government land holdings, including the
coveted Expo 86 site.

There was just one problem. The date was December 2, 1987, and
the deadline for expressions of interest in the Expo site had passed
more than a month earlier. A shortlist of bidders had already been
drawn up by BCEC, and Toigo wasn't on it.

McCarthy listened as Murphy—who had attended the meeting—
told her that a finance ministry official had also been present. The
official's minister, Mel Couvelier, had known about the meeting.
McCarthy had not.

McCarthy felt humiliated and angry. Vander Zalm must have kept
the meeting from her, she figured, because he knew it was wrong—
knew he was subverting the bidding process already under way in
order to help his friend. McCarthy thought back to the cabinet
meeting earlier that day. Vander Zalm had been sitting right beside
her in the cabinet chambers when he asked that an item be moved

up on the agenda because Poole, who attended cabinet meetings, had to leave shortly. So, it had been a secret meeting with Toigo for which Poole had had to leave.

The following day, December 3, McCarthy marched down to Vander Zalm's corner office. There, she launched into an emotional tirade about the meeting. "Why couldn't you tell me?" McCarthy demanded of Vander Zalm. "You knew David was leaving cabinet for that meeting. You and I had a private meeting in your office after cabinet; you could have told me then. It must have been a very big thing for you to lie to me."

"Come on, Grace, I think you're overreacting," Vander Zalm replied.

But McCarthy could no longer tolerate what she considered to be Vander Zalm sneaking around her back, getting BCEC staff to arrange special meetings for Toigo. She was tired of the interference in her ministry's affairs. It had gone on far too long.

The showdown between McCarthy and Vander Zalm had its roots in an early morning meeting held on May 29, 1987. Peter Brown, chairman of the B.C. Enterprise Corp., and Kevin Murphy, its president, strolled to a private meeting room in Toigo's B.C. Club, a swank restaurant on the Expo site. Vander Zalm had asked the two men to hear firsthand Toigo's proposal to develop a section of the 82-hectare site of the world's fair. Since the fair had closed in October 1986, the grounds had sat unused. The BCEC officials mistakenly assumed that McCarthy had been informed of the meeting by Vander Zalm since it had been arranged on his initiative.

BCEC had been established earlier in 1987 to dispose of half a billion dollars' worth of government land holdings, of which the Expo site was the most prized.

The site was at False Creek, a salt-water inlet that slices the city of Vancouver in half. Only eight years earlier the land had been a largely derelict area showing the effects of years of heavy industrial use: a shoreline contaminated with toxic waste and marked by mudflats, debris, and log booms. The area was bordered by a trendy market and theatre district to the west and a stretch of fashionable and high-priced condominium developments across the inlet to the south.

Brown, a high-profile but controversial broker on the Vancouver Stock Exchange who had a reputation as a consummate deal maker, had been asked by McCarthy to head the BCEC board. He knew the details of the Expo property through an earlier stint on the Expo 86 board, when he had been in charge of the fair's finances. Brown had also been a loyal friend of Social Credit, having raised millions of party dollars under former premier Bill Bennett.

His status changed under Bill Vander Zalm, who was suspicious of the Vancouver business establishment that supported Social Credit. The premier, self-styled friend of the little guy, vowed during his first few weeks in office that establishment power brokers of the past would no longer have special entrée to the premier's office. Everyone knew he meant people like Peter Brown.

Vander Zalm was also wary of Brown's flamboyant reputation. People joked that the dashing, dark-haired, dark-eyed Brown had a collection of Gucci shoes second only to Brian Mulroney's. He drove a Rolls-Royce Corniche and attended the most prestigious parties.

In 1986, Brown had thought about seeking the Socred leadership until a poll he commissioned showed that he had little support outside Vancouver. A political animal, Brown was able during Bill Bennett's reign to keep up with all the government gossip courtesy of his friends in the capital. Ostracized under Vander Zalm, he was reduced to phoning reporters, often from his bathtub at home, where he could be heard splashing around as he tried to get the latest political scoop.

Brown had annually raised more than half the party's funds. Now, filled with resentment, he wouldn't pick up the phone to raise a nickel.

BCEC president Kevin Murphy, who was also waiting for the meeting with Toigo on the morning of May 29, had a much lower profile in B.C.

He had been Expo 86's vice-president in charge of construction, and at age forty-six he had a well-earned reputation for turning troubled projects around. He had been the project director on a pulp mill in Iran during the final days of the Shah's reign. About the time Murphy began to work on a second mill, the Shah was overthrown. As thousands of Moslems flooded the streets, Murphy helped organize the evacuation of a planeload of American and

Canadian citizens before escaping himself.

Next, he had found himself in Argentina working for Atomic Energy of Canada, which was building a money-losing Candu reactor. Murphy successfully renegotiated the contract, working right through a military coup that installed right-wing dictator General Jorge Videla. His experience working amid political wars would serve him well as chief negotiator on the Expo lands sale.

It was now nearly 8:00 a.m. at the B.C. Club, a half-hour after the May 29 meeting had been scheduled to start. There was still no sign of Toigo. David Poole was there, though. Murphy found it extremely odd that Vander Zalm's chief political adviser would be attending a meeting with a private businessman, albeit one who was a good friend of the premier. Peter Brown was less surprised at Poole's presence. He had met Poole the previous month at a breakfast meeting with Vander Zalm in Victoria, during which the premier had surprised Brown by asking him why the corporation had not responded to Toigo's interest in one of BCEC's assets: a convention centre in the ski-resort community of Whistler.

Brown had said the corporation hadn't received an offer from Toigo, and then warned Vander Zalm of the political dangers of the government doing business with the premier's high-profile friend. Vander Zalm didn't see any problem, Brown later recalled. The premier's indifference to Brown's April warnings of the perils of dealing with friends was an omen of things to come.

Toigo, meanwhile, finally arrived at the B.C. Club thirty-five minutes late, setting a poor tone for the meeting. David Podmore, an official with Toigo's Whitbury Developments Ltd., outlined Toigo's development plans for the Expo site.

Podmore had made the same presentation to the cabinet on Toigo's behalf soon after the October 1986 election. Vander Zalm had also organized that presentation, which had raised the eyebrows of some ministers who questioned the premier's judgment in helping bring a friend's plan to cabinet. Little did they know that it wouldn't be the last time Vander Zalm would help Toigo in such a way.

At the B.C. Club, Toigo explained that he wanted to put up a world-class hotel and some restaurants that would be built around a theme park, using existing Expo 86 rides. While Brown looked on sceptically, Murphy pointed out zoning problems and the issue of contaminated soil on Toigo's proposed section of the Expo site.

David Poole said that the problems could be overcome. He stressed that the premier enthusiastically supported Toigo's plans and urged BCEC to act quickly.

Brown broke in. He told Poole he didn't like hiving off a piece of the Expo site; it should be sold as one chunk. And he said that once a deal with a good friend of the premier's became public knowledge, particularly a deal that wasn't the product of a fair public tendering process, the political fallout would be devastating.

Then he faced Toigo: "Look, we're not going to get staff going on this thing when we don't even know if you've got the money to buy the site."

"What do you mean?" Toigo shot back. "We've got as much money as you've got."

Brown and Toigo exchanged more angry words over the BCEC chairman's concerns about dealing with a prominent friend of Vander Zalm's. When tempers had cooled, Brown suggested to Toigo that since he only wanted to develop a piece of the Expo site, he get in touch with a local developer who was interested in purchasing the whole thing: Jack Poole, head of Bell Canada Enterprises Development.

It was advice Brown would come to regret offering.

Jack Poole (no relation to David Poole) didn't know Toigo well. But he did know that a connection with a friend of the premier's couldn't hurt at bidding time. In the summer of 1987 the two men formed a partnership.

It was an unlikely alliance: Jack Poole, the handsome and charismatic establishment Liberal, and Peter Toigo, the short, pudgy, outsider millionaire. Still, the combination of Bell Canada's resources and Toigo's connections made the pair a favourite to get the site. Soon the gossip in Vancouver's financial district was that the government had a pre-cooked deal with Toigo and Jack Poole for the Expo site. Local developers began approaching

BCEC officials with one question: "It's a done deal with Poole and Toigo, isn't it?"

In July 1987, representations of Hong Kong investor Li Ka-shing informed BCEC that they were no longer interested in entering the Expo site bidding game–which was expected to officially get under way in September–because they had heard that Toigo and Jack Poole were a lock. Li Ka-shing's people had to be assured personally by BCEC president Kevin Murphy that the tendering process would be fair.

Meanwhile, Toigo and Jack Poole decided at the end of July to take matters into their own hands, and they visited Vander Zalm personally at Fantasy Gardens. The premier professed excitement at their proposal, which incorporated Toigo's theme park plans with Jack Poole's vision of hotels and apartment complexes.

(A year later, Vander Zalm denied any knowledge of the Jack Poole-Toigo proposal. "I've never seen the deal, I don't know what it is, I've never asked and [Peter Toigo's] never told me," Vander Zalm told a group of reporters on April 28, 1988.)

On Wednesday, August 5, two months after he'd pushed Jack Poole and Toigo into each other's arms, Peter Brown phoned Kevin Murphy with some alarming news. He told Murphy he'd received a call from Jack Poole, who had said the premier had liked his and Toigo's proposal and couldn't see why BCEC couldn't proceed to cut a deal quickly.

This was crazy, Brown and Murphy, thought. In less than a month, BCEC was due to be advertising world-wide for expressions of interest in the Expo site. And here was the premier saying a quick deal could be cut with Jack Poole and Toigo.

Brown set up a meeting with Murphy for the following day at the Mandarin Hotel in Vancouver to review the Jack Poole–Toigo proposal, of which Brown had a copy.

What Murphy saw made him sceptical. The $160-million offer to buy the site was more like $60 million when the conditions Poole and Toigo wanted were considered. Murphy knew he could get a much better price.

On Friday, August 7, Murphy was finishing up a round of golf at the University of B.C. when he received a message from his office that a conference call was being arranged for later that morning with the premier and Peter Brown. Murphy returned to his office.

He ended up talking to David Poole, who told him the premier had seen the Toigo-Jack Poole proposal on the weekend and liked what he saw. Vander Zalm wanted the BCEC to "act on it" as soon as possible.

Murphy told Poole he could get the province a much better deal. Poole seemed surprised by Murphy's version of the deal; it didn't sound like the deal Vander Zalm had described. Vander Zalm had either misunderstood the Jack Poole-Toigo proposal or had been bamboozled.

The following week, the BCEC board convened, ostensibly to formalize the bidding process for the Expo lands; actually they wanted to prevent any further meddling by the premier's office in BCEC's affairs. Upon hearing about Vander Zalm's latest intervention into the Expo sale, BCEC director Keith Mitchell warned his fellow directors that the corporation should get ready for an inquiry down the road.

It was a seminal moment. Vander Zalm and BCEC had become enemies, and the government-owned corporation was going to make it as hard as possible for the premier to get a deal for Peter Toigo.

In September, the Expo site was advertised world-wide and a deadline of October 15 set for expressions of interest. By November, BCEC had selected a shortlist of eight for the bidding. One was Li Ka-shing, the Hong Kong multibillionaire.

Li was a self-made man whose story the premier could relate to; he had just happened to get a lot richer than the premier. Li had arrived in Hong Kong as a child from China and worked as a watchband salesman before starting his own plastic flower business at the age of twenty. The business grew into a property empire. Soon he owned Hong Kong's leading pharmacy and super-market chains. His most prominent Canadian deal had been the $500-million purchase of a controlling interest in Calgary-based Husky Oil Ltd. His personal wealth was estimated at $3 billion to $5 billion.

Intensely private, he permitted a few short interviews but other-wise left the Expo negotiations to his son Victor, a publicity-shy twenty-five-year-old, and George Magnus, Li's deputy chairman and chief deal maker.

In October, Vander Zalm had visited Japan and Hong Kong,

where he was introduced to Li. During the trip, Vander Zalm had made some telling comments to Vancouver *Sun* columnist Vaughn Palmer about the Expo deal. First, he said he had no qualms about doing a deal with Peter Toigo (who was now on his own, his partnership with Jack Poole having fallen apart when Bell Canada backed out after the stock market crash): "I would have to take some precautions for the sake of perception," said Vander Zalm, "but I still wouldn't have any trouble with it. That would be grossly unfair."

His preferences regarding a final bidder: "All things being equal, if there are two offers reasonably close, then I would prefer the Canadian one."

BCEC directors were not amused by Vander Zalm's comments, since they would no doubt make non-Canadian firms interested in the Expo site wonder whether it was worth pouring tens of thousands of dollars and resources into a proposal if a Canadian deal was going to get preference. BCEC had also been assured by cabinet in August that a Canadian company would not get preference.

For his part, Vander Zalm was increasingly irritated by BCEC's slow progress. A small businessman who had spent a lifetime making snap decisions, he couldn't understand why BCEC couldn't cut a good deal just as quickly, particularly when the taxpayers were shelling out $3 million a month to service BCEC's debt and pay salaries.

On November 10, a few days after Vander Zalm's return from Hong Kong, BCEC officials were summoned to report to the provincial cabinet on their lack of progress. Vander Zalm, it turned out, had a curious proposition. Instead of selling off the Expo site and the rest of BCEC's assets separately, why not a giant, one-time-only sale? He said that when he was in Hong Kong he had mentioned the idea to Li Ka-shing, who then offered $1 billion for the whole shot.

Kevin Murphy said that there was nothing legally preventing the government from changing the nature of the sale because the shortlisted proponents for the Expo site had not yet been notified that they were on the shortlist. However, he warned that scrapping the Expo sale might scare investors away from participating in a contest for a bigger package: how could they be assured that the terms of the sale, too, wouldn't be changed after they had invested time and money into proposals?

It was a big risk. If any change was going to made, the government would have to make it quickly. McCarthy was adamant that the current Expo sale not be changed because it had already been made public. Nonetheless, Vander Zalm asked his deputy, David Poole, to get together with Murphy to explore the possibilities.

A week later, Poole met with Murphy and Brown. Poole announced that Toigo had met with Vander Zalm on the weekend and informed the premier that he was interested in buying all of the corporation's assets.

Brown and Murphy wondered at the coincidence. The premier had mentioned the possibility of selling the whole corporation and suddenly his friend Peter Toigo was interested.

The next day, the BCEC executive committee–an inner group of directors that made decisions between the monthly board meetings–held an emergency meeting. The group was flabbergasted when told about the government's new plan. The directors thought it was ludicrous to consider changing the rules of the game at that point. Brown was dispatched to Fantasy Gardens to reason with Vander Zalm.

On Saturday, November 21, Brown met Vander Zalm in the premier's castle apartment. He told Vander Zalm he was worried about B.C.'s reputation abroad, worried that international investors would be wary in the future about getting into any government-sponsored bidding competitions if the current one was changed at this late stage. Brown pointed out that a shortlist had been selected and deadlines had been set.

After an hour-long meeting, Brown felt he had received reassurance that the Expo sale would not be scrapped in favour of a sale of all of BCEC. But it turned out the premier's and Peter Toigo's dream for that kind of sale was far from dead.

Meanwhile, what about the $1-billion offer from Li Ka-shing? Well, David Poole told Kevin Murphy the following week, it didn't exactly go like that. In fact, there had been no mention of $1 billion during the Hong Kong discussions.

Murphy later got a call from George Magnus, Li's agent on the sale. Magnus told Murphy that his boss certainly had not offered $1 billion for BCEC. However, Li was prepared to look at one big deal if it were a pre-emptive way to get the Expo site.

In late November, Murphy was in Phoenix, Arizona, for a short sun and golf holiday, trying to temporarily leave behind the trials of the Expo sale. That proved impossible. Murphy received a call from David Poole, who wanted to arrange a meeting to discuss the pros and cons of selling all of BCEC's assets at once. Murphy arranged for himself and his staff to meet with Poole on the afternoon of December 2, at BCEC's Vancouver offices.

On the morning of the meeting, Murphy's office received a call from Peter Toigo's secretary informing them that Toigo would be bringing some tax advisers along with him to the meeting that afternoon. Toigo? Tax advisers? What was all this, Murphy wondered. He immediately phoned Peter Brown to ask him whether he knew Toigo was going to be at the meeting.

Brown phoned David Poole, who told him that, yes, Toigo was going to be there. Poole also said that he wanted the corporation to supply Toigo with some basic financial information on the corporation, which Toigo was interested in buying.

Brown phoned Murphy back to tell him what was going on. Neither of them liked what they saw shaping up. Poole's presence at the meeting was the most blatant message yet from Vander Zalm that he wanted BCEC to pursue a deal with Toigo. Brown didn't want any part of it and decided not to attend. Murphy had similar qualms, but as BCEC president he felt he had to monitor the exchange of information.

Evidence that Vander Zalm was going out of his way to help Toigo was mounting: first there was the presentation by a Toigo representative to cabinet in November 1986 which Vander Zalm helped arrange; then there was the April 1987 meeting at which Vander Zalm asked Peter Brown why he had responded to Toigo's interest in the Whistler convention centre; then the meeting initiated by Vander Zalm a month later to allow Toigo to personally lay out his Expo site plans for BCEC officials; then Vander Zalm's request that BCEC act on Toigo's and Jack Poole's bid; and, when that fell apart, his idea to sell all of BCEC–after his friend Peter Toigo had expressed interest in buying it.

Brown had also found out from Poole that Alan Eastwood, a tax expert from the provincial ministry of finance, would be attending the meeting too.

Before the meeting began, Murphy and Poole held their own brief meeting.

"Now, I don't want you to be too negative in there," Poole told Murphy. "Don't bring up Toigo's relationship with the premier or any of that. Just give him some basic information on the corporation." Murphy told Poole that he was not at all comfortable with the surprise presence of Toigo.

Murphy walked into the meeting room and addressed Eastwood: "I can only assume your minister knows you are here."

Yes, Eastwood said, Finance Minister Mel Couvelier knew. Eastwood was to be the "eyes and ears" of the government.

"The more witnesses we have, the better," said Murphy ominously. Before the meeting began, Poole and Toigo locked themselves away in a separate room for what seemed an eternity. Finally, Murphy knocked on their door and told them to hurry.

Toigo opened the meeting by saying, "I'm interested in buying the whole corporation," adding that he thought a deal could be cut before the end of the year, twenty-nine days away.

The subject of BCEC's $150-million loan portfolio came up. BCEC wanted to know if Toigo was interested in purchasing it as well. "I thought the government was going to consolidate all those under finance, and package that out in a separate deal," said Toigo. BCEC staff were taken aback. Toigo obviously knew more about what was going to happen to the corporation's assets than the corporation did.

Even Murphy hadn't heard about packaging the loan, but he later found out that was precisely what cabinet had recently decided. It seemed to BCEC that Toigo had a pipeline into the government.

Murphy didn't endorse Toigo's plan to buy everything, but–at David Poole's urging–he didn't dash the millionaire's dreams either. Toigo wanted some more detailed information on which to base a firm bid, but Murphy said he'd have to get approval from the BCEC board to give it to him.

Later that day, David Poole phoned Murphy to reinforce where the premier's office stood. "We mustn't have any glitches," said Poole, adding that Murphy was to call him immediately if it appeared that BCEC's executive committee–which was to meet in two days–was not going to endorse the idea of selling the whole corporation at once.

Hence Grace McCarthy's fit when Murphy told her about the December 2 meeting. She was the minister responsible for BCEC, and both Brown and Murphy had incorrectly assumed that she had been notified of the meeting by the premier's office.

When she had confronted Vander Zalm in his office with what she took to be his lying to her and with her outrage at Toigo's special treatment, Vander Zalm had denied knowing exactly what was going to be discussed at the Toigo meeting. He claimed to have known that Toigo was trying to put together an offer, but not much beyond that. Frankly, the premier had told McCarthy, he didn't think it was a big deal.

The BCEC executive committee considered it a big deal indeed. At its meeting on December 4, the day after McCarthy had stormed into Vander Zalm's office, Kevin Murphy informed the directors that David Poole had ordered him to leave the meeting and call Poole if it looked as if the board was going to turn thumbs down on Toigo's proposal. After a few snorts of derision over Poole's instructions, the board passed a unanimous resolution prohibiting Murphy from making any call. The board decided not to give Toigo any further information because it did not want to disrupt the Expo sale.

As each day passed, the BCEC board became more independent of the premier's office. All highly respected and immensely successful B.C. businessmen, the directors were concerned not only about the Expo sale, but also about their reputations. One director, Chester Johnston, the sagacious former head of B.C. Hydro, wanted immunity from any lawsuits that could arise out of the sale and the way it was being handled by Vander Zalm's office.

In the meantime, word of the board's decision against Toigo

reached Vander Zalm. Soon Peter Brown was getting reports about the "explosion in the premier's office." Brown phoned Murphy to say he'd heard about a screaming match between Toigo and the premier. He'd also heard through a contact of Toigo's that the premier was threatening to fire the entire BCEC board and hire Vancouver entrepreneur Jimmy Pattison to be sole commissioner in charge of disposing of BCEC's assets.

"I guess you know what happened," said McCarthy to Murphy on the afternoon of December 9, after summoning him from lunch to attend an urgent meeting with her.

McCarthy recounted what had happened at the regular Wednesday meeting of cabinet that morning: Vander Zalm had brandished a letter which he said was an offer by Peter Toigo to buy all BCEC's assets. The premier had claimed that Toigo had substantial backers, and named Vancouver multi-millionaire financier Sam Belzberg as one of them. Toigo's offer was for $445 million.

The cabinet ministers had thought Vander Zalm was enthused about the proposal. They also noticed that he recounted details that were not included in Toigo's two-page letter. For instance, the letter contained no mention of such specific backers as Belzberg. (When asked about this episode later, Vander Zalm claimed not to have known anything about Toigo's proposal beyond what was contained in the letter.)

The cabinet meeting had gotten tense when McCarthy said she was opposed to negotiating with Toigo when the BCEC process for the Expo lands was already under way. She was supported by highways minister Stephen Rogers and attorney-general Brian Smith, but Vander Zalm had his backers, including tourism minister Bill Reid. The encounter portended a split in cabinet between ministers of the Bill Bennett era and the new Vander Zalm loyalists.

Cabinet had eventually decided that the Expo sale should continue as planned. However, firms that made the shortlist for the Expo site were to be informed that the government was considering selling the entire corporation and that they were invited to make an offer. "Those offers could be for all of BCEC, for all of BCEC less the False Creek lands or other variations," the cabinet directive stated.

(Vander Zalm would later tell reporters that Toigo's offer was killed by cabinet. In fact, cabinet had came close to embracing the Toigo proposal.)

When Murphy heard about the new wrinkle cabinet had slipped into the Expo sale, he was immediately worried that the government's erratic behaviour would scare off the shortlisted firms. "We might never get them back," he told McCarthy.

McCarthy said they should immediately talk to Vander Zalm, but she couldn't get past his gatekeeper, David Poole, who came up to her office instead.

Murphy asked Poole for details of Toigo's offer, which Poole said he had in the briefcase he was carrying.

"I'd like to get a copy of that," McCarthy piped up.

"Well, I'll have to get authorization from the premier before I can do that," Poole replied.

McCarthy couldn't believe it. She was the minister responsible for BCEC, and she couldn't even get a copy of Toigo's offer. She lit into Poole, telling him she resented the premier's interference in the Expo sale.

"I take my directions from the premier. I don't take directions from you, Grace," Poole snapped back.

Here was an unelected official telling a veteran cabinet minister to mind her own business. McCarthy hated it. And she was quickly coming to hate Poole. Soon their disdain for each other would become public.

On the spur of the moment, McCarthy decided to test her theory that Toigo was being regularly filled in on the secret details of the Expo lands sale by the premier and Poole. Remembering that Poole had left the cabinet room right after the BCEC discussion while the ministers moved on to the next item on the agenda, McCarthy asked Poole what Toigo had thought of cabinet's decision.

"Not much. He certainly wasn't very thrilled with it," Poole told McCarthy.

"You mean, David, that you left that cabinet meeting and phoned Mr. Toigo and told him about the decision cabinet took? That is absolutely disgusting," she said.

McCarthy needed no more evidence that Toigo was getting treatment normal citizens would never expect.

Poole left. McCarthy sat on her brown sofa, in front of an oak coffee table. Murphy sat across from her. With her left hand, McCarthy started to draw a circle on the couch with the point of her thumb and index finger pressed together. "Kevin, I can no longer accept that it's simple naivete on the premier's part," she said. "And when you rule out naivete, what you have left isn't very nice to contemplate."

Murphy had never seen McCarthy so shaken. They agreed to meet the next day with the BCEC senior management to discuss how to respond to the Toigo proposal.

It was now nearly three o'clock. Alone in her office, McCarthy walked slowly behind her desk. Water streamed down her windows as the rain refused to let up. The office was dark except for one corner of the room where a tiny desk lamp was on. McCarthy got several pieces of paper out of her drawer and began writing a letter. It began: "It is with a great deal of consideration that I tender my resignation from the government. I cannot continue to serve, given my knowledge of certain actions surrounding the disposal process of the B.C. Enterprise Corp." McCarthy wrote that it was "very apparent that Mr. Peter Toiga (sic) is not at arm's length in his relationship to our government. That he has had access to information and influence on the processes and policies of our government is totally inappropriate, and I cannot, in good conscience, overlook the ramifications of these actions and any that may follow in the future."

McCarthy took the letter to her secretary and told her to type it but not to breathe a word to anyone.

Canonized by her supporters in the Social Credit Party, McCarthy was credited with rebuilding the party after its shattering defeat in 1972 at the hands of Dave Barrett's NDP. She probably knew more Socreds than any person alive. And McCarthy realized that resigning from cabinet would have a devastating impact on the political institution she loved. But she felt she had no other choice.

That night, McCarthy and her husband attended a meeting of the BCEC executive committee. When the minister was in Vancouver, Ray McCarthy seemed to be constantly at her side, chauffeuring his wife in her 1972 Chevelle convertible. Nonetheless, his attendance at the meeting bothered some of the directors, especially when he kept interjecting that Toigo's letter to cabinet wasn't an offer. Some of the directors on the executive felt McCarthy's husband had no business being there and certainly no business offering his opinions.

The BCEC officials had studied Toigo's $445-million offer and didn't much like it. Taken at face value, they thought it wasn't a bad offer. But there were so many conditions and undefined terms—like the lease-back arrangement on the stadium—that it could also be a terrible offer.

BCEC management stayed at the corporation offices in Vancouver until midnight drafting a reply to Toigo's offer. The committee decided to focus its response on the negative impact that changing the sale process could have on a future sale of all the corporation's assets (which was what Toigo was interested in).

In its response, the committee wrote that Toigo's offer expired January 29, which could be accomplished by a concentrated effort on both sides "but would preclude a competitive basis for the sale." The committee felt Toigo's purchase price of $445 million was attractive on the surface, but it was only a starting point and the price would be negotiated down by Shato "for all encumbrances, liabilities, unknown factors which would discount value, and any other factor validly introduced as a result of due diligence. For example, soils problems could be used as a basis for discounting price and for asking for 'an indemnity.' " And the committee said there was no evidence of Toigo's ability to pay the $225-million down payment.

The committee felt that entertaining the Toigo proposal might irrevocably harm the Expo sale.

On Friday morning, McCarthy went to see Vander Zalm. She took a seat on the office couch, while the premier sat in a chair opposite.

"Bill, I hoped things wouldn't have to come to this but I'm afraid they have. I can just no longer tolerate what's been going on. Today was the last straw and I feel I have no choice but to resign."

McCarthy held up her letter of resignation. "Grace, I think you're overreacting," said Vander Zalm.

McCarthy cut him off. "What you're doing for your friend Peter Toigo is wrong, Bill, you must know that. There is a legitimate bidding process going on for the Expo site; Mr. Toigo had a chance to get in on it; he decided not to. He missed his chance. Now you're threatening to upset the whole thing by doing this crazy stuff."

McCarthy cut right to the question that worried her most. "Bill, what hold does Peter Toigo have over you? He must have something for you to be going to such lengths for him."

It was a damning charge for a minister of the Crown to be making about her premier. "Peter Toigo doesn't have any hold over me," Vander Zalm told McCarthy. "He's a friend with a legitimate offer and I felt I had to present it to cabinet. I would have been wrong not to."

The two talked for another thirty minutes. Vander Zalm told McCarthy he was going to talk to the BCEC board. "It won't matter, Bill, I can't go along with it even if you do talk them into it." Vander Zalm insisted on going to the next meeting, which was Monday morning. McCarthy decided not to press her resignation threat further, convinced that, once Vander Zalm met the board and realized how opposed it was to his plan, he would back off.

(Recalling the meeting later in an interview for this book, Vander Zalm said McCarthy had been very emotional but he didn't think she was seriously considering resigning.)

McCarthy had taken an enormous gamble. She and the premier hadn't been getting along. McCarthy was Vander Zalm's biggest stumbling block, and he must have been tempted to get her out of the way. But McCarthy felt that tendering her resignation was the only way to make Vander Zalm understand how serious matters were. She returned to her office and asked her secretary to put the letter in a safe place. McCarthy thought she might need it again someday.

That weekend, McCarthy phoned Attorney-General Brian Smith at his home in the upscale Victoria suburb of Oak Bay. "I am really getting worried about where this business with Peter Toigo is going," McCarthy said. "I really do believe that this might be the stuff of royal commissions and I wanted you to be officially aware of my concerns."

Once bitter rivals in the Socred leadership race, McCarthy and Smith were drawing closer together as the Expo land sale became more entangled in Vander Zalm's efforts to help his friend Toigo.

McCarthy wanted Smith to make note of the conversation and mark the date of her call–December 12. If the whole matter was ever the subject of an inquiry she wanted it known that she had expressed her concerns early to the province's chief law enforcement officer.

On Monday morning, December 14, the BCEC board had just begun its regularly monthly meeting shortly after 8:00 a.m. when in walked Vander Zalm, alone and unannounced. "Good morning, everyone," he said.

The directors were shocked into silence. Finally McCarthy asked one of her officials to get up from his chair so the premier could have it.

The awkwardness persisted. Finally, Kevin Murphy nudged chairman Peter Brown: "Maybe the premier came to say something, Peter."

"Oh, yes, Premier, did you have something to say?" Brown quickly offered.

In a slow, cautious manner, Vander Zalm told the board he'd had a chance to review the letter that had earlier been drafted by the BCEC management, outlining its concerns about changing the Expo sale to a giant sale of all of BCEC's assets. Vander Zalm said he understood BCEC's concerns, which led each director in turn to tell the premier what a disaster it would be to disrupt the current Expo sale. One director, however, chose to begin his speech with the line that the Toigo bid "could have been a good one."

"That's what I thought," said Vander Zalm enthusiastically. He then went on to extol the virtues of Toigo's giant purchase offer, particularly the fact that the province would receive $25 million cash at the front end of the deal. The directors felt Vander Zalm was fronting for his friend's bid, but he told them that he hoped no one misconstrued his motives in bringing the Toigo bid to cabinet. He said he'd bring any half-million-dollar offer to cabinet, whether it was Toigo's or anyone else's. And he said Toigo wasn't all that interested in the Expo site anyway; he had his sights set on the other BCEC-owned property. Vander Zalm said cabinet's December 9 directive "could be appropriately altered" and the Expo sale should continue as scheduled.

McCarthy wanted to get Vander Zalm's commitment to the Expo

sale in writing, in the event the premier had a change of heart down the road. The board had it quickly minuted: "It was agreed that the sale of False Creek would be independent from the sale of the [other] corporation shares and assets."

Eight months after BCEC was first directed by Vander Zalm to consider Toigo's Expo plans, the premier's friend was finally out of the picture. Or so McCarthy and the board thought.

By January 10, 1988, two companies were in the running for the Expo site–Li Ka-shing's Concord Pacific and the Vancouver Land Co., a consortium which Jack Poole had put together after Bell Canada bowed out. (Jack Poole had dropped Toigo because of the latter's controversial friendship with Vander Zalm.)

Another month went by with no interference from the premier's office. It looked as if Vander Zalm had indeed given up on the Toigo offer. But on February 3, BCEC chairman Peter Brown got a call at his downtown Vancouver investment offices. It was Vander Zalm's man, David Poole, phoning to notify Brown that Toigo's offer, which should have officially expired on January 29, was being extended at the request of government.

"David, what the fuck are you doing?" asked the shocked Brown. "Are you nuts? You're going to blow the whole fucking thing. The Expo sale is going to go down the fucking chute."

Poole was adamant. The offer stood, and Brown was to inform the board.

Vander Zalm didn't see any problem with extending Toigo's offer. First, he figured Toigo wasn't specifically interested in the Expo site but rather in BCEC's assets as a whole. So he didn't think that extending Toigo's offer would disrupt the Expo sale. But, more important, Vander Zalm felt there was a chance he and the cabinet wouldn't like the deal BCEC ended up getting for the Expo site. And if Vander Zalm didn't like it, he wanted to have Toigo's offer as a backup.

The BCEC directors saw it differently, of course. Toigo had been interested in the Expo site as far back as 1986, when he had first let cabinet know of his desire to develop the property. And then there had been Toigo's plan with Jack Poole which Vander Zalm had asked BCEC to act on. For Vander Zalm to say now that Toigo wasn't interested in the site was silly. The board was convinced that Vander Zalm wanted to scuttle the Expo sale so his friend could get the site by acquiring all of BCEC's assets.

The day after Brown received his call from Poole notifying him of the Toigo extension, the BCEC board gathered at 8:00 a.m. for its monthly meeting. Brown was fidgety as he brought the meeting to order. He then delivered the news: The Toigo offer was still alive.

Board members reeled in horror as the corpse rose from the dead.

"You've got to be kidding!" screamed one director. "Double-dealing," "sham," and other strong words were thrown around the room. In a week, BCEC was scheduled to receive the formal proposals from the two final bidders for the Expo site. The board demanded that McCarthy get cabinet to give BCEC full authority "in writing" to be the exclusive agent for the corporation and its assets so there wouldn't be any double-dealing on the side.

Murphy and his staff appeared before cabinet on Wednesday, February 10, to explain how the corporation planned to dispose of the remaining assets of BCEC after the Expo site was sold. Murphy said the corporation could get at least $500 million for its assets. "Oh, thank you very much, Mr. Murphy," said Vander Zalm huffily.

Vander Zalm appeared to be upset with Murphy for trotting out a figure that would make Toigo's $445-million offer look low.

The next day, BCEC chairman Peter Brown got a call from Vander Zalm, obviously frustrated by his lack of control over the BCEC board. "Peter, I'm going to appoint David Poole to the board."

It seemed obvious that Poole was being appointed to exert control over the board, but Kevin Murphy for one still felt it could work. He phoned Poole to congratulate him and asked how he wanted to implement the move.

"It's already taken care of," said Poole curtly.

He said it had been done via a cabinet order. Murphy explained that it couldn't be done that way; Poole would have to be elected.

Murphy could hear panic set in at the other end of the line. (In the end, however, a board member was kicked off to make room. The victim was Mike McGillivray, former president of the B.C. Development Corp., a now-defunct Crown corporation.)

On Monday, February 15, BCEC received the proposals of the two final bidders, Li Ka-shing and Jack Poole. Over the next two weeks, Murphy and his staff analyzed the two bids. Li was offering $102 million, about $20 million more than Poole. BCEC considered Li's development plans superior to the Vancouver Land Co.'s. Jack Poole's bid also depended on raising millions of dollars in a public share issue, only five months after the October 1987 stock market crash. If the public issue failed, the deal would not close. Poole also wanted the right to take any money he gained from the site and invest it elsewhere. The NDP was sure to make hay over that, BCEC staff thought.

For Kevin Murphy the choice was straightforward. He would recommend to the BCEC board that final negotiations take place with Li Ka-shing.

On February 19, McCarthy left on a 17-day trade mission to Japan, Hong Kong, and Korea, accompanied by her developer husband, Ray. The trip had been arranged for some time and was an opportunity for the minister to renew acquaintanceships with Far Eastern businessmen and establish new contacts in the region. While she was in Hong Kong, the Canadian trade commission's office received an invitation from Li Ka-shing for McCarthy and her husband to join the billionaire for dinner at his penthouse suite. McCarthy accepted the invitation. The McCarthys were accompanied at the dinner by staff from the trade commission office.

Grace McCarthy's presence at a dinner with one of the proponents of the Expo site so close to the date that the winner of the site was to be chosen provided fodder for her detractors. Months after the sale was completed, those in the premier's camp— who believed McCarthy was trying to destroy Vander Zalm—began quietly suggesting that a secret financial deal was struck at the dinner between the McCarthys and Li to make sure the Hong Kong developer got the site. McCarthy says that suggestion is ludicrous.

"We were accompanied the entire trip by staff from the Canadian trade commission's office. The suggestion that I or my husband would attempt to personally profit from my position is, quite simply, crazy."

Meanwhile, details of the two final bids were being kept secret, and Vander Zalm was getting anxious. He had David Poole tell Peter Brown that the premier wanted to be briefed on the bids.

Murphy and Brown were worried that if the premier were briefed, he would tell Peter Toigo, who they thought would either enhance his own bid or else fill in his old partner Jack Poole so that Poole could make last-minute changes to his bid before the final presentation to the BCEC board, which would take place in two days.

On March 9, Murphy learned that Vander Zalm was meeting with George Magnus and Victor Li the next day. Murphy was again worried that Vander Zalm would turn details of their bids over to Toigo. He phoned Magnus and made it clear that Magnus was not to discuss the bid with the premier. Magnus said it was simply a courtesy call.

By now, Murphy and the BCEC board were so convinced that Vander Zalm was fronting for Toigo that they didn't trust him to respect confidences. BCEC had effectively become a renegade arm of government; Vander Zalm had completely lost control of it.

After his and Victor Li's March 10 meeting with Vander Zalm, Magnus met Grace McCarthy in her Victoria office to brief her on the session.

Magnus told her that Vander Zalm was still pushing the idea of selling all of BCEC's assets at once. He reiterated the importance of "lots of cash up front" in any deal and then asked whether Concord Pacific's plans for the Expo site left room for local developers. Vander Zalm had mentioned Peter Toigo as someone who would be interested in developing part of the site.

Frantic over what she'd been told, McCarthy phoned Murphy, who had earlier declined a dinner invitation from Magnus because he thought it would be improper for the two to meet just before BCEC was to make a final decision on the Expo site. However, Murphy was so disturbed about Magnus's meeting with Vander Zalm that he decided he'd better hear firsthand about the premier's overture on behalf of Toigo. Murphy met Magnus in the latter's Pan Pacific hotel suite around 5:00 p.m. When the two men sat down, Murphy didn't let on that he had already been briefed by McCarthy.

Recounting the meeting with Vander Zalm, Magnus said that the premier had mentioned the possibility of local participation.

"Was he specific?" asked Murphy.

"Do you mean does his initials begin with P and end in R?" replied Magnus.

Murphy scratched his head.

"I mean, P.T.," said Magnus.

"You mean Peter Toigo," said Murphy.

"Yes, as a matter of fact he did mention him," said Magnus.

Murphy was amazed that Vander Zalm was so obvious in his attempts to get Toigo a piece of the Expo site action. The BCEC president was beginning to lose count of the number of times Vander Zalm had boosted Toigo's interest in the Expo site, but the tally by now was more than a half dozen.

The next day, March 11, newly installed director David Poole showed up for his first BCEC board meeting. He took chairman Peter Brown aside and gave him some startling news: the government had decided to extend Toigo's offer a second time.

Brown stared coldly at Poole and told him that if the true story of the Expo lands sale ever became public there would be a scapegoat and Poole would be it. It was a prophetic warning.

The BCEC chairman thought the best way for Poole to understand how the board felt about all the interferences was to have Vander Zalm's adviser announce the government's decision. Poole did, and the room exploded. Toigo's offer had risen from dead—again! What would it take to kill it, the directors wondered.

In minutes the directors were scheduled to hear the final presentations of the two finalists for the Expo site, both of whom had spent hundreds of thousands of dollars preparing plans. The board was then going to choose the winner. And here was Vander Zalm's right-hand man saying that an offer from the premier's friend to buy all of the corporation—including the Expo site—was still on the table.

The directors shook their heads in disbelief. Poole sat uncomfortably silent, looking as though he'd rather be under a dentist's drill. The board minutes stated: "It was felt that further consideration of the Toigo proposal would seriously affect the credibility of the corporation and the process."

The meeting went ahead. George Magnus on behalf of Li Ka-shing's Concord and Jack Poole on behalf of the Vancouver Land Company each made a last pitch.

Murphy and his staff then recommended Li's Concord bid. The board, however, said it wanted more than $102 million and double the $25 million Concord was prepared to pay up front. As well, the directors wanted payments over ten to fifteen years, not twenty as Concord was proposing. Eventually, the board passed a unanimous resolution recommending to cabinet that negotiations proceed with Concord Pacific. Poole abstained.

That weekend, McCarthy pulled out all the stops to ensure that cabinet accepted BCEC's recommendation to enter final negotiations with Li Ka-shing. To rally support among her cabinet colleagues, she brought groups of ministers into the Enterprise Centre throughout the weekend; she had George Magnus and Victor Li there to explain their plans.

During one session with a particular group of ministers, George Magnus's beeper went off. The message: Call Peter Toigo.

Magnus slipped away and phoned Toigo, who said he was going to be in Hong Kong on business with his son in a week and wanted to arrange a meeting with Li Ka-shing. Magnus didn't know what to say. He didn't want to reject Toigo out of hand because he didn't know what effect if would have on Concord's bid. A meeting was arranged.

When he returned from the call, he told McCarthy what had happened. She told him not to worry, that she would take the matter up with Vander Zalm.

The following Wednesday, March 16, BCEC recommended to cabinet that negotiations begin with Li Ka-shing. The majority of cabinet was in favour of BCEC's recommendation, but Vander Zalm didn't want to make a final decision; negotiations could wait a couple of weeks while Murphy tried to get a better price from Li. If Murphy could get more money and possibly some other sweeteners, Vander Zalm indicated, then cabinet might be ready to "officially" enter into final negotiations with Li. The instructions were the strangest Murphy had received in his negotiating career.

McCarthy sat beside Vander Zalm at the cabinet table, mystified. The premier's order to BCEC had been "speed over profit"; now he wanted to wait. She decided he was procrastinating to give his friend Peter Toigo a chance to visit Magnus in Hong Kong and try to cut himself in on the deal.

The next day, McCarthy phoned Vander Zalm to discuss Toigo's trip to Hong Kong. Vander Zalm, fully cognizant of Toigo's activities as always, said Toigo's son had a product he was planning to market over there.

McCarthy got to the point. "Peter Toigo better not go near Li Ka-shing's group in the midst of these negotiations," she said. "Things are at a very sensitive stage, Bill, and Peter Toigo could botch everything up. You've got to stop him."

"I can't stop Peter Toigo from going and seeing people. He's a private citizen," Vander Zalm replied.

McCarthy, furious, said, "Don't tell me he is not going to go there and not say that he has talked to the premier about it. It's as much as if you had sent your own envoy.

"I have to tell you he can't go. You have to stop him," McCarthy pleaded again. McCarthy told Vander Zalm that if the deal with Li Ka-shing fell through, there would be no deals left. Vander Zalm had already acknowledged that the Jack Poole bid didn't rate. Like it or not, McCarthy told Vander Zalm, Li's bid was the best they had.

"Well, Peter doesn't think it's a good deal," McCarthy remembers Vander Zalm saying.

Her eyes widened as the premier's words sank in.

"How does Peter Toigo know what Li Ka-shing's bid is? Nobody knows that but cabinet and the [BCEC] board," McCarthy shot back.

Vander Zalm recanted, "Oh, he doesn't know all the details."

"But you just said he thinks it's a bad deal," McCarthy replied. McCarthy felt she now had all the evidence she needed that Toigo was heading to Hong Kong with the knowledge that Li Ka-shing was going to get the Expo site and Toigo wanted a piece of it.

Vander Zalm still saw nothing wrong, but agreed to talk to Toigo before he left.

McCarthy had not merely been impudent, she had verbally

slapped Bill Vander Zalm around. Other premiers would have immediately demanded the resignation of any minister who spoke to them that way, but Vander Zalm promised to address McCarthy's concern. It's hard to imagine McCarthy having similar exchanges with the no-nonsense W.A.C. Bennett or his tough-minded son, Bill. Then again, she was probably never forced to.

At the same time, Kevin Murphy was having his own problems with the premier's office.

Earlier on the same Thursday that McCarthy phoned Vander Zalm, Murphy had met with McCarthy and David Poole in Victoria to get clearer instructions for his upcoming negotiations with Li Ka-shing.

Murphy was to try to get Li to add some sweeteners, including the possible purchase of all of BCEC's assets and the purchase of B.C. coal to fuel some of Li's thermal-generating plants in the Far East, before the government made a decision on whether it would enter final negotiations with Li. Poole described Murphy's mandate as a "fishing expedition."

Murphy was also to try to get Li to agree to some local participation in the development of False Creek.

"If Mr. Li wanted to include Mr. Toigo or Jack Poole, you wouldn't be opposed to that, would you?" David Poole asked Murphy.

Then David Poole, the former college administrator, started to tell Murphy, the veteran negotiator, what to say to Li. "Tell them that cabinet hasn't made a final decision, that price is a problem and both bids—including Jack Poole's—could be thrown out," said Poole.

"Listen, David, don't tell me how to fucking negotiate," said Murphy, a fiery Irishman who was wearing a green tie in honour of St. Patrick's Day. "I've got a little more experience at this than you do. I'm not going to be dancing on a string."

Then both Murphy and McCarthy wanted assurances that Toigo's bid was officially dead. "Listen," Poole told them, "The premier has dinner with him [Toigo] three nights a week. I have no idea what they're going to decide over a little red wine." Murphy and McCarthy exchanged glances. Even Poole, they thought, was cynical about Vander Zalm's utter lack of discretion.

Murphy's next problem would be Toigo's scheduled visit with Li Ka-shing, which he was informed of when he returned to his Vancouver office that St. Patrick's Day. Murphy received the news from BCEC director and legal counsel Keith Mitchell, who in turn had been advised by McCarthy.

Murphy feared that Toigo knew from Vander Zalm what the cabinet's position was vis-à-vis his bid. If so, he could arrive in Hong Kong and tell George Magnus what they needed to do to finally cement the contract: up their price and make room for local developers. Murphy felt that if he went over there after Toigo and told Li's people the same thing, Li would think everyone was in cahoots.

Late in the afternoon of March 17, Murphy, Keith Mitchell, and a small group of top corporation executives discussed what to do. They believed it was possible that Toigo was on his way to Hong Kong to use his "influence" with Vander Zalm in order to cut a deal with Li Ka-shing. BCEC lawyers were sent out to get the section of the Criminal Code dealing with influence peddling.

In Murphy's spacious Vancouver office, the group considered its options, which included wiring Li Ka-shing's top negotiator George Magnus before his meeting with Toigo. But the group felt that besides being a little too covert, such a request might scare Li Ka-shing away from B.C.

They thought about carrying on and trying to conclude a deal. But they were concerned there might not be anyone to negotiate with if action wasn't taken.

They considered going directly to the RCMP with their concerns, having the entire BCEC board resign in protest, and, as a final measure, having McCarthy resign from cabinet over the premier's interferences on behalf of Toigo.

Mitchell, who was a lawyer with the prestigious Vancouver law firm of Farris, Vaughan, Wills and Murphy, thought the best option was to go the attorney-general and lay out the group's concerns. The attorney-general could decide if there was enough evidence to warrant turning the matter over to the RCMP.

Murphy and the others knew that going to the attorney-general was an extremely serious matter. However, they felt that the consequences for them would be more serious if the deal with Li

Ka-shing fell apart and they had done nothing. If the whole story ever became public, they could be subject to charges of a cover-up and be crucified for not complaining to someone about the interference by Vander Zalm's office on behalf of Toigo.

The group made its decision. Murphy phoned McCarthy to say they wanted to go to the attorney-general; as minister responsible for the corporation, she would have the final say. She agreed.

Two hours later, Murphy phoned Li's agent, George Magnus, in Hong Kong.

"Are you planning to entertain Peter Toigo?" Murphy asked Magnus. "Well, not entertain," said Magnus. He did confirm a meeting scheduled with Toigo the following Tuesday at 1:00 p.m. Hong Kong time.

Magnus wanted to know which bid had won. Murphy refused to tell him. "It would make it easier to deal with Toigo if we knew where we stood," Magnus told Murphy.

The remark seemed odd, Murphy thought. Why should that information make any difference?

If there were no final decision, Concord didn't want to offend Toigo, although Magnus had serious concerns about the wisdom of meeting with a close friend of the premier at so delicate a time.

"George, is your concern that Mr. Peter Toigo might be coming to influence peddle?" Murphy asked bluntly.

There was a long pause. "Kevin, the answer to that can only be yes. You put your finger on our concerns," said Magnus.

After consulting with McCarthy, Murphy returned to the BCEC offices around midnight and phoned Magnus again.

"George, you will not be doing Mr. Li any favours if you meet with Mr. Toigo," he told Magnus.

Still, Murphy wasn't convinced Magnus knew how serious the matter was. The BCEC president went home but couldn't sleep. All he could think about was the Toigo meeting in Hong Kong.

He arrived at BCEC headquarters early the next morning and fired off a telex to Magnus. The message was simple: Any meeting with Peter Toigo would be a breach of the confidentiality agreement that Li Ka-shing had undertaken when he entered the bidding for the Expo site and thus any future negotiations would be immediately halted.

It was a bold move. If the meeting did go ahead, and Murphy suspended talks with Li, there would have to be a public explanation that would be explosive.

It took Magnus less than an hour to respond: The meeting would not go ahead.

After the fact, Murphy phoned BCEC chairman Peter Brown to tell him Mitchell had gone to the attorney-general. "Oh, shit, couldn't you have done something else?" said Brown, who thought the move was an overreaction.

Two days later, Grace McCarthy was spending Sunday evening working on government business in the den of her posh Vancouver home. Shortly after 9:00 p.m., the phone rang. It was the premier.

After a few minutes of pleasantries, Vander Zalm said he'd just had a call from David Poole, who had spoken to an angry Peter Toigo in Hong Kong. Toigo was irate that his meeting with Li Ka-shing's people had been cancelled.

"Grace, we're going to have to talk about this. This is appalling."

Vander Zalm complained to McCarthy about the activities of the BCEC board and suggested that Kevin Murphy was carrying out a vendetta against Peter Toigo. Vander Zalm said he was tempted to fire the entire board and appoint Vancouver multi-millionaire Jimmy Pattison as an independent commissioner.

"Well, Bill, I'm sorry it's had to come to this, but if Peter Toigo is going to involve himself like this, insert himself into government business, we're going to have a difference of opinion," said McCarthy.

She refused to back down. Vander Zalm hung up in frustration. For the second time in less than four months, McCarthy decided events were getting out of control and her position as minister in charge of the Expo sale was being eroded. She decided to resign. The next day she drafted her second letter of resignation, which she planned to announce at a news conference.

"In these past few days certain information has come to me that suggests that another party, unconnected from government and our professional staff, has attempted, with the premier's knowledge, to enter the negotiation process with one of the proponents."

"Although this interference in the process has been halted, it is, nonetheless, known to me and is unacceptable to me as the minister responsible. . . . Neither can I condone the fact that the premier, having the same knowledge would, and has, found such conduct acceptable. I therefore, tender my resignation as a minister of the Crown."

Again, McCarthy had her secretary type it up. But McCarthy would decide again to hold off making the announcement because she wanted to see the sale through. She felt if she resigned, it might open the door for Toigo.

On Monday evening, the BCEC board was scheduled to meet to discuss cabinet's directive. David Poole phoned Murphy to inform him about the decision cabinet had taken earlier that day regarding the Expo sale. He said Murphy was not to negotiate a final deal with Li Ka-shing.

"You can't negotiate. Just go on a fishing trip. See if you can open up discussions for the sale of the whole corporation," Poole told him.

"Where does Toigo fit into all this?" Murphy asked.

Poole said Toigo was out of the picture, then added: "But don't quote me if he pops up again." Once again, Murphy marvelled at Poole's matter-of-fact attitude toward his boss's close relationship with Toigo.

Shortly after 7:00 p.m., the BCEC board gathered at the Enterprise Centre. Murphy and chairman Peter Brown decided the board should be told that Keith Mitchell had gone to the attorney-general on Friday.

But neither Murphy nor Brown wanted David Poole, now a BCEC director, to know what they had done. If they told the board, it would have to be recorded in the minutes and Poole would find out.

Before Poole was hooked up to the meeting by phone, Brown and Murphy decided that the meeting wouldn't officially start until Grace McCarthy arrived. Before she did, Murphy explained to the others why Keith Mitchell had decided to go to the attorney-general, a decision the group ratified. The board's endorsement of the move would only appear on the "unofficial" version of the minutes and not the official version which Poole would ultimately see.

Meanwhile, the eighteen-month fight of the BCEC, its board, and the minister responsible for it against the premier's office and Peter Toigo was about to go public.

Word of Toigo's offer was leaked to Vancouver *Sun* columnist Vaughn Palmer. Toigo then decided to publicly promote his offer through another of Palmer's columns. The people could decide if his bid was a good one.

Interestingly, the offer Toigo made public contained different numbers than the one Vander Zalm had put before cabinet in December. Toigo was now saying that his offer was $500 million for BCEC, not the previously mentioned $445 million.

When Kevin Murphy heard about the new, improved Toigo offer, he immediately thought back to the cabinet meeting in February when he had told the premier that the book value of BCEC's assets was $500 million and the premier's reaction, "Oh, thank you very much, Mr. Murphy."

Now, Toigo's public offer jibed with the numbers the corporation had given cabinet in February.

But Toigo's going public brought new dangers for the premier. He gave the green light for BCEC to go public too. So began the first public civil war in Social Credit's thirty-five-year history.

CHAPTER 10

The Investigation

The voice on the phone sounded desperate. It was early Friday morning, April 8; Vander Zalm had just taken a call at his Victoria office from his friend Peter Toigo.

"You got to get me out of this! This is terrible," Vander Zalm recalls Toigo telling him. "Everybody suspects me of something and I haven't done a damn thing. How do I get out of this?"

A report on Vancouver radio station CKNW that morning had said that Toigo was under investigation by the RCMP. This was the same investigation prompted by BCEC's concerns about Toigo's Hong Kong visit and the pattern of special treatment BCEC felt Toigo was receiving from Vander Zalm.

Vander Zalm wasn't entirely surprised by the report.

CKNW's newsman George Garrett had tried to verify the story with David Poole earlier in the week; Vander Zalm had consequently called attorney-general Brian Smith to his office the Wednesday before the report aired.

Smith had sat across from Vander Zalm in the premier's office and told him "that as justice minister I couldn't comment on investigations. I explained the problem that if I commented on one investigation then I'd be forced to comment on them all, and you can't have that."

Smith, of course, knew that not only was Toigo being investigated; so was the man seated across from him. He wasn't about to tip off either of them while the investigation was in progress.

Two days later the report aired and Toigo phoned Vander Zalm.

"[Toigo] called and said, 'If there is an investigation into me, tell me about it,'" Vander Zalm recalls. "'And if there is no investigation, then please clarify this, because now, investigation or no investigation, as long as that statement is out there, some people think I'm guilty of something.'

"He said: 'It isn't fair. I am here doing business, paying my taxes; why should I be treated this way? Even the worst criminal doesn't get treated this way.'"

Vander Zalm went to the airwaves the same day in Toigo's defence. On CKNW's morning talk show—then hosted by Gary Bannerman, a friend of both the premier and Toigo—Vander Zalm accused the BCEC board of leaking the story.

"My God, what's happening in this country? It's not very good," he told Bannerman over the telephone from his Victoria office. "They [the BCEC board] don't mind making enemies, these people."

Poole phoned the attorney-general to see if he would publicly confirm that there wasn't an investigation. Smith said no.

Poole called the deputy attorney-general, Ted Hughes, down to his office. Was there an investigation? Hughes parroted his boss.

Finally, Vander Zalm called Grace McCarthy down to his office. Was it true that the BCEC board had complained about Toigo to the attorney-general?

McCarthy knew it was true, but like Smith she didn't want to give Vander Zalm a chance to quash the investigation. She told Vander Zalm the BCEC board had not gone to the attorney-general to complain about Toigo. Technically, she was correct because it was Keith Mitchell who had gone to Smith to air BCEC's concerns about Toigo's trip to Hong Kong and his relationship with the premier. But his actions had been ratified by the board. McCarthy had deceived Vander Zalm to protect the investigation—which he might try to shut down by firing Smith—and her good friend Mitchell, whose law firm did lucrative work for the government.

Toigo, meanwhile, had been assured by Vander Zalm that Smith would issue a release clearing Toigo's name.

"The attorney-general will be making a statement shortly clearing the whole thing up," Toigo told a Vancouver *Sun* reporter.

Around 3:30 p.m., Smith received a call from Vander Zalm on his speaker-phone. Vander Zalm had prepared a release which said the attorney-general had not been asked by the BCEC board to investigate Toigo. McCarthy's supersubtle answer had led the premier to assume he had the facts right.

"I don't want my name associated with that release," said Smith. "I've told you my position, and I should tell you, Premier, that this is a sphere that your office ought not to be entering." Smith added he was only doing what any minister of justice would do in not discussing investigations.

"You're not a real minister of justice, or you'd do justice to Mr. Toigo," Vander Zalm said.

Smith wrote Vander Zalm's words down. He did not want to forget what he had just heard.

Vander Zalm eventually issued a release under his own name, saying McCarthy had assured him that the BCEC board had not complained to the attorney-general about Toigo. It did not quote the attorney-general.

Vander Zalm thought the matter was closed. He didn't know that, as he prepared to leave his Victoria office that day to return to Fantasy Gardens, one of the RCMP's top investigators was checking out the allegations against Toigo in a top-secret file he'd been assigned in late March. Inspector George Vander Kracht soon realized while scanning the file that the investigation would focus not solely on Toigo but on the premier himself.

On April 8, the same day that Vander Zalm had struggled to help clear Peter Toigo's name, his association with the Delta millionaire was being questioned elsewhere. The Vancouver *Sun* broke the front-page news that David Poole had arranged a meeting for Toigo on December 2, 1987, with staff from the B.C. Enterprise Corp., so that the premier's friend could get financial information on the corporation's assets.

The day before the story broke, the *Sun*'s Palmer and Mason had caught up to the premier as he was walking out of the main legislative building to his office in the west annex.

The premier stood in the breezeway linking the two buildings, armed with a load of binders and other government documents, as the *Sun* pair, acting on a tip, badgered him for nearly twenty minutes about his and David Poole's efforts to help Toigo get the Expo lands.

"Toigo's never had special treatment," Vander Zalm said. "He's never sought special treatment. And he's never been given special treatment."

Vander Zalm said he'd done nothing wrong in taking Toigo's offer to cabinet, after telling Palmer a few days earlier that he didn't know how the offer had come to cabinet. The premier also disclosed that he had warned Toigo, two days before Toigo left for Hong Kong, to meet with Li Ka-shing's officials, not to say anything that might "influence" the government or BCEC in any way. Finally, Vander Zalm defended Poole's role in setting up the special BCEC-Toigo meeting the previous December.

The morning the *Sun* story broke, reporters gathered outside the offices of the Social Credit caucus shortly before ten o'clock, awaiting MLAs heading into the house. The television cameras rolled when economic development minister Grace McCarthy, responsible for the Expo sale, emerged wearing her usual broad official smile.

McCarthy told the reporters that Poole should never have arranged the fact-finding mission for Toigo.

"There's no question I have not been happy with some of the things the B.C. Enterprise Corp. has had to tolerate, and that's one of them," said McCarthy.

She did not mention that the finance minister had been told about the Toigo meeting ahead of time but she had not.

David Poole didn't disappoint reporters looking for a provocative quote in response.

"I am a member of the [BCEC] board—equal member of the board to her and will participate as such."

Poole's contempt for "her"—McCarthy—was never more evident. The bitter behind-the-scenes battle over the Expo sale had left him with a genuine distaste for "her." He'd come to believe McCarthy was out to get Vander Zalm and had enlisted BCEC to help her do it.

Poole thought Vander Zalm was supreme and that cabinet

ministers were there to be servants of the premier's office. Poole's haughty response to McCarthy's jibe at him confirmed to many Socreds that power had gone to his head. "He's got to go," said one Socred MLA at the time.

That weekend, a *Sun* reporter phoned BCEC president Kevin Murphy at his home to find out whether he had–as Poole told reporters–"enthusiastically" attended the December meeting with Toigo.

Murphy said no. He had made his "grave reservations" known to Poole.

Thus, in Monday's *Sun*, across the top of the front page, the premier's chief political adviser was essentially accused of lying–or at least of having a faulty memory. Later that week, Vander Zalm denied a published report that he'd personally asked BCEC chairman Peter Brown why he had not responded to Toigo's interest in the Whistler convention centre. Vander Zalm would later admit that yes, maybe he had raised the matter with Brown.

In the legislature, the member known as The Ice Man–the NDP's Bob Williams–had found an irresistible issue. Williams was the Opposition's most feared critic. He had been forests minister during the NDP's brief term as government in B.C. between 1972 and 1975, and his composed but searing attacks on government mismanagement were fuelled by hatred for Social Credit.

Shortly after two o'clock on the afternoon of April 12, House Speaker John Reynolds convened question period, fifteen minutes set aside in the day for the Opposition to ask the government questions. Williams led off, even more fearless in the debating chamber, where he had immunity from libel or slander.

"Do you know what insider information is all about, Mr. Premier?" Williams said to a hushed house. "I ask you, Mr. Premier, what kind of hold does Mr. Toigo have on you?"

The Socred benches were silent. The question was ruled out of order before Vander Zalm responded. However, Williams had dared to ask the question many were wondering about; the question Grace McCarthy had asked Vander Zalm five months earlier in his office.

Each day, the Expo lands sale was becoming a bigger circus. The *Sun* had now documented at least ten occasions on which Vander

Zalm or his right-hand man, David Poole, had intervened on behalf of Toigo. On one of those occasions, in 1987, cabinet had killed a deal to sell the Expo rides to an Ontario-based company in order to accommodate Toigo's interest in the rides. Toigo's plan for the rides never went anywhere, and they sat rusting, costing taxpayers $700 000 annually to service the interest charges on the borrowed money which had paid for the equipment.

There were daily dust-ups between Vander Zalm and his ministers or government officials. Ministers were paranoid about the daily leaks to the media, including the secret goings-on in cabinet, that were aimed at discrediting Vander Zalm. Finance minister Mel Couvelier stormed into one cabinet meeting accusing McCarthy's assistant, Jim Bennett, of leaking damaging material to the *Sun*. When Brian Smith's ministerial assistant was seen talking to an NDP MLA who was one of the government's fiercest critics, it was immediately reported to the premier's office by a Socred politician sympathetic to Vander Zalm.

Socred party members were also upset. In mid-April Vander Zalm's office received a fourteen-page fax from the party office in the Vancouver suburb of Richmond. The fax was a breakdown of letters, fundraising responses, and nearly 1000 telephone calls headquarters had received from April 1 to April 15. The responses ran three to one against Vander Zalm. Many were like Mr. and Mrs. G.R. Mackintosh's of West Vancouver; the Mackintoshes wrote that they would not vote for Vander Zalm in the next election because "we feel he is a danger to this province and he should be removed."

Responses to fundraising letters were particularly distressing because they came from party members, not NDP hacks phoning headquarters for fun. They were also distressing because people were mailing back complaints but no money.

Members of the Socred caucus were getting the same negative feedback from their constituents. Caucus morale was plummeting even farther than it had over the abortion crisis. Socred politicians began gathering in small groups in the legislative dining room to discuss the party's mounting leadership crisis.

Staff morale in the premier's office was also down as the government's policy agenda became mired in all the controversy.

There was no damage control plan in place. But at least one of the premier's aides recognized that something had to be done.

On April 14, Bob Ransford put the final touches on an extraordinary, highly confidential memo to his boss, David Poole. Poole's well-connected executive assistant had talked to business leaders, Socred party members, and political experts who had all conveyed the same perception of the government: that it was being led by a one-man band—a premier who "was out of control and who has no idea of where he is headed."

The memo said that some of the party faithful were openly talking about replacing Vander Zalm, while others were talking about starting a new party. The public attacks on Vander Zalm by his caucus were unprecedented in the history of the party. (Kim Campbell, then the Socred MLA from Vancouver-Point Grey, now a federal cabinet minister, told a reporter: "There's a lot of unhappiness out there. There's a lot of concern in caucus. Unfortunately, there are very few checks and balances on the first minister in our parliamentary system.") Even during the party's dark days of 1983, when tens of thousands of protesters marched in the street under the opposition banner of Solidarity, Socred MLAs had not publicly criticized their leader, Bill Bennett.

Ransford said in his memo that whether or not Poole or Vander Zalm wanted to admit it, the messages flowing from the government were perceived to be:

1. Vander Zalm "has no regard for his colleagues and the role that they should play in a democratic government."
2. Vander Zalm "is motivated by and draws his support from a small group of extremists who remain anonymous."
3. "Religion and personal moral values are more important to Vander Zalm than economic stability."
4. Vander Zalm is "naive and takes his business advice from Peter Toigo. Toigo is the premier's source of political financial support and the premier is deeply indebted to him."
5. "The Expo lands controversy was more than the straw that broke the camel's back, it was a telling commentary on Vander Zalm's single-mindedness and disregard for his own and his party's political future."

6. Vander Zalm "shows no respect for the office he holds and the traditions of the province."
7. The premier "has no respect for women in politics, government or business."

Ransford told Poole that, after eighteen months, it was time the premier's office drew up a long-term plan to deal with public policy decisions and a political plan to deal with damage control. He suggested that Vander Zalm assume a lower media profile and let ministers make announcements instead of making them himself all the time. Ransford said caucus "needs to be stroked, not informed and lectured to." He suggested the premier call caucus members in periodically for random input and advice.

As a former assistant to Progressive Conservative MP Gerry St. Germain, Ransford understood how to stroke a caucus. "How do you think Mulroney kept his caucus in line during the first couple of years?" Ransford would say to Poole. And then he would tell him how Mulroney and St. Germain, who was chairman of the Tories' massive 200-member-plus caucus after the 1984 election, had set up regular meetings with small groups of MPs who were given a chance to air concerns directly to their leader. The meetings gave the impression, at least, that Mulroney cared, and kept MPs from going public with their concerns.

In one brutally frank four-page memo, Ransford had said it all. He had summed up perfectly Vander Zalm's autocratic and often flighty governing style. His solutions were precisely the ones veteran Socred ministers and the party's rookie caucus chair, Carol Gran, were urging.

Ransford discussed the memo with Poole, who listened intently and then promised to pass on Ransford's recommendations to Vander Zalm. But within days, the memo was forgotten. And soon it was obvious that it had gone the way of the wastebasket. The same mistakes were still being made.

As the second week of April drew to a close, an embattled Vander Zalm looked forward to a planned weekend foray into the Kootenays, in southeastern B.C. It was one of Vander Zalm's favourite regions: he had always received warm welcomes there.

He visited a high school in Trail, a small, working-class town dominated by a Cominco smelter. When Vander Zalm walked into the gym to address students and answer questions, he was surprised to hear boos and catcalls. A student asked if Vander Zalm had the right to impose his moral views regarding abortion on the rest of the province.

"If you're asking should we attempt to influence the morals of the province, then the answer is yes." Another chorus of boos rang out.

The following morning, Vander Zalm got up early to address a prayer breakfast hosted by the local mayor. It was the kind of believing audience with whom Vander Zalm felt at home. He told members of the Christian Business Men's Committee of Trail that people everywhere would find it easier to cope if they got to know Jesus Christ.

After the breakfast, a reporter asked if single mothers on welfare–women who had just had their payments cut by the government days earlier–would find it easier to cope if they believed in Jesus.

"I think we'd all find it easier. . . ," said Vander Zalm. "Certainly those that suffer, say, from the pressure of an unwanted pregnancy, will find it much, much easier to cope with the situation if they have faith in Jesus Christ."

It was another reminder of how Vander Zalm mixed his personal religious beliefs with public policy. And in the most secular province in Canada, his comments were swiftly denounced by the NDP and anti-poverty organizations. "Belief in Jesus Christ is not going to put bread on tables," said NDP leader Mike Harcourt.

Vander Zalm returned to Victoria on Tuesday morning, upset with the media treatment he'd received over his comments in Trail and increasingly bitter over what he saw as the public crucifixion of his friend Peter Toigo.

When his white Ford LTD pulled into the driveway near the back entrance of his office, a crowd of reporters was waiting. The morning scrum had been a routine start for the day since he had become premier in August 1986. But on this day, Vander Zalm brushed by reporters, blurting that he had nothing to say, and bounded up the stairs. It was the first time he hadn't stopped to chat.

In the legislature that afternoon, New Democrat Moe Sihota asked Vander Zalm if he'd be prepared to resign if it could be proved that he had given "Toigo secret government information," such as details of Li Ka-shing's bid on the Expo lands. Vander Zalm scoffed at Sihota's suggestion.

After question period, Vander Zalm walked down the corridor toward his office, pursued by reporters tripping over each other as they shouted questions at him, their arms draped over his shoulders, their microphones inches from his face. It was an odd sight, this moving mass of bodies and television lights. Legislature staff who happened to be heading out of their offices would see the slow-moving human blob and quickly step back into safer surroundings.

Vander Zalm's once good-natured responses were now filled with bitterness: "You don't care what the facts," said Vander Zalm, dropping his verb as he was wont to do. "You'll go and write the story your way anyway."

The New Democrats, meanwhile, remained preoccupied with the Big Rumour rampant throughout the legislature's corridors and the Vancouver business community: that Vander Zalm owed Toigo some personal or corporate financial obligation and that was why he went to such lengths to help his friend get the Expo site.

Vander Zalm's Fantasy Gardens was known to be under a mountain of debt–about $6 million–and there were reports from people running stores in the Gardens that business was down badly because of Vander Zalm's political unpopularity. There were estimates that the Vander Zalms required $800 000 a year just to service the Gardens' debt. Where were they getting the money? If Vander Zalm wasn't getting direct cash infusions from Toigo, then was Toigo using his multi-million-dollar empire to guarantee Vander Zalm's loans?

Then the *Sun* revealed that Toigo's main holding company, Shato Holdings, held the business licence for a restaurant in Fantasy Gardens. Though Vander Zalm insisted Fantasy Gardens belonged to his wife, his financial disclosure statement listed a 30 per cent interest.

Television crews were at Fantasy Gardens in a flash, interviewing Toigo's daughter, Louise Green, who ran the restaurant, which she said had been purchased for her to run on her own. Vander Zalm was furious. He said that if his wife, Lillian, who was running the Gardens, wanted to lease to Shato Holdings she had every right to.

The provincial cabinet met in Vancouver to ratify the sale of the Expo site to Li Ka-shing. But the excitement that one might have expected around the cabinet table was nowhere to be found. There was more relief than anything, with most ministers privately hoping that the announcement of the sale would end the mind-numbing assault on Vander Zalm, who was looking tired, the bounce in his step gone, the megawatt smile burnt out.

The glitzy unveiling of Li's plans for the site should have been a moment of glory for Vander Zalm. The Expo lands was the flashiest item on Vander Zalm's privatization list, and the government expected to get positive exposure from it when it was announced. Instead, the afternoon ceremony would focus attention on the polemics that had engulfed the sale from start to finish. Although Vander Zalm wouldn't admit it, the fault was mostly his own.

With his mood soured, the last thing Vander Zalm wanted to do was stand beside Grace McCarthy, BCEC chairman Peter Brown, and corporation president Kevin Murphy at the unveiling and have to pretend he was happy about being in their company. But Poole, urged by Murphy, convinced Vander Zalm to show up.

At the unveiling, held at a theatre on the Expo site, the lights were dimmed and a shrouded model of Li Ka-shing's plans was revealed to the 500 guests of the government.

The model included futuristic office towers rising forty-five storeys with their own communications satellite, and an island-dotted waterway running along the development's boulevard. Vancouver Mayor Gordon Campbell called it breathtaking.

BCEC directors, who had stood up to Vander Zalm for months, looked on with a mixture of relief and triumph. When it came time for pictures, the jewellery-laden McCarthy, her famous red coiffure meticulously set, grabbed Vander Zalm's hand. The gesture was supposed to symbolize that she and the premier were united.

"I feel great and I feel great having the premier here and if this will help to dispel any idea that there has been a separation of our thoughts for this place I can tell you that we're together and delighted," said McCarthy, knowing that as she spoke an RCMP investigation was under way.

"There were difficult moments but that's all behind us now," said Vander Zalm, unaware he was being investigated.

In the final deal, Concord Pacific doubled its initial payment to $50 million and increased its total (in 1988 dollars) to $125 million. The nominal value, however, the amount paid out over the fifteen-year term of the deal, was $320 million.

The final package also included bonuses ranging from $7.5 million to $32.7 million, depending on the zoning density approved by city hall. For its purposes, the government assumed a bonus at the mid-point, giving the province $145 million for the land–the nominal value being $430.7 million.

The day after the signing four gallery reporters each received a phone call from David Poole with a very unusual invitation. The four–Baldrey of the *Sun*, Clem Chapple of BCTV, Daphne Bramham of the Canadian Press news agency, and Ian Jessop of radio station CKNW–were invited to interview Vander Zalm and ask him any questions they wanted.

The deal was that they tell none of their fellow reporters.

Poole, whose idea it was, felt Vander Zalm should respond in a controlled setting to questions about Toigo from representatives from the province's four major media outlets. That way, Vander Zalm could get his message out without being subjected to a media mob.

The four reporters first gathered in Chapple's office, in an armory behind the legislature, to discuss Poole's bizarre overture. The group discussed the possibility that they were being set up. But they had been assured that the session would be on the record, so they decided to go–and not to tell any other reporters.

Shortly before eight o'clock, under the shield of darkness, the four entered the premier's annex through the back door and were led by staff into Vander Zalm's office, where they took up chairs around a round oak table.

In a departure from the atmosphere of trust that had marked Vander Zalm's early days in office, when he would meet reporters alone, this time the premier's aides–David Poole, Bob Ransford, and Bill Bachop–sat behind the group listening.

Vander Zalm lit his pipe and began.

"I don't mind telling you that I've obviously been very troubled by all of the publicity and all the statements and all the suggestions and all of the questions over the last number of weeks," he said, his arms leaning on the table, his two hands cupping his pipe.

"Troubled not so much for myself but troubled obviously because, well, I guess the example is I phoned home today and asked my daughter, 'How are things?' The phone rang ten times before she answered and she said: 'Thank heavens it's you, dad, because we've had nothing but crazy calls all day.' "

For the next half hour, Vander Zalm for the first time candidly discussed the extraordinary pressure he, his family, and his friend Peter Toigo had been under for the last month. He talked about how he had met Toigo and how their two families had become close. He admitted that his repeated interventions in the Expo sale on behalf of Toigo had probably been unwise, but still insisted he had done nothing wrong.

Vander Zalm looked beat as the white smoke from his pipe swirled before his face. Earlier that day, he had been through a similar truth session with his caucus.

The premier's story was a great one for the four reporters who had been invited to hear it. What they didn't know was that waiting outside the premier's back entrance were seething colleagues from other news outlets who hadn't been invited. When the four reporters left Vander Zalm's office, they were met with the glare of television lights.

The next day, the president of the press gallery, CBC radio reporter Barry Bell, sent an angry letter to the premier protesting the exclusive late-night rendezvous with the Gang of Four, as they were quickly dubbed. The premier's office defended the decision, saying it could invite whomever it wanted. Nonetheless, an attempt by Vander Zalm to clear the air about his association with Toigo had become another schmozzle.

Vander Zalm's link with Toigo remained the dominant political issue in the province. Good-news government announcements were completely overshadowed. On May 10, for example, Vander Zalm cut the ribbon on a $30-million rebuilding project at Vancouver General Hospital. He walked down from the podium to a waiting throng of reporters only to be confronted with more questions about Toigo. This time they concerned his friend's place on the Premier's Economic Advisory Council.

"It's ridiculous this keeps coming up again and again," Vander Zalm protested. Vander Zalm still didn't understand that it was his judgment that was being questioned, not the actions of his friend.

The advisory council was a government-appointed group of national and international businessmen who gathered twice a year to advise Vander Zalm on economic matters. At one meeting of the premier's council, business immigration was discussed. Later it was learned that, after the meeting, B.C. had lobbied Ottawa to relax the program's rules. It was disclosed that Toigo had not, while sitting on the council, revealed he was a director of a syndicate set up to attract foreign investment under Ottawa's business immigration program. (Toigo had not violated any conflict-of-interest guidelines because there were none governing the council. And there was no evidence that Toigo profited in any way from B.C.'s lobbying efforts. And in August 1988 he had said his presence on the council was more trouble than it was worth and resigned.)

Then a much more serious controversy began to dog the government.

BCTV, the province's highly rated and most-watched television station, began running nightly stories about irregularities in the conducting of a plebiscite involving the Knight Street pub in Vancouver.

Toigo had built the pub while there was a moratorium on pub licences. After construction was completed the moratorium was lifted. Charles Giordano, Vander Zalm's former campaign manager, ran the government-required neighbourhood referendum to see if enough people approved of a pub operating in their area. After the pub began operating, some people in the area didn't believe the required 60 per cent of their neighbours had actually voted in favour of the pub. Soon, BCTV was revealing evidence of forged signatures; of thirteen people in one house signing ballots; of relatives of the pub manager signing ballots. The minister in charge of approving pubs, Lyall Hanson, and the general manager in charge of liquor licensing, Bert Hick, ran for cover.

As each story aired, there were accompanying pictures of Toigo, Giordano, and Vander Zalm–the web of friendship. The previous disclosures of Vander Zalm's special treatment of Toigo had heightened interest in the Knight Street pub affair.

When Toigo was upset over the abuse he felt he was taking in the media, he generally phoned the premier's office to talk to Vander Zalm. He often got through without any problem. On May 24 he phoned at 8:45 in the evening. David Poole's executive assistant, Bob Ransford, answered the phone. Toigo wanted to talk to either Poole or Vander Zalm, both of whom were tied up in a meeting.

"This is the last day of taking this and doing nothing," Toigo screamed into the phone, as Ransford furiously jotted down notes. "The harassment has gone far enough, especially on this pub thing. I told David [Poole] last week that they should have done something and they didn't. They could have stopped it then but instead they let it drag on." Toigo didn't elaborate on how Vander Zalm could have stopped the story.

Toigo said police and media were harassing pub staff. When Ransford mentioned that it had been on the news again that night, Toigo blurted, "I didn't know you ran [the government] by the six o'clock news."

In May, as his popularity plummeted to new depths, Vander Zalm was forced to consider an election. Not a general election, luckily for him, but a by-election in the province's South Okanagan riding of Boundary–Similkameen, a Socred stronghold.

The premier's office had notified Allan Gregg's Decima Research of the impending by-election and asked for some fresh polling information. Early on May 11, the same day Vander Zalm called the by-election for the following month, Decima reported.

The Ontario-based agency had polled 250 residents in Boundary–Similkameen by telephone between May 4 and 6: the NDP had 47 per cent of the decided vote, the Socreds 44 per cent, and the Liberals 6 per cent.

Those figures represented a 13 per cent drop in Socred support since the election of 1986. And this was the heartland of Socred country, a 13 000-square-kilometre riding from the Cascade Mountains in the west, through the southern Okanagan Valley, across the hills of the Interior dry belt and the Monashee Mountains to the north, reaching the western side of the Lower Arrow Lake valley. Though riding boundaries had changed over the years, the area had voted Socred since 1952.

The NDP candidate, Bill Barlee—a popular local historian, author, and television personality—focused his campaign almost exclusively on the premier, seldom mentioning his nominal challenger, Socred Russ Fox, a likeable small-town banker.

Decima's Ian McKinnon advised the Socred strategists to keep the by-election a local campaign, as opposed to focusing on the provincial issues which Vander Zalm represented, and to identify family life supporters—who backed Vander Zalm—and profile the premier mainstreeting and knocking on doors as opposed to giving speeches defending his personal actions and his government's policies.

The Socred campaign was put in the hands of Brian Battison, a young political strategist from Penticton who had been recently brought into the premier's office as a troubleshooter. Besides the Vander Zalm factor, Battison faced a tough issue: free trade. Boundary-Similkameen was grape-growing and wine-making country, and under free trade—which Vander Zalm loudly supported—there were concerns that the local wine industry would be wiped out.

Vander Zalm promised aid, but it was little comfort to growers faced with ripping out their vines and looking for other work.

Vander Zalm vowed to make five appearances in the riding during the five-week campaign, confident that his presence would help the Socred cause. His advisers knew it would probably hurt more than help, but they didn't have the heart to tell him. The Vander Zalms loved the Okanagan. Lillian's mother lived in Penticton, Boundary-Similkameen's largest centre, and Vander Zalm had taken a keen interest in the area's development. If there was one constituency he felt wouldn't let him down, it was this one.

But by the end of May, Battison and Bob Ransford knew they were losing. The polls showed it. Just after seven o'clock one evening, Battison and Ransford went into David Poole's office, where Battison phoned former Social Credit premier Bill Bennett in Kelowna. Battison had worked at Socred headquarters when Bennett was premier.

Battison told Bennett the Socreds were heading for certain defeat, to the surprise of the former premier, who said he'd bet someone a steak dinner that the Socreds would win by at least 2000 votes.

Battison asked Bennett–as Ransford and Poole listened to the conversation on the speaker-phone–if he would allow his name to be signed to a letter urging voters to reject the idea of voting NDP as a way of sending a message to Vander Zalm.

Bennett chortled and said he'd retired from politics and had passed up numerous previous opportunities to speak out publicly, particularly during the Coquihalla Affair.

That barbed reference was to an inquiry ordered by Vander Zalm into a $500-million cost overrun on the Coquihalla Highway, a beautiful four-lane ribbon of blacktop in the province's Interior. It had been extremely damaging to Bennett, whose office was linked to efforts to hide the overruns. Bennett had almost been sub-poenaed to testify. Vander Zalm had done nothing to defend Bennett at the time, and Bennett felt no obligation to help Vander Zalm out now. Besides, he told Battison, Vander Zalm had had plenty of messages sent his way and had chosen to ignore them. Perhaps what he needed was a stronger message, like a loss in Boundary-Similkameen.

The following day, June 1, Battison and Ransford received the latest polling numbers. The NDP's lead had soared to 53 per cent, compared to 39 per cent for the Socreds and 8 per cent for the Liberals. Vander Zalm's forays into the riding were turning people off. Battison, Ransford, and Poole kept the numbers to themselves. They didn't want to demoralize party workers.

The Socreds, meanwhile, were spending gobs of money in a losing cause. Most of it–$150 000 by the end of the campaign–was being spent on advertising. During one reconnaissance into the riding, Battison and Ransford visited a Penticton radio station to hear some Socred election ads that Ransford had written and dropped off a week earlier for voicing. It was a Friday afternoon, and the sixty-second radio spots were scheduled to start running the next day.

Ransford didn't like what he heard. The Socred message was lost in the actor's dull recitation of the script.

Ransford looked at Battison. "You and I are going to do the ads over again."

"Are you nuts?" Battison said.

"No, we can do it. I've done it before," said Ransford, a former radio reporter.

The two aides to the premier walked into the radio station's sound room and sat behind two large microphones, while an even larger tape recorder rolled. Battison and Ransford were supposed to be two guys in a casual conversation.

"So who you voting for?" Battison says.

"Well, I'm thinking I might vote for the NDP guy, and send the government a message," says Ransford.

"Yea, I was thinking about doing that," Battison says back. "But I got to thinking, it just doesn't make sense. Russ Fox is a bright guy, and he'd be a voice inside government, a voice that could make a difference."

After Battison explains that a vote for Bill Barlee would be wasted in Opposition, a converted Ransford cuts in.

"You know what? You're right. I'm with you. I'm voting Russ Fox."

It took the bold duo nine takes to finally get it down without laughing or fluffing their lines. People on the campaign eventually recognized the voices of the premier's aides, but the media didn't. For Battison and Ransford, who was working on the by-election while collecting a healthy taxpayer-financed salary in the premier's office, the stunt would provide hours of future entertainment as they recited the ad from memory over a few beers.

While the Socred campaign was in disarray, the NDP had run a tight, well-financed campaign with a charming, folksy candidate fully in charge.

On by-election night, June 8, a crowd gathered at Russ Fox's Penticton campaign headquarters, a room overlooking an empty, iceless curling rink. The public, unaware of the latest polling results, was still expecting a squeaker. While Socreds knew people in the area were mad at Vander Zalm, no one believed the people would turn their backs on their party.

Shortly after 8:15 p.m., the first polls put the NDP ahead. Ten minutes later the NDP had expanded its lead. Within thirty minutes of the polls closing, the unthinkable was being witnessed: an NDP landslide.

Socred MLAs at Fox headquarters were stunned, but none more than Ivan Messmer, the former Penticton mayor who held the other of the riding's two seats. He was given the thankless task of phoning the premier's office with the results.

Barlee had taken 53 per cent of the vote, just as Decima's last poll had predicted. Fox managed only 35 per cent, four points less than Decima's final dismal projection. The Socreds were down 10 000 votes from the election in 1986. It appeared that not only had Socreds refused to vote for their own party, they had voted NDP!

It was the most humiliating by-election defeat in the party's history. Strangely, Socred supporters milling about Fox headquarters with plastic glasses of beer or harder alcoholic soothers seemed almost relieved. Maybe the loss would finally convince Vander Zalm he had to change.

Russ Fox arrived, with his teary-eyed wife, and thanked his supporters. He refused to blame Vander Zalm for the defeat. But Socred party director Jess Gee had no hesitation: "The premier has to change, clearly."

In Victoria, the premier and a small group of politicians were gathered in a private room in the legislative dining hall for a dinner in tribute to B.C.'s retiring lieutenant-governor, Bob Rogers. As the group prepared for dessert, the door suddenly burst open and in walked Vander Zalm's deputy, David Poole, bearing the bad by-election news. With his right index finger, Poole gestured to Vander Zalm to meet him outside.

Without stopping to apologize or bid adieu to the guest of honour, Vander Zalm obediently left the room and a table of stunned guests, including Socred House Speaker John Reynolds and NDP Opposition Leader Mike Harcourt, who attempted to give His Honour a dignified send-off. (Rogers was supposed to vacate his post on July 15 but was asked to stay until September, reportedly because of Ottawa's concern over Vander Zalm's future.)

Vander Zalm huddled with Poole, Bob Ransford, and his press secretary, Bill Bachop, in Poole's corner office. During the campaign, he had dismissed Decima's polling results as "dumb," always putting more faith in his own powers than in polls. But he couldn't dismiss this result.

The aides urged Vander Zalm to strike a conciliatory note when he went outside to meet the reporters waiting at the foot of the stairs leading to the back door of the premier's office. It was agreed that Vander Zalm would tell the media that the people of Boundary-Similkameen had sent the government an important message and he was going to listen. The group then walked out the back door to meet reporters.

"Well, premier, the people of Boundary-Similkameen have sent you a pretty strong message tonight. Are you now prepared to change your style of governing?" he was asked.

"I can't change," Vander Zalm began. His aides exchanged nervous glances behind his back. "I don't intend to make any changes at all. I can't change my moral views. I can't compromise my moral convictions on particular issues."

Vander Zalm said he would "sleep well" knowing that what he was doing was right for the province. And he warned that the riding might get poorer representation for voting NDP.

David Poole and the rest of the premier's staff looked ill. In the time it had taken the premier to walk twenty steps from Poole's office, he had abandoned the conciliatory plan. Moreover, he had insulted the voters of Boundary-Similkameen by suggesting they were less moral than he was.

He had demonstrated an arrogance and defiance his supporters refused to believe existed behind the famous smile. It was a telling episode: it showed Vander Zalm could get indignant when he was let down, when his charm with the voters failed. His tone convinced many Socreds that their party was going down in flames with a kamikaze at the controls.

"How can you be defiant when your family just walked out on you?" Socred MLA Harold Long told reporters the next day when asked about Vander Zalm's comments. Other Socred politicians supported Long, saying Vander Zalm had to change.

The premier, however, remained defiant, accusing the media of destroying British Columbians' pride in their province.

"You're destroying pride, you're destroying optimism, you're creating pessimism, and we all lose by this," he told reporters, once again identifying his misfortunes with those of the province.

By mid-June the RCMP's investigation into BCEC's complaints was winding down.

Under the Criminal Code, the section that deals most closely with the allegations BCEC had levelled was Section 110, Frauds upon the Government. "Everyone commits a crime who directly or indirectly gives a government official or any member of his family a loan, reward, advantage or benefit of any kind as consideration for cooperation, assistance, exercise of influence in connection with the transaction of business relating to government, whether or not . . . the official is able to cooperate, render assistance, exercise influence or do or omit to do what is proposed. . . ."

Everyone commits an offence who "having or pretending to have influence with the government or with a minister of the government or an official, demands, accepts or offers or agrees to accept for himself or another person a reward, advantage or benefit of any kind as consideration for cooperation, assistance, exercise of influence or an act or omission," in connection with government business.

Peter Toigo was going to meet an associate connected with Li Ka-shing. The fact that officials with BCEC, or the official Toigo was going to visit, believed that the premier's friend might be going to influence peddle, wasn't enough to get a criminal conviction. For starters, the police needed evidence of a financial benefit passing between Toigo and Vander Zalm.

The case that the attorney-general's department handed over to the police lacked the evidence necessary for a criminal prosecution. There was no evidence of a financial benefit conferred on Vander Zalm by Toigo.

After an exhaustive search of Toigo's and Vander Zalm's financial records, the RCMP could find nothing that tied the two men together. The closest the RCMP got was a tip that Toigo, through his company Whitbury Holdings, had purchased some park benches at an auction of Expo 86 assets in November 1986. The benches were delivered to Fantasy Gardens.

The RCMP found out that Lillian Vander Zalm had attended an auction of Expo 86 items at which David Podmore, representing Toigo's Whitbury Holdings, was also present. Lillian wanted several park benches that were up for grabs but didn't have money along with her to pay. So Podmore, on behalf of Whitbury, wrote out a cheque for $2200 for the benches, which were later delivered to Fantasy Gardens.

RCMP Inspector George Vander Kracht went to Maynards Auctioneers to seek permission to go through their files to find the invoice of the sale. Maynards said it would be all right with them as long as Vander Kracht got permission from the B.C. Enterprise Corp., which was in charge of Expo 86–related records. Ironically, Vander Kracht had to phone BCEC president Kevin Murphy to seek his permission to go through the invoices.

Murphy gave the okay. Vander Kracht spent days searching through thousands of invoices before he found the one for the park benches. But then he discovered that Lillian had later paid Whitbury back the borrowed $2200. The benches were not a gift from Peter Toigo.

The RCMP interviewed all the principals, including Li Ka-shing's agent George Magnus, who confirmed to Vander Kracht his conversation with Murphy in which Magnus expressed his concerns about Toigo's coming to Hong Kong. But those were merely Magnus's fears. The meeting didn't take place; there was no proof Toigo was going to influence peddle despite the pattern of special treatment from Vander Zalm evidenced by BCEC officials.

Vander Zalm, meanwhile, still had no knowledge that he and Toigo were under investigation. He couldn't have imagined it because he didn't believe he'd done anything wrong. He did believe that McCarthy and Smith were out to get him, and an incident on June 15 would convince Vander Zalm forever that his conspiracy theory was correct.

Deputy attorney-general Ted Hughes had received a call from McCarthy's assistant, Jim Bennett, who told Hughes he had someone he wanted to bring to the deputy's office, someone who might have something interesting to say. He did not tell Hughes what the subject was.

The person Bennett was bringing to Hughes's office was Ken Mowers, a Victoria real estate agent. Bennett had once shared office space with Mowers and had discovered that he did real estate deals with Toigo. Bennett thought Mowers might be able to shed some light on Toigo's business dealings and urged him to attend a meeting with the deputy attorney-general.

Mowers was curious enough to attend, but soon after he got there it seemed apparent to him that the meeting was arranged to get dirt on Toigo. Mowers was asked, for instance, where Toigo's money came from. Mowers then recalled Bennett saying: "If we don't get something on Peter Toigo in two weeks, Brian Smith is going to be out of a job." Bennett says he didn't say he wanted to get Toigo but may have speculated that Brian Smith could soon be out of a job and his replacement might shut down the investigation.

Ted Hughes felt the Mowers meeting was a waste of time. The man had no information pertinent to the RCMP investigation. He did not even bother passing it on.

Toigo learned about the meeting Mowers was summoned to and of Jim Bennett's alleged remark about him, and passed the information along to Vander Zalm, who now believed McCarthy and Smith were in cahoots to get him by getting Toigo.

Rumours of a major cabinet shuffle peaked in late June. It was said that Vander Zalm was going to split up the ministry of the attorney-general and fire Brian Smith.

Both rumours were correct.

Vander Zalm planned to have a solicitor-general in charge of police and corrections, and an attorney-general in charge of legal and constitutional matters. The official reason given for this by the premier's office was that such a system was more efficient and was used in Ottawa and several provincial jurisdictions. More important, however, it allowed Vander Zalm to expand the size of his cabinet and add to the number of people that would be too beholden to him to take part in any palace coup.

Vander Zalm was planning to sack Smith over the latter's decision to publicly embarrass Vander Zalm on the abortion appeal decision and Smith's refusal to carry out Vander Zalm's request to issue a news release to clear Toigo's name.

Brian Smith had considered resigning after his dust-up with Vander Zalm over the Toigo news release, but he wanted to stay to ensure that the RCMP investigation was completed. Smith told others that he felt Vander Zalm was going to fire him and install a crony in the job who would deep-six the investigation.

On the morning of June 28, Brian Smith put the finishing touches on his resignation speech. It was the last possible chance Smith would have to dramatically announce his decision in the legislature, which was about to adjourn for the summer. He knew he was going to be fired in the cabinet shuffle that would happen any day. Smith wanted to quit rather than be fired; that way he could control the drama and the headlines.

The premier and his supporters would always believe Smith decided to quit because he had found out the night before that the investigation was over.

At two o'clock on June 28, Smith walked into the legislative assembly carrying only a brown manila envelope. He sat down, nervously pulled a sheaf of white paper from the envelope, and slid it underneath the brown wrapper, nervously tapping on it with his fingers as he gave members of the press gallery shifty-eyed glances.

As question period unfolded, Smith's nervousness became evident. The young page, who was continually beckoned by the attorney-general, shot members of the press gallery a quizzical look after delivering Smith's fourth glass of water.

The other sign that something was amiss was the presence in the gallery of Smith's new wife, Barbara, who only showed up for special occasions.

The suspicious press watched from a gallery directly above the speaker of the house. "He's going to do it, he's going to resign," one reporter said.

After question period, Smith raised his microphone and began to get to his feet. But Speaker John Reynolds recognized another minister first, then another, then another. Finally, Smith was recognized. He announced he had a ministerial statement to make.

"For over five years I have had the honour to hold the post of attorney-general," Smith began. ". . . I now find that I can no longer carry out my duties as I clearly do not have the support of the premier and his office, who do not appreciate the unique independence that is the cornerstone of the attorney-general's responsibilities in a free parliamentary democracy. Therefore, I am submitting my resignation as attorney-general and am stating that I do not wish at this time to be considered for another cabinet post in this administration."

For the next five minutes, Smith outlined his reasons for leaving, while Vander Zalm, slouched in the chair right beside Smith's, sat emotionless, his chin resting on his right hand. Someone had sent Vander Zalm a note earlier, telling him that Smith's wife was in the gallery, and Vander Zalm had suspected then that something was up.

Asked what went through his mind once he realized what Smith was doing, Vander Zalm recalls, "I thought this is another trial you go through, part of what you live with. . . . It will go away like all other things and [one must] carry on and be strong."

Smith told the legislature he believed Vander Zalm was planning to weaken the independence of his ministry by splitting it up and appointing someone to the position who was not a lawyer. He mentioned his differences with Vander Zalm over abortion and Peter Toigo.

He ended his speech with a line destined for the headlines: "I am resigning as an act of honour," a paraphrase of his hero Richard McBride's resignation speech in 1901. (McBride later came back to become B.C.'s longest-serving Tory premier.)

Provincial Secretary Elwood Veitch immediately became acting attorney-general and met with Smith for fifteen minutes after his resignation. Veitch, whose thoughts on the law were represented solely by a joking reference that judges were idiots, denied that there was any crisis in the government.

Vander Zalm and Poole drafted a response which the premier released the following day when he met with the media. He noted, among other things, that at no time did Smith discuss his concerns with Vander Zalm.

"Mr. Smith's stated reasons for resigning have no basis in fact," said Vander Zalm, who in fact had intended to fire Smith two weeks later and split his ministry.

Smith's stated reasons for resigning were taken at face value by most of the major media outlets. However, Victoria's weekly *Monday Magazine* took a more sceptical view and suggested that Smith had merely positioned himself to take over as premier should scandals eventually force Vander Zalm out of office.

It wasn't as simple as that. Smith had finished second at Whistler, taking all the establishment votes with him. But he had been loyal during Vander Zalm's first year in office. Why else would he have dreamed up such atrocities as the sedition writ and the abortion spy caper? Certainly not to help his future leadership chances. But his relationship with Vander Zalm had begun to unravel over the premier's stand on abortion, and had deteriorated completely during the BCEC scandal.

With the Socred caucus seriously questioning their leader's ability, an RCMP investigation of Vander Zalm was certainly convenient for someone who still aspired to the throne. But the fact is that Smith had little choice but to turn BCEC's complaints over to the RCMP. If it had ever been learned that he sat on all the evidence of interference that had been handed to him, he would have rightly been accused of a cover-up. He would have been finished as a politician.

As much as Brian Smith's resignation hurt Vander Zalm politically, the premier wasn't sorry to see him go. With everything that had happened between them, there wasn't much of a friendship left. In less than a week, Vander Zalm would be faced with a more painful resignation from his cabinet, this one by an old friend.

Three hours after Smith resigned deputy attorney-general Ted Hughes was lying in a Victoria hospital following a knee operation when he was visited by RCMP Inspector George Vander Kracht, RCMP Superintendent Dennis Moore, and special Crown counsel Len Doust. The RCMP said they had found nothing untoward in Vander Zalm's relationship with Toigo. They told Hughes that they planned to interview Vander Zalm and Toigo to officially wrap up the case.

There would be suggestions later when it became public that the investigation wrapped up the same day Smith resigned, that Smith had waited to hear that news before leaving cabinet. Clearly that wasn't the case as Hughes didn't find out the case was closed until after Smith resigned. Nonetheless, Smith's resignation was no surprise to his former deputy, to whom he had read his resignation statement the day before doing it for real.

Fall From Grace

The bright sun bounced off the sleek body of the government's blue-and-white Cessna Citation jet as it sat on the tarmac, waiting for its important cargo. It was 8:00 a.m. on July 5, 1988, and the B.C. cabinet ministers boarding the jet in Vancouver for the fifteen-minute dash to the government hangar in Victoria were a little unsettled. Today they were to be told what would happen to them in the following day's cabinet shuffle.

"Good morning, all," said a chipper Bill Vander Zalm as he boarded the plane. Economic Development Minister Grace McCarthy and other ministers exchanged pleasantries with the man holding their future in his hands.

Each minister and prospective minister had been given an appointment to see Vander Zalm. Like nervous school children heading off to visit the school principal, one by one they left their legislative offices, walked across the cement breezeway to the premier's annex, and took a seat in a waiting area until they were summoned.

The cabinet shuffle was an important one for Vander Zalm. He desperately needed to demonstrate leadership, to put together a loyal group of ministers who would support him in the event of any uprising among the disenchanted in his caucus.

It was nearly eleven o'clock when Grace McCarthy entered the premier's office. She was as anxious as she'd ever been about similar meetings under two previous Social Credit premiers. She had enjoyed the economic development ministry as much as any ministry she'd ever held, and she wanted to keep the portfolio. But the sixty-year-old Socred icon was attending her last meeting as a cabinet minister.

Vander Zalm began by offering McCarthy the provincial secretary's job and the ministry of tourism, as well as responsibility for being the government's spokesperson on multiculturalism. The two ministries were ones McCarthy had held before. McCarthy was told that another minister would be put in charge of selling BCEC's remaining assets. McCarthy was immediately concerned it would be a rookie, who wouldn't stand up to Vander Zalm if he tried to interfere in the sale process, perhaps on Toigo's behalf. She was less than thrilled. Before giving Vander Zalm an answer, she asked him a question:

"What are you going to do with David Poole?"

"I know you have a personality conflict with him," Vander Zalm returned.

McCarthy said it had nothing to do with personality conflicts; Poole was simply unqualified for his job. His meddling on behalf of Toigo and other developer friends had hurt the government, as had his embarrassing public policy comments (such as "The United States of British Columbia"). It wasn't only McCarthy who wanted Poole gone, it was the entire Socred caucus.

"We could not get elected outside of this term," McCarthy said, staring into the eyes of the man she had encouraged to run for the party's leadership two years earlier. "We could not get elected today. Why is that? You're getting so far removed you don't trust anybody in cabinet; you're not getting good advice.

"You are getting advice from somebody [Poole] who has got two years' experience or less, and your friend, Peter Toigo–that's who's running the government."

Vander Zalm said McCarthy was being unfair, that he did consult his cabinet. McCarthy wouldn't budge. She said morale in the civil service was terrible.

"Bill, I haven't had a deputy in six months while I wait for David Poole to pick one for me. It's preposterous," McCarthy said, adding that in the past ministers had been perfectly capable of finding their own deputies.

She suggested that Vander Zalm place Poole in Socred party head-quarters, which was in disarray after being without an executive director for months. Vander Zalm said he had somebody else in mind for the executive director's job and was going to be announcing the appointment in two weeks.

McCarthy felt that, with Poole still around, the government's problems would continue, along with its popularity slide. McCarthy was a survivor with excellent political instincts. If she stayed in cabinet she'd go down with the sinking ship. She told Vander Zalm she wasn't going to accept a cabinet post.

"You don't mean that," said Vander Zalm.

"Yes, I do, Bill," she said.

At this stage of her political career she wasn't so desperate to stay in cabinet that she would return to ministries she could run with her hands tied behind her back. And she didn't like the prospect of sitting around the cabinet table while another minister of economic development carried out the plans of which she was so proud.

"Grace, you are upset, I know," McCarthy recalls Vander Zalm telling her. "You've probably not had any lunch. Why don't you go get some lunch and think about it?"

It wouldn't be Vander Zalm's last patronizing comment about the most powerful and respected woman in his government.

McCarthy walked out of Vander Zalm's office to find Transportation Minister Stephen Rogers and a couple of other ministers waiting. McCarthy's meeting with the premier had gone on longer than expected, and there was now a lineup.

Rogers was next. Before Vander Zalm had a chance to speak, Rogers told him that he was prepared to step aside to make room for a backbencher who hadn't had a chance to serve in cabinet.

Vander Zalm would have none of it; he wanted to fire Rogers.

"Stephen, you've done a good job in your ministry but I'm afraid I can't let you stay. In a cabinet you need loyalty, and from what I hear you haven't been too loyal."

Vander Zalm was referring to reports of a meeting of Rogers's Vancouver South executive committee at which the acerbic and cynical MLA—who liked to refer to Vander Zalm and Lillian as Zalm and the Headband–had criticized Vander Zalm's leadership and mused about how his leader could be dumped.

But Vander Zalm was the last one to be talking about dis- loyalty. Rogers had been in the cabinet that Vander Zalm had branded as "gutless" in 1982, and in the same Socred caucus that Vander Zalm said hadn't had the "moxie" to fight alongside him during the abortion row. Rogers didn't bother pointing out the contradiction.

The meeting lasted about thirty minutes, with Rogers attempting to explain what he'd said at the constituency meeting and why he had said it. Unmoved, Vander Zalm said he was sorry to have made the decision, but it was necessary. Stephen Rogers was gone.

Meanwhile, McCarthy had returned to her office firm in her decision to leave cabinet. She contacted a couple of key aides to advise them of her decision. Then she spent a couple of hours attending to unfinished ministry business, making her last executive decisions under Bill Vander Zalm. At about 2:30 p.m., her secretary put through a call from the premier's office.

"Grace, I've got to know what you've decided. Your decision impacts on everyone else," said Vander Zalm.

"Have you changed your mind regarding David Poole?" said McCarthy.

"No," said Vander Zalm.

"Well, I'm sorry, then: neither have I," said McCarthy.

The impact of what she had done suddenly hit her. She wondered what she was doing tending to ministry business when she had to decide how to announce her resignation. Her aides arrived, and it was decided to make the announcement that day because the next was the cabinet shuffle and her reasons for leaving would be lost in all the other news of the day. If she waited, she would also be open to charges that she was trying to upstage Vander Zalm's cabi- net shuffle.

McCarthy re-read the letter of resignation she had handed Vander Zalm the previous December. It brought into focus why she was leaving. She then started to write.

Around three o'clock, McCarthy's ministerial assistant, Jim Bennett, breathlessly announced to members of the press gallery that his minister would be making an important announcement later that afternoon. Most realized instantly that McCarthy was leaving cabinet. Given the atmosphere of open hostility between her and the premier's office, why else would she be holding a news conference? The unknown was whether she'd been fired or had decided to leave on her own.

Anticipating that McCarthy might quit to embarrass Vander Zalm and enhance her own leadership chances, David Poole had put Neil Vant, an unassuming MLA from B.C.'s Cariboo region, on notice the day before that Poole might need to see him the afternoon of July 5. McCarthy's resignation had a domino effect on Vander Zalm's cabinet plans. Vander Zalm decided to make Vant transportation minister, a position earmarked for Cliff Michael, who held the post in an earlier cabinet before being fired over a conflict-of-interest controversy. Michael became government management services minister, responsible for Crown agencies. Bill Reid, who was supposed to get that job, ended up with provincial secretary and tourism, the dual post McCarthy was to have.

Shortly after five o'clock, reporters crowded around McCarthy's desk as she announced that she could no longer serve in Bill Vander Zalm's cabinet as long as "arrogant" unelected officials like David Poole were determined to interfere in the operations of her ministry.

"I, therefore, tender my resignation as a minister of the Crown," McCarthy said, stopping briefly to fight back tears, "a position that I have carried with pride, knowing the trust inherent in that office." After two earlier false starts, McCarthy was actually resigning.

She hoped her resignation after seventeen years in cabinet would send Vander Zalm a message that the Social Credit Party would not accept that any one person had "ownership over the fate of this province."

Before the cameras and most reporters left, the man who had announced his resignation from Vander Zalm's cabinet a week earlier, Brian Smith, arrived to give McCarthy a very public hug of support. As the cameras whirred, the two political renegades held hands as Smith mourned his colleague's decision.

"This is a terribly serious event that just occurred," he said, calling his one-time leadership rival the "conscience" of the Social Credit Party and a woman of "great bravery."

This maudlin and contrived display of affection helped fuel the theory that the two were in cahoots to get Vander Zalm.

Smith and McCarthy had met several times, and would meet several more, to informally discuss how Vander Zalm was destroying the party and what could be done about it. But there is no evidence of a concerted plan by them to dump Vander Zalm. Unquestionably, both knew that their resignations would stimulate the clandestine movement for a review of Vander Zalm's leadership. But neither had the will to become the leader of such a movement.

Their dilemma was this: The leader of a review movement would automatically enter an unofficial leadership contest with Vander Zalm. If the review bid failed, then whoever led it would have lost to Vander Zalm. If the review leader was a Socred politician like Smith or McCarthy, he or she couldn't continue to serve in the Socred caucus after openly trying to dump the leader.

In the end, neither Smith nor McCarthy wanted to take the chance. Both decided to wait and see if Vander Zalm resigned of his own accord or was eventually forced to resign over some scandal. Then they would be in a position to run for the leadership without having been seen as leading a review movement that could split the party.

News of McCarthy's resignation spread quickly.

Hope Rust, president of the party, heard it on her car radio driving home. "When I heard it I thought, My God, what could happen next?"

Carol Gran, Socred caucus chair, said Vander Zalm would have to do something quickly to restore confidence in his leadership.

Reporters gathered outside Vander Zalm's office for his official response to McCarthy's decision. The premier's usually neatly combed hair was straggly. Speaking in a low, joyless tone, Vander Zalm said that while he regretted McCarthy's announcement he was standing solidly behind Poole. "Mr. Poole and I have a wonderful working relationship and will continue to have."

However, "It's no secret that obviously Mrs. McCarthy is dearly loved by many Social Credit so we'll definitely need to convince the membership it was her decision."

McCarthy's resignation was much more serious than Smith's

because of the phenomenal support she enjoyed in the party and because people knew she was not a quitter. As well, because her resignation so quickly followed Smith's it created the impression that the sky was falling in on Vander Zalm.

NDP leader Mike Harcourt, not about to understate the case, said it was time for an election: "The affairs of ordinary men and women of British Columbia are being neglected as this government collapses."

The Vancouver *Sun* said: "The effect on British Columbia—even taking into account our history of political wackiness—is unsettling and potentially dangerous. We're rapidly achieving a dubious reputation as Fantasy Province World."

The next day, July 6, cars carrying cabinet ministers, and those soon to be, began arriving at the lieutenant-governor's estate shortly before 10:00 a.m. To reporters counting ministers outside the mansion, it appeared that cabinet was increasing in numbers, rather than decreasing as Vander Zalm had promised.

Sure enough, Vander Zalm announced that he was increasing his cabinet from seventeen members to twenty-two—the largest in the province's history. He was promoting eight backbenchers and firing only one, Stephen Rogers. There was no one in the cabinet from the province's largest city, Vancouver; some said this was a snub for not electing Vander Zalm mayor in 1984. But Vander Zalm had intended to put Vancouverite McCarthy in cabinet; once she turned him down he decided to reward a loyalist, Neil Vant, rather than any of the Vancouver MLAs, who had all been critics of his leadership.

It wasn't really surprising that Vancouver was a hotbed of anti-Vander Zalm sentiment. Vander Zalm had been totally indifferent to the powerful Vancouver business establishment. The city slickers were also embarrassed by their premier and his castle home in Fantasy Gardens. And in a city where women made up a large part of the workforce, Vander Zalm's view that a woman's place was in the home did not help him. Neither did his strident pro-life stance: Vancouver was centre of the B.C. pro-choice movement.

In his shuffle, Vander Zalm failed to promote any women, despite the obvious talent of MLA Kim Campbell and Carol Gran. After the ceremony, reporters wanted to know why municipal affairs minister

Rita Johnston remained the only woman in his cabinet. He re-
acted angrily.

"Oh, my goodness. I don't think the women of the province are
as picky as you."

The most notable new face in cabinet was Kamloops's Bud Smith,
the shrewd political fixer who had crossed the floor to Vander Zalm
at the 1986 leadership convention. Smith, a lawyer, was named
attorney-general. He quickly made it clear to reporters he believed
in independence of the office, a warning to Vander Zalm not
to try forcing him to issue statements on behalf of friends of
the premier.

Vander Zalm had rewarded loyalty. Backbenchers like Howard
Dirks from Nelson, Angus Ree from West Vancouver, and Jack
Weisgerber from Fort St. John had all kept their mouths shut when
their colleagues were criticizing Vander Zalm during the abortion
and BCEC furor. Vander Zalm wanted to consolidate the numbers
around him to fight the forces of division in his own caucus.

Following the swearing-in ceremonies, the new ministers mingled
in a dining room upstairs at Government House. The deputies
assigned to the ministers by David Poole were waiting in a room
downstairs. The plan was for Poole to bring the deputies up and
introduce them to their ministers. Then Vander Zalm would give a
rah-rah speech about how the government had been through some
tough times but things were going to get better and everyone had to
stick together.

Poole introduced the deputies, but when it came time for the
speech Vander Zalm backed out. He told Poole to give it; he wasn't
in the mood. Reluctantly, Poole carried out the order, knowing how
bad it looked: The deputy who was being criticized daily for having
too much power and being arrogant was not only telling the new
cabinet ministers who their deputies would be but also giving a
speech telling them they had to stick together and play as a team. A
few weeks later one of the new deputies would remark to Poole,
"I knew the instant you made that speech who was really
in charge."

There were numerous organizational changes in the premier's
office and the bureaucracy, all made without the cabinet's or the
caucus's knowledge. Poole insisted on secrecy. At one meeting of

the premier's staff prior to the shuffle, an aide to Poole had suggested that caucus and cabinet be advised ahead of time about the changes. Poole had exploded: "Listen, if anybody doesn't want to go along with the way we're doing it, then they can just pack their bags. This is the way it's going to be done."

The change most talked about was the announcement that Peter Bazowski, a former deputy minister of health, provincial Ombudsman, and head of the RCMP in B.C., was joining Vander Zalm's office as an adviser who would take on special projects.

While it wasn't quite clear what Bazowski would do, his appointment seemed to signal that Vander Zalm was listening to those who were saying he had to bring professional bureaucrats into his office.

But despite all the changes, Poole's power remained undiminished. He would still run the civil service and be Vander Zalm's chief political adviser.

Grace McCarthy spent her first day as a backbencher accepting bouquets delivered to her door.

"It's like being in the flower business again," beamed the former florist's shop owner, as she allowed reporters and camera crews to record the evidence of her popularity. After seventeen years as a cabinet minister, McCarthy's were probably the most impressive patronage networks in B.C.

As the large clock in McCarthy's living room chimed four, Vander Zalm was preparing to speak to the Social Credit board of directors in a conference call organized by party president Hope Rust. The directors had been shocked by McCarthy's resignation and wanted an accounting from Vander Zalm.

In recent months the board had met with Vander Zalm on a few occasions to ask for an explanation of his actions, particularly over the abortion fiasco. The directors, who had the power to call for an emergency convention to review the party's leadership, were becoming increasingly alarmed about the declining support for Vander Zalm in the various regions of the province. Here they were again, forcing Vander Zalm to defend his actions.

Vander Zalm, talking over the speaker-phone in his office, tried to explain what he had offered McCarthy, but his explanation again revealed his supercilious attitude toward the most successful woman in the history of the Social Credit Party.

He told the directors that he had offered McCarthy the provincial secretary's ministry–which was in charge of protocol, lotteries, and some government services–and tourism because "I felt she could travel and attend those fancy functions she enjoys so much. It was something she would be good at." Some of the directors listening at Socred headquarters were friends of McCarthy's. They rolled their eyes at Vander Zalm's patronizing comment.

Vander Zalm promised to send a letter to all Socred party members explaining the recent resignations.

Rust said she and Vander Zalm were prepared for a flood of resignations over the veteran minister's abdication from cabinet. "The premier and I had a long talk yesterday about Grace and feel we could stand 20 000 membership resignations" out of the party's 90 000 members. Rust said McCarthy's support was shallow outside her Vancouver constituency, then added:

"We don't know whether to be more concerned about her or Brian or a union between them."

Rust said she'd asked party constitutional expert Les Peterson for a ruling on how ten constituencies could call for a leadership review as was allowed in the party constitution. But even if they could, Rust was not prepared to let it happen.

"I'm going to take the stand that it has to be the general membership and by a 75 per cent margin," Rust said.

Meanwhile, Vander Zalm had, surprisingly, handed the phone call over to his deputy, David Poole, who was being blamed across the country for McCarthy's resignation. The pressure Poole was under began to show. When one board member asked if Vander Zalm hadn't learned anything from the last six months of controversy, Poole broke in: "Where was this big brave board when the premier was here? Why didn't you ask that question before?"

The board member shot back: "We weren't told he was only going to talk to us for ten minutes, then leave."

Poole had again demonstrated that all he cared about was Vander Zalm–the board and the party meant very little to him. He didn't understand that the Social Credit Party was bigger than its leader.

Poole's arrogant performance would heighten calls in the party for his resignation.

The conference, which had been called to mollify party members, resulted in disaster. A verbatim account ended up in the hands of the *Sun*'s Vaughn Palmer, who published two columns on it that were highly embarrassing to Vander Zalm.

The board eventually accused one of its own, Jim Maclean, party director for the Vancouver region, of surreptitiously taping the conversation and leaking it to Palmer.

Maclean was a McCarthy supporter and known anti-Zalmite who would later play a key role in attempting to organize a secret ballot on the premier's leadership. At a July board meeting, ostensibly called to discuss the party's upcoming convention, Bob Ransford of the premier's office, who was seated beside Maclean, said, "We all know who did it. The person just doesn't have the guts to own up to it."

Everyone stared at Maclean, who later sent a letter to the party brass expressing his distaste at the meeting and the tactics which were employed. "I feel that there was no need for you to disguise the meeting's intent and no basis for the allegations of disloyalty which were made," Maclean wrote.

Vander Zalm and Poole realized that the reorganization and cabinet shuffle hadn't been enough to quell the dissent in the party. On Friday, July 8, they called Bob Ransford, Bill Bachop, and Brian Battison into the premier's office to discuss their options. The premier's aides urged Vander Zalm to wage war on his enemies McCarthy, Brian Smith, and the BCEC management. One way of doing that was to dig up as much dirt on those people as possible. And they urged Vander Zalm to get Peter Bazowski to do the job.

The following week Vander Zalm met with Bazowski, and asked him about carrying out an investigation into BCEC and the Expo lands sale. Vander Zalm didn't think the corporation's officials–especially the president, Kevin Murphy, and chairman, Peter Brown–were as innocent as they had led people to believe. The premier believed that if there was a thorough investigation of BCEC, it would turn up some shenanigans among the same top officials who'd gone to the former attorney-general to complain about Vander Zalm's friend Peter Toigo. It might also expose some of the activities of Grace McCarthy, who the premier's office also believed wasn't as clean as she came off in the Expo lands controversy.

Bazowski was being asked to be a one-man commercial crime squad. He turned the assignment down flat.

Bazowski's icy refusal ended the meeting abruptly. Vander Zalm didn't ask the former head of the RCMP about investigating McCarthy's former ministry or seeking advice on what to do about Brian Smith, the other assignments the premier's staff had come up with for Bazowski. Before the end of the month, Bazowski would be relieved of his duties.

As the summer heated up, so did the dissent in the Socred ranks. The man who had promised from a Whistler mountaintop two years earlier to bring a new style of government to the province now had people begging for a return to the old days.

Retired Socred premier Bill Bennett, who'd maintained a discreet silence about the mess Vander Zalm was making of the party Bennett and his father had built, was routinely getting calls at his home in Kelowna from people begging him to return as leader. Retired Socred cabinet ministers gathered informally to discuss the dismal state of affairs.

Socred headquarters was a shambles, having been without an executive director for six months. Party president Hope Rust was forced to deal on her own with the mounting disenchantment. When she asked for suggestions, Jacee Schaefer, a skilled political strategist and top Socred campaign organizer, prepared in early July a confidential ten-page memo.

Schaefer called for a new campaign team as well as a strong executive director. She advised Vander Zalm to "rebuild and guard that area of 'mystery' B.C. voters expect of a premier—don't be so accessible to the media."

Schaefer echoed the sentiments of virtually all Socreds: Vander Zalm wouldn't be in half the trouble he was in had he talked to the media less. That was true to an extent. Vander Zalm's reputation as a one-man band came in part from his inclination to speak to reporters on any subject, regardless of which minister's turf it was.

However, media access had nothing to do with Vander Zalm's bigger problems, such as his stand on abortion and his indiscretions on behalf of Toigo. Vander Zalm tried to blame the media for his problems, refusing to look inward at the real source.

Schaefer also recommended a less visible role for unelected officials. She didn't have to mention Poole by name. "Voters need to be assured that it is their elected representatives, cabinet ministers and the leader making the decisions of the province. Not the advisers."

Good advice. Like Ransford's memo earlier, it was ignored.

On July 11, one week after McCarthy's resignation, underground rumblings of a rebellion to oust Vander Zalm became public when Vancouver South MLA Russ Fraser, who had been a cabinet minister under Vander Zalm for a short three-month period, became the first Socred politician to call for a review of Vander Zalm's leadership. Fraser cited seven other like-minded Socred MLAs–Grace McCarthy, Brian Smith, Stephen Rogers, caucus chair Carol Gran, and backbenchers Kim Campbell, Dave Mercier, and Graham Bruce. The group would be branded the Gang of Eight.

Fraser's call for a review touched off a debate over a provision in the party's constitution allowing for a "special" convention if at least ten constituency associations demanded it. At such a convention, a special resolution dealing with leadership could be placed before the delegates, but needed 75 per cent approval to pass.

As the rebellion within his party grew, Vander Zalm's attention was focused elsewhere. The day after Fraser's call for a secret ballot, Vander Zalm was forced to sit down with an RCMP officer to discuss his relationship with Peter Toigo.

Just one week earlier, on July 4, Vander Zalm had been unusually solemn as he slipped into the passenger seat of the government's white LTD.

From Fantasy Gardens, it was a fifteen-minute drive to RCMP headquarters, located on a quiet street near Vancouver's serene Queen Elizabeth Park. Accompanied by his aide-de-camp, Bill Kay, Vander Zalm walked through the main doors of the RCMP station around 11:25 a.m. and announced his arrival to the sergeant at the front desk.

The RCMP officer made a routine call to Wilson's office to verify the meeting, then escorted Vander Zalm and Kay to Wilson's third-floor offices. Vander Zalm was immediately ushered into Wilson's corner suite. Kay stayed in the sparsely decorated waiting lounge.

Vander Zalm sat on a grey chesterfield, while Wilson plunked down on a matching loveseat. A round coffee table separated the two men. In his brown Mountie uniform, the fiftyish Wilson, who was generally friendly and soft-spoken, appeared much more serious than the caricature of him hanging on the beige office wall.

Days earlier, Vander Zalm had been devastated when Peter Toigo told Vander Zalm to go to the RCMP because the premier himself was being investigated. What had led Toigo to the RCMP?

Toigo's suspicions had been aroused when he heard about the meeting at which Ken Mowers, Toigo's Victoria real estate friend, was told that Brian Smith had only limited time as a cabinet minister unless some dirt could be dug up on Toigo. After that, Toigo had found out from a third party that the RCMP were asking questions about the purchase of park benches by his company for Lillian Vander Zalm as part of an investigation into Toigo and Vander Zalm. Toigo had immediately set up a meeting with the RCMP's Wilson on June 30 to find out what was going on. As a result of that meeting, Toigo told Vander Zalm to contact the RCMP because the premier was being investigated.

Vander Zalm set up the meeting with Wilson to get more details.

"What the heck's going on?" Vander Zalm asked Wilson.

Wilson confirmed that there had been an investigation into Vander Zalm's relationship with Toigo, but said that the RCMP had found no evidence of misconduct. But before the RCMP could close the file, Vander Zalm would have to be interviewed.

"This is crazy," an exasperated Vander Zalm said. He was angry that the RCMP would launch an investigation based on what he saw as some specious and politically motivated complaint to the attorney-general. Was it that easy to get a person, let alone a premier, investigated? Vander Zalm wondered.

Vander Zalm failed to understand that the RCMP wouldn't have launched an investigation if it hadn't felt that the complaints by

BCEC warranted further investigation. As well, it had been Ted Hughes's decision to turn the matter over to the RCMP, and Hughes, a former Supreme court judge, was one civil servant for whom Vander Zalm had immense respect.

A week later, in the boardroom at Fantasy Gardens, Vander Zalm sat across from the RCMP's George Vander Kracht for the interview necessary to close the investigation.

Vander Kracht asked such questions as: "How long have you known Mr. Toigo?" "What is your relationship with Mr. Toigo?" "Have you ever had any financial dealings with Mr. Toigo?"

Vander Kracht asked about the Expo land sale and the purchase of the park benches, Vander Zalm was completely relaxed, thought Vander Kracht, certainly not uncomfortable with the questions.

The ninety-minute interview over, Vander Zalm still couldn't attend to the brewing party revolt because there was now a fresh newspaper report that David Poole had intervened on behalf of yet another friend who wanted to purchase valuable government land.

Ex-BCEC chairman Peter Brown told the *Sun* about a May 7, 1987, breakfast meeting he had attended with Poole and land developer Bill Langas, who had been acting as an agent for another developer interested in a seventeen-hectare site in Burnaby, one of Vancouver's suburbs.

Before the meeting, Poole had told Brown that his friend Langas and the developer Langas represented were "very good friends of government," and that the premier didn't care "if you give them the land." Brown said that at the meeting, Poole had openly discussed in front of Langas the details—including the amounts being offered— of other bids BCEC had received from the Burnaby property. Brown reportedly was appalled by Poole's lack of discretion.

Vander Zalm told reporters that he had instructed Poole to intervene on Langas's behalf because the latter was getting the runaround from BCEC. Langas was an old friend of Poole's and a long-time supporter of Burnaby cabinet minister Elwood Veitch.

The developer Langas was acting for never got the land, but the incident provided another startling example of the way Vander Zalm did business: Friends of government got preferential treatment.

Nevertheless, Vander Zalm was particularly indignant about

BCEC president Kevin Murphy's characterization of the Poole-Langas meeting as improper.

"Mr. Kevin Murphy has a bit of a game of his own, I gather," said Vander Zalm on Thursday, July 14. Vander Zalm's choice of words was intriguing, but he refused to elaborate. What no one else knew at the time was that Vander Zalm knew that Murphy, in part, had instigated the RCMP investigation.

Day after day, British Columbians awoke to some new scandal or controversy surrounding Vander Zalm and his party.

The meeting with Vander Kracht over, Vander Zalm and Toigo talked about what to do. Toigo wanted to go public with the fact that the RCMP had been investigating the premier's affairs, not his. But the fact was the RCMP had been investigating both of their affairs.

Toigo wanted to clear his name and expose the strategies of Vander Zalm's enemies–Brian Smith, Grace McCarthy, and the gang at BCEC.

It was an enormous political gamble. Vander Zalm worried that the revelation that he was being investigated might tear the Socred party apart even more. On the other hand, exposure might clear the air, bringing his enemies' tactics out into the open.

Finally, Vander Zalm agreed with Toigo's plan to go public.

On July 14, Toigo came to the offices of the Vancouver *Sun* for a meeting with the paper's managing editor, Gordon Fisher. He told Fisher he'd gone long enough without responding to the various allegations–specifically that he had gone to Hong Kong to do something wrong–and he wanted to set the record straight. Fisher said the paper would be glad to tell Toigo's story on the condition that everything was on the record.

Fisher suggested that reporter Mark Hume do the interview. Before agreeing, Toigo said he wanted to check Hume out with other sources. Hume passed the test, and showed up with a photographer the following day, July 15, at 3:00 p.m. at the address of Toigo's head office.

There they found a thin, tacky building attached to a neighbourhood pub and drive-in beer and wine store. Once inside, the two were escorted into a small room, barren except for a picture of the globe on the wall. They couldn't believe that this was where Toigo based his multi-million-dollar empire.

Hume was escorted into a tiny boardroom where Toigo was sitting with his son, Ron. It was the same room where Toigo had held his first meetings with Vander Zalm three years earlier about their possible partnership in Fantasy Gardens.

Toigo held a sheet of paper with an opening statement typed on it. His hand shook slightly as he began reading it aloud. Tiny beads of sweat formed at the edge of his hairline.

"I think we've gone as long as we can leaving nothing said," Toigo began, breaking three months of self-imposed silence.

"I feel I'm the victim of vicious rumour and innuendo that are certainly unfounded. So I've decided at this time to hopefully set the record straight."

Toigo spent the next two hours discussing his relationship with the premier and his involvement in the Expo lands sale.

Toigo said that he had never intended to disrupt the Expo sale; he had wanted the BCEC assets with or without the Expo site although his written offer to government had included the Expo lands. He said he had not gone to Hong Kong specifically to meet with officials of Li Ka-shing; he had been going there anyway with his son and had thought he would fit in a meeting with Li's people while he was there. (Toigo never spelled out for Hume why he had wanted to meet with Li's people.)

As for his friendship with Vander Zalm, Toigo said he had never expected any favours from the premier and that the friendship had not gained him any advantage. In fact, he said, it had probably harmed his business opportunities.

Toigo claimed that every investigative reporter in the province had, for the previous four months, looked into every aspect of his life since his birth and had found nothing improper or immoral.

Then he turned to the April 8 report of a police investigation into his affairs.

"I can now assure you that there was no investigation by the RCMP into Peter Toigo, Shato Holdings, or any of our companies," Toigo said angrily. "But there was an investigation. And it is a sad statement to have to make, but I can state, uncategorically [sic], that the investigation launched by the attorney-general's department was to investigate our premier."

Hume's eyes widened. He couldn't believe what he'd just heard.

"[Vander Zalm] was devastated to learn about it," Toigo said, as he went on to castigate the motives of Grace McCarthy and Brian Smith, suggesting that the two were working hand in hand to dump Vander Zalm from office, having never accepted the verdict of the delegates at the 1986 Socred leadership convention.

"That's what this is all about. A couple of losers who are willing to destroy, destruct, to get the power back. It's as simple as that."

When the interview ended, Hume told Toigo he was going to have to speak to Vander Zalm about the RCMP investigation. Toigo said that was fine, Vander Zalm would be expecting his call.

Late that evening, Vander Zalm had not called Hume back, despite the numerous messages Hume had left for him. Without speaking to Vander Zalm, the reporter could not corroborate Toigo's story about the RCMP investigation. Finally, it was decided to run the interview with Toigo in the next day's paper without any reference to Vander Zalm and the RCMP investigation, and to try to talk to the premier on the weekend for Monday's paper. Hume thought the *Sun* had the information about Vander Zalm on an exclusive basis anyway.

But Toigo had also given the story to CBC-TV, which went out to Fantasy Gardens that weekend to get Vander Zalm to confirm that he'd been investigated by the RCMP. The CBC thus revealed the news first, on its Sunday 11:00 p.m. report.

Vander Zalm finally returned a *Sun* reporter's call on Sunday afternoon.

"The RCMP interviewed me about one week ago," Vander Zalm told the reporter over the phone from Fantasy Gardens. "The charge was influence peddling and I know where it came from."

Vander Zalm said the investigation had been initiated by former attorney-general Brian Smith and officials from BCEC. "Brian Smith was not alone in this. It was BCEC with the A-G working together, and it's real messy," Vander Zalm said. "It's a big story. It could kill me but it could save me, too."

"It's a pain in the butt, I'm glad it's behind me," the premier added in one of his more humorous mixed metaphors.

Vander Zalm complained that he was getting "crucified" over Smith's and McCarthy's resignations, knowing all the time what was going on behind the scenes. "But I had difficulty talking about it because I didn't want to tear the party apart even further.

"It's a pretty sad state of affairs when you have people in government and outside government saying things and then you investigate the premier and the premier doesn't even know about it," said Vander Zalm.

"You must have been furious," the reporter said.

"I was disappointed. I never get very angry but it was tough. It's been frustrating knowing about it and sitting on it but I think it's more important that we keep the party together. But it's been bad, sure."

On Monday morning, the incredible tale from Fantasyland had crossed the country. Only Vander Zalm, jaded observers of the wacky B.C. political scene noted, could think that news of an RCMP investigation into his affairs would save his political bacon.

Grace McCarthy, besieged by reporters, said that Vander Zalm was merely trying to deflect criticism of his leadership style by revealing existence of the RCMP probe. But, she said, his action had only helped turn the province into a "circus and laughingstock."

Brian Smith met reporters in a oak-panelled meeting room at the legislature to respond to Vander Zalm's charges.

Smith said the investigation was instigated on a "solid body of evidence" and not because of political motivations. He explained how the investigation had been launched after his deputy, Ted Hughes, forwarded to the RCMP allegations that the attorney-general's ministry had received from two highly placed individuals, whom Smith refused to identify but news organizations quickly identified as BCEC's Kevin Murphy and Keith Mitchell.

"I hope [Vander Zalm] is not seriously thinking that a group of people sat down and hatched a plot to try and get him out of office on the basis of some allegation," said Smith.

The NDP said Vander Zalm should have turned over the "reins of power" as soon as he found out he was under investigation. And they demanded that the government release the RCMP report to clear the air.

"We're not dealing with an ordinary citizen here, we're dealing with the premier of B.C.," NDP leader Mike Harcourt said. "I can't believe it. They've got detectives on one another. They've got files a foot thick on each other. I mean it's just crazy. Who's minding the store while these guys rumble?"

Rumble, indeed. Regardless of how one viewed the latest revelation–a sinister attempt by McCarthy and Smith to get Vander Zalm, or a legitimate investigation of questionable dealings by the premier and his friend–it was clear that the province's governing party was in a state of crisis. The next step was secret meetings to organize a coup.

Quelling the Palace Revolt

"**D**avid, they're just out to get you," Vander Zalm told David Poole when he arrived at his legislative office for work on July 19.

Twelve hours earlier, Vander Zalm had met with fifty Socred riding executives from Vancouver Island. For more than two hours, one executive member after another had berated him for running a one-man show and for relying too much on Poole and not enough on his ministers. Virtually everyone in the room demanded Poole's head.

It was the toughest going-over Vander Zalm had ever received. But it demonstrated the serious divisions in his party. Such an uprising by riding executives, traditionally minor functionaries, was unprecedented.

"It was a pretty wild time," remembers Poole. "We began to recognize that the pressure and focus on me, some of which was directed purely at me for what I had done and some of which was deflected from the premier, was not going to go away."

Vander Zalm had thought that bringing in Peter Bazowski as a special adviser would be enough to satiate cries for a professional bureaucrat in the office. But Bazowski simply wasn't working out. Vander Zalm didn't like him. He thought Bazowski talked too much about past accomplishments with the RCMP and as a bureaucrat.

Poole hated Bazowski. Poole told people Bazowski was more concerned about perks than anything else. (Bazowski had demanded
the number one parking spot in the deputy ministers' parking area.)
But at the root of Poole's hatred was his knowledge that Bazowski
was telling Vander Zalm to get rid of his principal secretary.

But Bazowski wasn't the only one offering that advice. Members
of the Socred caucus and cabinet also felt that Vander Zalm's
problems would continue as long as Poole was running the show
out of the premier's office.

Vander Zalm and Poole decided to raid the finance ministry
for deputy Frank Rhodes, a highly respected civil servant who had
played a major role in steering Bill 19 through the legislature.
Rhodes was to take over Poole's responsibilities as chief policy
adviser and head of the civil service. Poole would continue as
principal secretary, his mandate to serve as the premier's chief
political adviser and liaison with the business community and
the party.

At least, that was what Vander Zalm told reporters at a news
conference on July 20, the day after his run-in with the Socred
riding executives: "I believe these changes will answer concerns
and result in a clear division of responsibilities."

In fact, Vander Zalm and Poole were not planning any real
changes. There had been an understanding reached with the forty-
four-year-old Rhodes, a consummate bureaucratic survivor, that he
would clear any policy matters through Poole first before taking
them to Vander Zalm.

Vander Zalm also announced a powerful new "planning and
priorities committee" of nine cabinet ministers who would advise
the premier on the political side of public policy issues. There had
been planning and priorities committees under Bennett, but they
had seldom met and had had little influence. The committee Vander
Zalm was announcing was actually going to meet regularly and
wield power.

The idea was finance minister Mel Couvelier's and it was strongly
supported by attorney-general Bud Smith. Both felt that the committee would show that decisions were being made by a group, not
just one man. More important, it put both leadership aspirants in
powerful positions within the government.

Bazowski, it was announced, was leaving the office on September 1, and Bob Ransford, Poole's dutiful executive assistant, was bailing out for the private sector.

Ransford genuinely liked Vander Zalm and felt he had enormous potential as a leader. But although Vander Zalm had courage and convictions, he lacked political savvy, and ultimately that would destroy him, Ransford thought.

Ransford also respected Poole for his ability to get things done. What Poole and Vander Zalm had accomplished in eighteen months, Ransford says now, would have taken more cautious administrations years to achieve. But in their haste they paid a heavy political price, which Ransford had warned them about as far back as the spring of 1987. But his advice had been ignored, and that frustrated him.

Ransford understood that everyone in the premier's office, not just Poole, had become tainted by six months of scandals, and the sooner Ransford removed himself from the premier's office the sooner his reputation could be restored.

(Ransford and Poole visited Gary Moser, of the government's personnel department, to arrange a severance package. "It's very unusual for someone to be getting severance who's decided to leave government," Moser said. Nevertheless, Ransford got five months' severance pay.)

Vander Zalm was sorry to see Ransford leave. He enjoyed the young aide's tenacity. "He was a real political animal," Vander Zalm recalls. "He could figure things out politically. If there is one regret, it is that we should have had Ransford more involved in the process, closer to the front end of things. He would have been a good adviser on political issues."

Meanwhile, Vander Zalm finally filled the executive director's position at Socred headquarters. The executive director was responsible for Socred party operations. The job had been vacant for six months. Before that, the position had been filled on a temporary basis by Lorne Valensky, a young political strategist from Ontario. But Valensky had been sacked for allegedly not being loyal to Vander Zalm. He'd apparently not informed the premier's office of brewing Socred dissent in the Fraser Valley.

Before Valensky, Poole had held the executive director's position for a few months. Prior to that it had been vacant since 1983, when Jerry Lampert had held the job.

Now Vander Zalm was announcing that Dale Drown, a thirty-four-year-old political consultant, had agreed to a three-year contract for $70 000 a year plus expenses. The contract also included a new mid-sized car supplied by the party and a maximum $10 000 interest-free loan–to be paid back within six months–for the purchase of a new home.

Drown had not been Vander Zalm's first choice. In fact, the search had been a nightmare. On May 30, 1988, for example, Charlie Giordano, one of Vander Zalm's leadership campaign managers, was told he would be getting the job. He had not been the first choice of the executive search committee put together by the Socred party, but the premier wanted Giordano.

Two others who had been in the running were told that they would be Giordano's assistants. All three were told that the jobs wouldn't be announced for a month. But in the interim, Giordano became more embroiled in the Knight Street pub scandal, and Vander Zalm decided against giving him the job. Giordano was devastated.

Reaction to the changes were mixed. Grace McCarthy said she hoped they weren't merely cosmetic. However, caucus chair Carol Gran, who three weeks earlier had hung up on the premier for his shabby treatment of her and the caucus, saw the changes more positively: "It's a good start."

Vander Zalm had hoped the latest reorganization would immediately release some pressure, but in a week the heat was back on. For a change, the focus wasn't on Vander Zalm but on one of his enemies–Brian Smith.

On Monday, July 25, Vancouver *Sun* columnist Nicole Parton met Smith at a downtown Vancouver office where she confronted him with evidence of the government's spy operation on the pro-choice movement. Smith confirmed it all.

Vander Zalm was quick to deny any knowledge of the covert Watergate-style operation. He even denounced it as a "police-state tactic."

The whole affair probably helped Vander Zalm, ending Socred thoughts about dumping Vander Zalm in favour of Smith, the second-place finisher at Whistler. For Vander Zalm, the spy scandal was divine retribution for the trouble Smith had created for him with the RCMP investigation.

There was widespread speculation that the story was leaked to Parton by the premier's office to discredit Smith. But Parton wouldn't reveal her source.

The spying operation allowed another nemesis of Brian Smith's—the new attorney-general, Bud Smith—to settle an old score. The two Smiths despised each other, their mutual disdain dating back to the leadership convention where an agreement to support each other had fallen through and both had felt double-crossed.

When reporters asked Bud Smith about the spy operation, he called his predecessor stupid and savagely denounced his action as an unconscionable intrusion into the lives of B.C. citizens. Thus, besides publicly humiliating a person he didn't much like, Bud Smith was also planning for that day down the road when the two might face each other again in a leadership race. Bud Smith wanted the man behind the spy operation to look as bad as possible. However, many Socreds felt that he had overdone it.

Meanwhile, Bill Vander Zalm had to deal with the Socred caucus meeting, scheduled for August 10-11 in Courtenay, a beautiful resort community three hours north of Victoria on Vancouver Island.

The meeting was shaping up to be the most important caucus meeting held by the Socreds since the one in 1952 when W.A.C. Bennett was chosen to lead the party. This time, leadership was again on the caucus's mind.

Many Socred politicians were convinced Vander Zalm had to go if they were to stand any chance of re-election. At the very least, Vander Zalm had to get rid of Poole. Despite the recent reorganizations in the premier's office, caucus members believed that as long as Poole remained, the premier would seek his advice only, and the problems would continue.

And problems there were. The polls had Vander Zalm at 19 per cent. People were leaving the party in droves. Party donations were way down. Caucus members were openly criticizing Vander Zalm and calling for a secret ballot on his leadership.

The message the caucus planned to deliver to Vander Zalm in

Courtenay was simple: shape up or ship out. If Vander Zalm remained unrepentant, some caucus members believed they had the power to go to the lieutenant-governor with a new leader, saying they'd lost confidence in Vander Zalm. But while a lieutenant-governor may listen to such an entreaty, he is not obliged to adhere to their demand.

Vander Zalm knew he had to do something to quell the dissent.

For the past month, as the pressure on Vander Zalm to make changes mounted, he and Poole had drawn closer together, more defiant and determined.

Although Poole loved his job and the man he worked for, the daily pressure and press attention was affecting not only him but also his family. His wife, Barb, couldn't stand seeing her husband attacked daily in the press. His parents, who lived in the Vancouver Island city of Nanaimo, noticed that the plastic letters on a roadside restaurant sign had been rearranged to form a derogatory statement about their son. Barb's parents, who lived in Qualicum, just north of where the caucus meeting was to be held in Courtenay, stopped going to church because of comments being made about their son-in-law.

"I never fooled myself in the last year," Poole remembers now. "I knew that I was in an impossible position and my days were numbered. Your days are numbered from the first day you start."

Poole informed Vander Zalm that he had begun to work on a letter of resignation. "Are you sure you want to do this?" Vander Zalm asked him.

"Premier, we've got no choice," Poole said.

Vander Zalm and Poole now saw what three weeks earlier they had closed their eyes to: If Poole didn't go, they both might end up evicted from the premier's office by a caucus coup. Poole understood, perhaps more clearly than Vander Zalm did, that the two had been masters of their own demise; in their haste to change the face of British Columbia they had forgotten all about politics.

"We let the political side of the operation slide, no doubt about that," reflects Poole.

For Vander Zalm, losing Poole was tough.

"You develop a very deep affinity. You become very dependent upon one another. You share the problems and the glories. It is a sharing process and he and I shared a great deal for a couple of years. It is very tough to see someone like that having to leave. He had to leave. There was no choice for him. He was cornered."

Vander Zalm also felt bad for two other reasons; he knew that people were taking their anger out on Poole because it was easier and more acceptable than criticizing the leader. Vander Zalm also realized that Poole was being crucified for carrying out his orders, as was evident in the Expo lands sale.

On Tuesday, August 3, David Poole stayed at the office late, working on his letter of resignation. It was a maudlin testimony to the deep emotional bond that had formed between the two men.

"It was probably two years ago when I first met you but it was not until some time after, that I came to know you and began to fully understand the type of genuine, committed, caring person that you are," Poole began. "And it's this knowledge, more than anything else, that make this, my letter of resignation, so difficult to write."

In four pages, Poole hailed Bills 19 and 20, Vander Zalm's "courageous" stand on abortion, privatization, changes in the civil service. Poole regretted that he and Vander Zalm hadn't better communicated their accomplishments. He ended his letter by saying "Our friendship will remain a treasured part of my life."

The next day, Poole let Vander Zalm read the letter. The premier was moved, although at the press conference his public response was not nearly as emotional as Poole's. Vander Zalm instead defended his aide's record and expressed admiration for his courage in stepping down "because he believes it is in the best interests of myself and my government."

Vander Zalm also used the occasion to take a shot at Grace McCarthy, Brian Smith, and others: "He never flinched or ducked away from those decisions and his responsibilities even though he knew they would bring attacks from some politically motivated individuals."

Vander Zalm made one thing clear: the decision was Poole's; he had not been fired. Later, this seemingly harmless declaration would fuel a major scandal that would ignite shortly after Poole had left office. Meantime, Vander Zalm said that Poole would be stepping down on September 30.

Socreds everywhere rejoiced. Their relief was almost palpable. Carol Gran predicted that the Socred caucus meeting in a week's time would go more smoothly than had been feared.

Grace McCarthy, however, said Vander Zalm would still have to prove that he was prepared to change his governing style. McCarthy, like a number of Socreds, felt that Vander Zalm, not Poole, had been the problem. Vander Zalm's detractors said he would always be controversial, because he relished attention and governed in such an ad hoc way. A case in point was the Alex Hankin parole board fiasco.

Around the time of Poole's resignation, news broke that Vander Zalm had phoned a member of the B.C. parole board in 1987 to complain about a decision to grant day parole to former Squamish Five terrorist Julie Belmas. The parole board member who had received the call, Alex Hankin, later had his board appointment revoked.

Hankin was a devoted Socred and the former president of Vander Zalm's Richmond riding association, as well as the riding's chief fundraiser during the 1986 election. Besides his seat on the parole board, Hankin had also held a government-appointed position on the Richmond hospital board.

At first Vander Zalm denied making any phone call to Hankin. Then he admitted phoning Hankin to complain that he and others were not happy with the board's decision. The incident reinforced the public's growing impression that Vander Zalm spent his time interfering in government on behalf of friends.

Vander Zalm's defence of his phone call to Hankin looked terrible. After first denying making a call to Hankin, then later admitting it, Vander Zalm tried to justify his action by saying that Hankin was worried that the Belmas parole had cost him a spot on the hospital board. However, as a Vancouver *Sun* editorial pointed out, Hankin had been dropped from the hospital board four months before he took part in the Belmas decision.

The Hankin incident highlights a disturbing Vander Zalm characteristic. When confronted with a damaging story involving himself, his first instinct is often to deny it. The examples were everywhere: denying that he had said his caucus members lacked moxie during the abortion debate, then later having to admit it when confronted with taped evidence; denying any knowledge of how Peter Toigo's offer to buy BCEC had gotten on the cabinet agenda, then later admitting he had personally brought it to cabinet; denying ever seeing Toigo's and Jack Poole's proposal to buy the Expo site, when in fact he had asked staff to act on it; denying he had asked Peter Brown, over breakfast, why he had not responded to Toigo's interest in the Whistler convention centre, then later admitting that maybe he had mentioned something about Toigo.

Vander Zalm's propensity for disavowal had made many journalists sceptical of his denials.

The Hankin story followed Vander Zalm to the Courtenay two-day retreat. He didn't want to talk about it. Chased down hallways and up stairwells by reporters, Vander Zalm shouted behind him that he had nothing to say.

After one particularly heated chase, Vander Zalm, with his aide-de-camp, Bill Kay, in tow, reached his hotel room, frantically opened the door, and yelled to Kay to close it as quickly as possible.

When both men were safely inside, Vander Zalm grabbed his aide's arm and said, "Bill, we're going to get through this. We are." He then collapsed on a couch. Kay, who had spent thousands of hours with Vander Zalm, had never seen him so upset.

In the calm of his hotel room, Vander Zalm had time to think about the caucus meeting. He thought Poole's resignation had deprived his opponents of important ammunition.

"The purpose of that meeting was to put everything on the table," recalls Vander Zalm. "And for me to give an overview of what happened over the preceding number of months and my explanation for some of those things. And then to have everybody come at me. I was prepared to sit there and listen, for two days if need be." He wouldn't be disappointed.

As Socred politicians decked out in golf shirts, summer slacks, and deck shoes filed into a small convention room in the roadside hotel, the mood was definitely tense. Absent was the easy banter with the media, who were there in full force to record the showdown.

For ten hours that stretched into the next day, Vander Zalm quietly listened to a sometimes brutal assessment of his leadership.

Stephen Rogers, the cabinet minister fired by Vander Zalm, dragged out unflattering gossip that he'd heard about the premier's friend Peter Toigo and the premier's wife's business dealings. Vander Zalm didn't flinch; he just sat and stared at Rogers. Rogers's colleagues were stunned by his cheap shots. Instead of hurting Vander Zalm, Rogers's comments had rallied support for the premier from MLAs who were sympathetic and who admired Vander Zalm for the calm, rational manner in which he dealt with the attack.

The speech judged by most to be the most effective came from Norm Jacobsen, a quiet, extremely unassuming politician from the conservative Fraser Valley.

Jacobsen, a former truck logger, focused his speech on the state of B.C.'s forests, which he used as a metaphor for Vander Zalm's problems. The forests needed to be cared for and nurtured. A leader has to constantly tend to members of his party to regenerate their enthusiasm. If they are ignored, they too will die off. Everyone in the room was touched by the passion of Jacobsen's remarks.

Vander Zalm's response was conciliatory. He admitted his mistakes and promised to be more careful in the future about what he said and did. He promised to rely on the advice of the new, inner cabinet and said he was confident that a new communications strategy would repair the party's tattered image by telling British Columbians all the good things that had been accomplished by the government.

While publicly Vander Zalm had been blaming his problems on the media, now he was finally conceding that he himself was to blame. One of the great contradictions about Vander Zalm was and would remain his willingness to listen and change on some occasions and his unwillingness to do so on other occasions. Vander Zalm could be both stubborn and inflexible and contrite and responsive.

As a result of the Courtenay meetings, a new committee of Socred backbenchers would review all ministry budget requests to ensure that ministry priorities conformed to the government's–and caucus's–long-term priorities. It was a tremendous concession for Vander Zalm to make; no other Canadian premier had ever allowed his caucus in on the budget-making process.

But never before had a Socred leader had to humble himself before his colleagues in a desperate act of contrition and compromise in order to save his job.

Vander Zalm and Carol Gran emerged at meeting's end to tell reporters the caucus had reached a consensus on how to solve its internal problems and that a "majority" of the caucus members supported their leader.

"You will see more unity in caucus and my personal feeling is you will see very little dissent," said Gran. Others were less certain. "It's up to the premier to deliver," said Russ Fraser, who earlier had led the call for a secret ballot.

In a party where loyalty had long been a tradition, the Socreds had given Vander Zalm a second chance. He had won supporters who respected him for admitting the problems he had created and admired him for stoically taking such verbal abuse over his leadership. There was also a fear that any internal effort to dump their leader might cause a backlash in the party, like the one that had split the federal Tories in the 1960s over a campaign to dump their leader, John Diefenbaker.

Vander Zalm had survived, but he was on probation. His next big test was supposed to be the party convention in two months' time, when he would have to answer to the party at large for his actions of the past several months. Instead, he was in trouble by the conclusion of the Courtenay meeting.

Vander Zalm was asked by reporters about the wish of an unwed mother from North Vancouver that Vander Zalm be the godfather of her month-old son. The mother, Serina Hinde, had said that her boy owed his life to Vander Zalm, who, through his strong anti-abortion stand, had convinced her to carry the baby to term despite objections from the father.

Most politicians would have avoided Serina Hinde like scurvy. Not Vander Zalm. He said he would be honoured to be at the baptism as the child's godfather.

The next day, the *Province* heralded the news that "Zalm"– as the tabloid referred to the premier–had agreed to act as godfather. But the paper had also dug up the fact that the woman was a stripper. So Vander Zalm agreed to be godfather to an unwed stripper's son.

Socreds everywhere cringed. As noble as the premier's motives were, he once again appeared to be a flake.

The baptism went ahead at the small Holy Trinity Catholic Church. Lillian carried the baby outside after the service, wrapped tightly in blankets. "God works in mysterious ways," said Vander Zalm.

(The story would have a tragic end. A month later, while Vander Zalm was out of the country on vacation, the baby died in his sleep.)

As Vander Zalm's jet lifted off on Wednesday, August 18, for a first ministers' conference in Saskatoon, a confidential report by provincial ombudsman Stephen Owen into the Knight Street pub affair arrived in the hands of *Sun* columnist Vaughn Palmer. The report would prove devastating, particularly for David Poole.

The report revealed that Poole had asked the head of the liquor licensing branch, Bert Hick, to put Charlie Giordano's firm on the list of companies approved by the government to conduct a pub referendum.

Giordano was Vander Zalm's former campaign manager. He had earlier been selected executive director of the Socred party but lost the job before it was announced because of media revelations surrounding the Knight Street pub vote.

According to the ombudsman's report, Poole had told Hick that Giordano was an "on-side guy" and should go on the list. Under B.C. laws at the time, any application for a neighbourhood pub has to be approved by 60 per cent of the people within a six-block radius of the pub's location. And the vote has to be conducted by an accredited polling firm.

Following Poole's call to Hick, Giordano's firm, Delta Media Services, had been put on the government's accredited list of firms over the objections of Hick's deputy and against Hick's own prior intentions.

Peter Toigo had leased the pub site to a woman named Valerie McRobbie. The report said Toigo, on or about October 15, 1986–during the provincial election campaign on which Toigo served as Socred fundraiser–phoned the then deputy manager of the liquor branch and threatened to have him fired if

McRobbie's pub application was not given preliminary approval.

The report quoted Toigo as saying, "You will be sorry. You have turned me down once too often."

It was Toigo, a good friend of Giordano (their homes were a block apart), who phoned Poole and told him Giordano needed work. That led to Poole's call to Bert Hick.

The ombudsman also attacked an earlier investigation carried out by the government's own labour ministry into the allegations of wrongdoing, an investigation which claimed to have found nothing wrong.

(It would later be revealed that the labour minister, Lyall Hanson, knew about Poole's controversial phone call to Hick weeks before his ministry released its report on the matter. The ministry's report, which was widely criticized as a cover-up, made no mention of the incident. In fact, when the report was released at a news conference, Hick was asked if Poole had ever tried to put pressure on him regarding the pub licence. Hick said no. Hanson, who was sitting right beside Hick, realized Hick was lying but did nothing about it. Hanson didn't feel Poole's call to Hick warranted any action, yet when Brian Smith was made aware of it while he was still attorney-general he considered it so serious that he turned the information over to the RCMP, which was investigating the Knight Street pub affair at the time.)

On the return flight from Saskatoon to Victoria that Friday, Poole and Vander Zalm talked about the report and its implications. Both agreed that Poole should leave office immediately rather than waiting until September 30. He would probably be dogged by the media during his remaining time anyway over the Knight Street pub scandal; he didn't need that.

Poole cleared out his office that weekend, taking down his favourite picture of himself and the premier, which showed them, both laughing, outside Government House at the cabinet swearing-in following the 1986 election.

As Poole shoved personal papers into a large brown briefcase, something Quebec Premier Robert Bourassa had said to him days earlier in Saskatoon kept ringing in his head: "You're the best example of a scapegoat that I have ever seen."

In the spring of 1989, Poole told the authors of this book that he believed he would have still been principal secretary had he and Vander Zalm brought Frank Rhodes in earlier to head the civil service. "We waited too late," said Poole. He said that if he had one regret it was "that we didn't handle the politics better. The premier never paid enough attention to either the house, the cabinet or the caucus in his previous life. It was more important to just get things done.")

On Monday, August 23, Vander Zalm announced that Poole had resigned early in the wake of the ombudsman's report.

"Dave's the type of guy who gives 100 per cent in whatever he does and he thought he couldn't do that any more because of what's happened," Vander Zalm told reporters.

Bert Hick, the liquor branch manager, was fired that day as well.

The promise that governments make to their citizens—to carry out business objectively, ignoring the influences of friends or third-party advocacy—had been broken yet again by Vander Zalm's government. Where the public may have been confused by the arcane details of the Expo lands fiasco, it had no trouble understanding the wrongdoing involved in the Knight Street pub affair.

It was all the more damaging because of Vander Zalm's promise, made following his sweeping election victory in 1986, to bring to government a new ethics and integrity.

"I believe it is vitally important that those who are elected to public office assume the responsibility of behaving and acting in a manner that sets the highest standard for the community at large," Vander Zalm had said upon being sworn in as premier.

He had let his people down badly.

As for Poole, it meant that his exit from government would be all the more shameful. He would be remembered not for his and Vander Zalm's accomplishments, but for devastating evidence that he was—as one commentator put it—an open faucet to friends.

For Socreds, the report was demoralizing. The fresh start promised at Courtenay was over already.

That week Vander Zalm went out to Poole's home in a tony Victoria subdivision. Vander Zalm recalls the evening: "We reminisced and talked and cried on each other's shoulder a little bit."

Poole needed a new job. Everyone he approached in B.C. had the same response: not in a million years. Poole remembers those lonely days.

"Either they couldn't hire me because they were concerned about what their board would say or they just wouldn't do it themselves. The notoriety was too much. And the affiliation with Vander Zalm was a very negative trait."

Poole and his wife, Barb, had planned to spend the rest of their lives in B.C. "Now, we were, in effect, being driven out of the province. People said: 'You may be a hell of a nice guy, but you have got to get out of here.' "

One person who wasn't ready to turn his back on Poole was Peter Toigo. He offered Poole a job as head of Shato Holdings' Ontario operations out of Toronto.

Poole was sceptical. He knew what people would think if he took the job: that he had been in cahoots with Toigo all along. Poole told his former aide, Bob Ransford, "I could never take that job." Eventually, however, he realized Toigo's was the only substantial job offer he had.

Poole was also worried about how taking a job with Toigo would reflect on Vander Zalm, who recalls receiving a telephone call from his former aide.

"I don't want to hurt you," Poole told Vander Zalm. "I don't want people to read things into this. But he [Toigo] is the one guy who sort of sympathizes with me and my position and what I have had to go through."

Vander Zalm told Poole that he need not worry about how it might reflect on him.

"David, you're no longer in government. You don't owe me, and I don't owe you. We've been good together, we've worked well together, but you have your own life to lead. If you feel that you would like to work for Peter Toigo, who am I to say you can't work for Peter Toigo?"

David Poole packed up his belongings and moved to the Toigo job in Toronto. But even when he was thousands of miles away, Poole wouldn't be able to stay out of the news in B.C.

Although Vander Zalm had managed to stave off a caucus revolt at Courtenay, there was still profound discontent in the party.

By September, dissident Socred riding executives from Vancouver were meeting regularly to plot the overthrow of Bill Vander Zalm. They didn't have much time; the party convention was a month away.

The group was spearheaded by Bill Enefer, Socred riding president of Vancouver South, and also included riding presidents Alistair Palmer, of the upscale constituency of Vancouver–Point Grey; George Anderson, representing Grace McCarthy's riding of Vancouver–Little Mountain; and Jim Maclean, a Socred director in charge of the five Vancouver-area ridings.

The group began meeting in earnest after McCarthy's resignation. Enefer, Anderson, and Maclean were all supporters of McCarthy. As well, Enefer was president of a riding whose two Socred politicians, Stephen Rogers and Russ Fraser, had been among Vander Zalm's strongest critics. While in cabinet, Rogers had enjoyed regaling meetings of his riding executive with the latest "horror" story from Victoria. It was at one such meeting, attended by party president Hope Rust, that Rogers laid out all of Vander Zalm's problems as a leader and why, in essence, he had to go for the good of the party. Rust reported Rogers's comments to the premier's office, and subsequently Rogers lost his ministry.

Palmer was being regularly filled in on all the atrocities in Victoria by Kim Campbell, the Socred politician who represented his riding. Palmer's opposition to Vander Zalm would be immortalized in a simile: "It's like when you put your cat down. You don't like to do it, but it's got to be done."

Throughout the summer the dissident riding executives had met at various Denny's restaurants throughout the city; over burgers they came up with the idea of holding a secret ballot on the second resolution read at the convention. Traditionally, the second resolution calls on delegates to "confirm and reiterate" confidence in the premier and government. Since the days of former premier W.A.C. Bennett, the second resolution had always been a formality, something delegates passed with a show of hands right after pledging allegiance to the Queen.

Maybe this time, the riding executives reasoned, enough people would vote against the resolution to force Vander Zalm to call a leadership review. They agreed to take the angle that Vander Zalm and other members of the Socred caucus had to support a secret ballot because it was exactly the democratic measure the government had made sure was included in Bill 19 to combat intimidation tactics by union leaders.

Now the group needed to work on prospective convention delegates. But who *were* the delegates? Only the premier's office and party headquarters had access to the list, and they weren't giving it out to anyone, precisely because they were afraid it might land in the hands of someone like Enefer.

Enefer did, however, secure a delegate list from the 1986 leadership convention, figuring that many of the same people would be heading to Penticton. He sent everyone on the list a package of press clippings condemning Vander Zalm and a covering letter calling on the delegates to support a secret ballot on Resolution No. 2.

Enefer's letter was soon leaked to the media. Socred politicians were asked by the media where they stood on a secret ballot. Not surprisingly, all of the Vancouver-area Socred politicians–Stephen Rogers, Russ Fraser, Kim Campbell, Grace McCarthy and her seatmate Doug Mowat–endorsed the secret ballot concept. As well, Brian Smith, Burnaby's Dave Mercier, and Penticton's Ivan Messmer also endorsed a secret ballot.

Vander Zalm seemed almost blasé about the secret ballot movement. He figured some minor support for a leadership review existed in the Okanagan, but most of it was centred in Vancouver and Victoria, specifically Brian Smith's nearby riding of Oak Bay. At most, Vander Zalm estimated that 250 to 300 delegates out of the 1300 expected to attend the convention might be prepared to vote for a secret ballot.

However, that 25 per cent of convention delegates comprised largely the urban, upscale, professional, and moderate wing of the party. How could Vander Zalm expect to win an election with that wing of the party sitting on its hands?

Vander Zalm didn't seem to realize that Social Credit was in danger of being reduced to a rural, Interior, right-wing rump.

"I'm not worried at all," said Vander Zalm, refusing to speculate on what vote percentage it would take for him to survive a secret ballot on his leadership. Commentators agreed that the premier needed 60 per cent to avoid a complete loss of face.

The design of the unofficial button of the anti-Vander Zalm forces showed a barred circle–the well-known symbol for no smoking, no parking, etc.–superimposed over a shovel. The shovel was the symbol that Vander Zalm had adopted as his own in the years after he had said people on welfare ought to "pick up a shovel." Enefer at one point considered setting up a popcorn machine at the convention registration desk; delegates would be handed bags of popcorn with Ban the Shovel buttons attached.

A few days before the convention, Enefer and friends came up with the idea of holding a meeting of all the Vancouver-area convention delegates and MLAs. The event was disguised as a pre-convention rally, but its purpose–to focus attention on dissent–was evident.

The evening got off to an inauspicious start when Enefer decided to use the death of an eighty-one-year-old Social Creditor to take a shot at Vander Zalm.

Annie Hughes had been made famous by *Sun* columnist Denny Boyd's profile of the feisty Socred octogenarian, who was going to tear up her Socred membership because of Vander Zalm. When Vander Zalm was made aware of the column, he contacted Hughes and promised her a cup of tea at Fantasy Gardens. She recanted on her threat to tear up her membership, although she later complained to Boyd in a subsequent column that she still hadn't had her cup of tea with Vander Zalm. She would die within days, without her promised meeting with the premier.

Hence Enefer's cheap-shot opening: "It's too bad Annie Hughes had to die without her promised cup of tea."

McCarthy, Rogers, and Fraser each gave a rah-rah speech that avoided any direct Vander Zalm bashing. But McCarthy's seatmate, Doug Mowat, who wasn't able to attend because of business in Toronto, had a letter read which said that thousands of people were turning in their Socred memberships because of Vander Zalm.

Then came Alistair Palmer's emotional and macabre tribute to Kim Campbell, who days earlier had announced that she was resigning to run for the federal Conservatives. Palmer was virtually in tears as he told the gathering that it was Vander Zalm's fault Campbell had left, which was entirely true.

He then ended his speech by saying that when Vander Zalm got up to the podium to deliver his speech to the party convention in a few days, Palmer would imagine "an empty podium with a single rose–the rose will represent Annie Hughes; the empty podium will represent Kim Campbell."

He was booed off the stage. The dissidents' rally was a disaster.

The anti-Vander Zalm movement was faltering for several reasons. First, it lacked a leader. Neither McCarthy or Brian Smith, the two obvious choices to lead a revolt, was prepared to put her or his neck on the line to oust Vander Zalm. Leading the movement meant potentially alienating thousands of party members who believed in loyalty to the leader and who regarded any efforts to dump him as treasonous. Such a movement could result in a deadly split in the party.

If Smith or McCarthy wanted to someday take another run at the party's leadership, they couldn't afford to alienate members by leading a secret ballot movement. Instead, they would quietly give their approval to the Socred executives who were organizing the anti-Vander Zalm campaign.

The second reason the movement was doomed to fail was the decision by the Socred caucus to give Vander Zalm a reprieve at Courtenay. If the politicians whose future livelihoods depended on Vander Zalm could give him a second chance, then the convention would have to as well.

The pre-convention rally by the Vancouver Socreds had merely confirmed what Vander Zalm had been suggesting all along, that opposition to his leadership was centred primarily in Vancouver. That set up a Vancouver-versus-the-rest-of-the-province showdown at Penticton. And there were a lot more delegates going to the convention from the rest of the province than there were from Vancouver.

Finally, pro-Vander Zalm forces were at work. Cabinet ministers had been touring the province, giving speeches to Socred constituency associations urging unity at Penticton. As well, Socred president Hope Rust supported the premier and she was constantly on the phone to party supporters and executives across the province pressing Vander Zalm's case and monitoring the activities of the anti-Vander Zalm forces.

Arrangements were also being made to airlift a group of prominent Vancouver businessmen, such as Century 21 founder Peter Thomas, to the convention to demonstrate that the business community was also behind the premier.

Meanwhile, a powerful group of prominent B.C. businessmen, including Vander Zalm's nemesis, Peter Brown, was preparing to leak a $70 000 poll it had commissioned from Martin Goldfarb. The six men who had chipped in to pay for it wanted Socreds to know before the convention just how despised Bill Vander Zalm was by British Columbians.

The poll was leaked simultaneously to the Vancouver *Sun* and the Penticton *Herald* two days before the convention was due to open on the condition that the papers not identify those who had commissioned it.

The poll suggested that 50 per cent of British Columbians felt Vander Zalm should step down before the next election. It also said that those polled thought the Socreds should hold a leadership convention. Goldfarb's personal assessment of the numbers was that "people in B.C. hate Bill Vander Zalm."

A few days before it was leaked, Goldfarb's poll had been delivered to Vander Zalm in person by a former cabinet colleague, Don Phillips, who had become an extremely successful government lobbyist. Phillips was part of a group of former Socred cabinet ministers concerned about the future of the party under Vander Zalm, with whom all had served.

Vander Zalm ignored Phillips's package of information, dismissing it as he does all polls. But before the convention started, the government leaked its own poll, purporting to show that 70 per cent of British Columbians thought Vander Zalm should remain as leader.

The result was highly suspect. It came from the same Vancouver pollster–Les Storey–who had released a poll months earlier which showed that Vander Zalm was in deep trouble. As well, the government didn't leak the entire poll but just a couple of selected questions. Nonetheless, the leak had its desired effect, drawing attention away from the Goldfarb poll.

On the eve of voting day in Penticton, Vander Zalm and Socred president Hope Rust hosted a dinner for the party's fifty riding presidents. Enefer arrived late. As he walked to his table at the front of the room, he could hear the whispers: "What's he doing here?" "Hey, there's the traitor."

Vander Zalm gave a short speech and asked for questions. A riding president from Vancouver Island called Enefer a disgusting traitor. Enefer planned to get up and respond when Vander Zalm announced the end of question period.

Enefer left for a cocktail party at the convention centre. As he mingled he received more snide comments. "Why don't you go home!" one delegate said.

The great showdown was set. But everyone in the anti-Vander Zalm camp knew that the dissidents didn't have nearly enough support to force a secret-ballot vote on Vander Zalm's leadership. In the lobby of the Delta Lakeside hotel on the eve of voting day, Grace McCarthy bumped into two reporters. "It's all over, isn't it?" she said, referring to the likelihood of a leadership review. "It's back to the politics of arrogance."

Just after ten o'clock the next morning, Vander Zalm strode purposefully to the podium on the convention stage. He received a loud and sustained ovation. He flashed a wide grin. His wife Lillian sat in the front row on the convention stage, her eyes locked adoringly on her husband.

Bill Vander Zalm touched the edges of the speech notes on the rostrum in front of him, making sure they were all in order. He was now ready to deliver perhaps the most important speech of his career.

"Before I prepared my speech I had lots of people wanting to give advice, some good, some not so good," Vander Zalm began.

"One bit of advice was, 'Don't speak about the Opposition, don't talk about the media, and don't mention God.' Well, I don't worry too much about the first two, but as for God, he's pretty influential, he got me through some pretty tough times."

The convention delegates looked horrified. If Vander Zalm

started on his personal religious views, the A-word was sure to come up. And abortion was the last thing the premier's supporters wanted him to mention.

But Vander Zalm chose a safer route, launching into the twin themes of his speech, courage and conviction.

"My friends, strength is gained by overcoming adversities, not by giving in to them . . . too many politicians, in times of criticism and adversity, lose courage, abandon conviction, and show weakness."

He outlined his government's accomplishments–reducing the size of the provincial deficit, Bill 19, a thriving economy, major hikes in retail sales and exports. He made an oblique apology for his arrogant response to the Boundary-Similkameen by-election loss. And then he addressed the dissension in his own party, appealing for an end to the public feud.

"I am concerned about those within this party who take our family disagreements into the public arena as their issues," said the man who once publicly called his cabinet colleagues gutless. "They are doing the work the Opposition could never do."

The delegates jumped to their feet, erupting in an ovation.

As his speech continued, Vander Zalm quoted Benjamin Disraeli, Rudyard Kipling, W.A.C. Bennett, Abraham Lincoln, and Margaret Thatcher. The heavy use of quotations seemed strange for an admitted nonreader. Had he or someone else looked them up in Bartlett's?

He dismissed the negative polls, saying that the NDP always soars in the polls between elections but never on election day.

"Social Credit has been buffeted by political storms before and we always come out stronger and even more united than ever," Vander Zalm said.

As he finished speaking, Vander Zalm received another standing ovation. Even some of his detractors were clapping. He received an emotional embrace from Lillian. Most agreed it had been a good performance.

"He pressed all the right buttons," said a cabinet minister who was concerned about Vander Zalm's leadership. "He confessed his sins, he asked for forgiveness, he talked about all the good things we've done and appealed to an end to all the bullshit in the party."

It was now time for the vote on the second resolution. Vander Zalm and Lillian took seats in the front row on the convention floor. After pledging allegiance to the Queen, resolution chairman Peter Hyndman, a former Socred cabinet minister under Bill Bennett, read out the resolution.

Mickey Patriluk, a Kelowna delegate chosen by the dissidents to prove province-wide opposition, stood ready at one of the four microphones on the floor; she notified Hyndman she was going to move an amendment, asking that a vote on the motion of confidence be a secret ballot. Then Don Phillips, in a move that galled even the most hard-edged cynics in the party, gave a thunderous speech endorsing Vander Zalm. Only days earlier, the political lobbyist had delivered the Goldfarb poll to Vander Zalm to show the premier how much he was hated in B.C.

After fifteen minutes of procedural wrangling, a vote on the motion was taken. It was defeated, but more than 30 per cent on the floor had voted for a secret ballot. After that, Hyndman called for a vote on the motion without amendment. This time, Vander Zalm received endorsement from 1036 delegates, with 37 against and more than 200 abstaining.

Vander Zalm was jubilant, as were his many supporters who began to chant "Bill, Bill, Bill" in an echo of Whistler.

McCarthy told reporters that the failure to have a secret ballot was a "sad day for democracy."

"Why don't you knock it off, Grace? Haven't you done enough damage already?" one woman yelled above McCarthy's comments to the press.

Bill Enefer, the man who had spearheaded the secret ballot movement, accepted the result with bemused resignation. "Hey, we had fun doing it. And I think we focused a lot of attention on the leadership question. I think Vander Zalm was forced to listen. Maybe things will be better as a result."

Vander Zalm was too smart to be smug about the result. On the question of whether there should be a secret ballot, more than 30 per cent of the delegates had voted yes—not an insignificant showing for a leaderless movement.

The premier now understood that he would have to make real changes in his governing style in order to remain as leader. He was obliged to his inner cabinet for their efforts to ensure that there were no nasty surprises at Penticton. In return, Vander Zalm was going to consult his ministers more before making decisions, and he would have to hand them back some of the power he had usurped. It seemed that Bill Vander Zalm was entering a new phase in his leadership, one void of controversy. But just one week later. . . .

Bill Kay chauffeured Vander Zalm to a downtown Vancouver hotel to give a long-ago-scheduled speech on ethics to a Christian group.

"Every government will claim to have ethics," Vander Zalm told the forum, sponsored by a right-wing Christian organization, Campus Crusade for Christ. "But by what standards? To adopt pure Christian standards will be a continuing battle, and the closer we come to Christ the busier the devil gets.

"Real leadership comes from someone with a real purpose continuing on to fight and win when your overwhelming majority is you and your Lord Jesus Christ."

Then the coup de grâce: Vander Zalm compared his struggles to those of Christ.

"Can we as a Social Credit government be politically popular if we follow the precepts I've outlined for you? It won't be easy . . . but good things weren't meant to be easy. Christ didn't have an easy way. He came into the world poor. He never travelled far from home. He was taunted and ridiculed. He never had a [university] education. He would have been low in the polls. But he left a tremendous impression on the world."

The speech was videotaped and 1300 copies distributed across B.C. Not unexpectedly, a copy reached the *Sun* in early November and became front-page news, the strongest evidence yet of Vander Zalm's zealotry. It shocked supporters and detractors alike. Supporters wondered how he could have allowed the Christian organization to distribute the video, knowing that it would likely end up in the media. And why such a controversial speech just a week after promising his party in Penticton that he was going to stay out of trouble?

Detractors wondered how he had the nerve to deliver a speech on ethics–the same man who had tried to help his friend strike a $500-million deal to buy government land, who had tried to convince the attorney-general to compromise his office on behalf of that friend.

This controversy paled before an even worse one. The *Sun*'s Vaughn Palmer broke the news that David Poole had left government with a $97 500 golden handshake, which soon became rounded off in the telling to an even $100 000: a nice number that the average working stiff could relate to.

By the time Poole had left government after twenty-two months of service he had become the symbol of everything that was wrong with the Vander Zalm administration. British Columbians phoning hotline hosts couldn't understand how someone like Poole could get $100 000 for leaving his job voluntarily.

It would later be learned that the government had also kicked in about $50 000 to top up Poole's pension contribution, bringing his total farewell package to about $150 000.

"Yep, I guess government's got a pretty neat deal," said Vander Zalm when asked to defend the amount of the severance package. It was the kind of flippant response that did not sit well with the public.

Even though Poole was now thousands of miles away, he was still front-page news in B.C. The severance issue would dog Vander Zalm into the following year when he would claim, contrary to the facts, that he had fired Poole and therefore his former aide was entitled to the severance amount.

In a way, it was fitting. The year had started with the abortion fiasco in January and was ending with the Poole severance controversy—bookends around a year of scandal and discontent.

On an early December weekday, Vander Zalm put on his heavy knee-length navy-blue winter coat and slowly made his way to the front of the legislature. Vander Zalm was taking part in a cross-Canada Christmas-tree-lighting ceremony. At 4:00 p.m., the prime minister and all the provincial premiers would simultaneously hit the switch on Christmas lights bedecking trees in front of the House of Commons and the provincial legislatures.

In Victoria, it was unusually dark. The sky was grey and there was a stiff wind. As he stood on the top steps of the legislature, Vander Zalm looked old and tired. Below him, about fifty demonstrators had gathered, protesting everything from government logging practices to welfare cuts. But Vander Zalm seemed oblivious. He seemed, in fact, to be lost in a daydream. The man who had once been regularly mobbed by an adoring electorate now seemed alone. A cluster of protesters and a handful of office workers ordered to show up for the ceremony were all that he could draw.

As he hit the switch lighting the mammoth fir tree on the legislature's front lawn, Bill Vander Zalm was probably still wondering how things could have gone so disastrously wrong.

Paradise Lost

On a sunny afternoon in late January 1989, a discouraged Bill Kay walked with a reporter through the garden outside the premier's office complex and pondered his boss's future.

"He just isn't interested anymore. The enthusiasm isn't there," Kay sighed. "The bureaucrats have taken over. He doesn't seem to care any more."

Vander Zalm had blown it. Another election was drawing inevitably closer–it had to be called by the fall of 1991–and the only question was whether the premier would step down voluntarily or defiantly hang on.

Over the 1988/89 holiday season Vander Zalm went through some lengthy soul-searching, much of it at home at Fantasy Gardens, talking to Lillian and the kids. He spent far fewer hours on the job than he normally did.

"I didn't read many newspapers or even watch any newscasts for several months," Vander Zalm recalls. "I hadn't done that before. I had to get away from all of it and it helped. It was like therapy."

Quitting crossed his mind only briefly, he says. "But I think there is still so much to do, still things I want to accomplish."

He had just spent six months fighting for his job and winning. But sticking around was not as easy as it sounded.

In early February, Vander Zalm left for Europe on another business and holiday trip with Lillian. Back home in B.C., the plotters were up to their old tricks.

A few Socred MLAs and their party supporters attempted to plant wild stories about coups and resignations in the minds of reporters, some of whom dutifully reported them.

One story–spread by, among other people, Stephen Rogers–had several government MLAs crossing the floor, the whole revolt being guided by Bud Smith.

Such groundless speculation made its way onto a few airwaves and into a few newspaper stories. It made the MLAs who had started the stories more than happy, and kept alive the image that Vander Zalm was a weak leader, no longer in charge of his own caucus.

But when none of the talk resulted in action, it simply pointed once again to the fundamental flaw in the attempts to dislodge Vander Zalm from the premier's office: No one was willing to make the first move and be the one to step forward and present himself or herself as the leadership alternative. No one wanted to be the Dalton Camp (who in the 1960s led the move to dump John Diefenbaker as federal Tory leader, in the process ruining his own hopes for the leadership) of B.C. politics.

Meanwhile, Vander Zalm seemed almost oblivious, incapable of enforcing caucus discipline. He still preferred the hale and hearty role, backslapping everyone in public and brooding quietly in his office or back home at Fantasy Gardens.

"I can't be ruthless. I don't hold a grudge. I feel sorry for people before I get mad at them. I can be decisive about what needs doing but not in any ruthless way or hard," he told the authors.

Vander Zalm had, however, changed the way he dealt with the media. Now he rarely commented on issues better dealt with by his ministers. His answers sounded like carefully scripted lines fed to him by his handlers. He avoided scrums, sometimes walking briskly past reporters who greeted him when he arrived with Bill Kay each morning. For the first time in his life, he was being quiet.

His trip to Europe was a moderate success. He led a B.C. delegation to the prestigious World Economic Forum in Davos, Switzerland. Clad in matching bright yellow-and-blue ski jackets and sporting B.C. and Canadian flags everywhere they went, the twenty-one-person B.C. delegation made quite a splash, wooing 1000 senior businesspeople in the effort to convince them that B.C. would be the place to be in the 1990s.

Vander Zalm enjoyed every minute of the visit; he was a salesman again, hawking his wares and showing off the province's beauty.

The forum helped refire Vander Zalm's engines. He returned with a little more pep, a little more enthusiasm for the battles that lay ahead. The legislature was due to open soon; a "good news" budget would be unveiled; and it was almost springtime, when the flowers would be in full bloom in Victoria and back home at Fantasy Gardens.

But Vander Zalm was no longer able to mould government policies in his own image. The cabinet's powerful planning and priorities committee–created in the fall of 1988 in the wake of the botched attempts by Vander Zalm and Poole to govern by themselves–had slowly taken over. The eight cabinet ministers on that committee now ran the province.

The "P and P" committee was steered by finance minister Mel Couvelier and attorney-general Bud Smith. Other members were two old Vander Zalm allies, Jack Davis and Rita Johnston, as well as Lyall Hanson, Stan Hagen, and Elwood Veitch. Between them, they had enough contacts to dominate the caucus, the party, and the rank and file.

No longer could Vander Zalm decide government policy on a whim, or in response to a reporter's question; there was now a process to be followed. He had become a bit player.

An example of Vander Zalm's new detachedness: the previous November, he had seen some cameramen walk into the legislative press theatre for a news conference being held by Couvelier. Vander Zalm had poked his head in and said quietly, "I just wondered what was going on," before walking back to his office.

His relations with the Socred caucus had improved marginally. But the caucus, still stinging from the abortion and Toigo affairs, were wary of the premier's leadership. They too wondered how much longer he'd be around. Some of them were also growing increasingly worried about their own chances of re-election. They didn't want Vander Zalm to drag them down in his quest for vindication from the people.

Even before the legislature opened, Vander Zalm faced a big test—and this time it wasn't from his own caucus.

On a sunny afternoon in early March, Vander Zalm showed up at the campaign office of Michael Levy, the Social Credit candidate in the by-election in Vancouver's posh Point Grey riding. Levy and the Socreds were trying to retain the seat left vacant by Kim Campbell, who had successfully moved to federal politics. Since the previous August, the government had been trying hard to recover support, but it hadn't made any headway.

Not only that, but Levy had won the nomination on an anti-Vander Zalm platform, a damaging and embarrassing spectacle for the premier and the party.

Vander Zalm walked tentatively into Levy's office. Several MLAs and cabinet ministers were there already. Levy had been a vocal critic of the premier; despite recent attempts to make amends, the encounter was awkward. After some pictures and light-hearted bantering, the two men left for a round of campaigning.

Vander Zalm and Levy knocked on two doors and visited a senior citizens' home. How things had changed. Vander Zalm, the master campaigner who would walk miles to kiss a baby, was now reduced to visiting three hand-picked places. There were more journalists than voters on the quick tour. Vander Zalm, looking uncomfortable most of the time, said very little.

He knew the by-election was being touted as a referendum on his leadership, and he knew his party was in trouble in Point Grey. Levy had had trouble raising money and attracting campaign workers. The volunteer sign-up sheet in Levy's office had only three signatures on it. Socred party people had had to be brought in from outside the riding just to run the office.

In the March 15 vote, Vander Zalm and his party were trounced by the NDP, both in Point Grey and in Nanaimo. Vander Zalm tried to maintain a brave smile, but, as he said, "A thumping is a thumping. It doesn't feel very good."

While Nanaimo was a blue-collar town that usually supported the NDP, the posh blue-blooded neighbourhoods of Point Grey were anything but. The riding had been all-Socred from 1975 to 1986, when the NDP grabbed one seat. Before the mid-1970s, it had been traditionally Liberal. Now Vander Zalm had succeeded in turning it into a dual-NDP riding.

But a close look at the poll results shows that the loss was even worse than most observers had expected. The Socreds had at least run a close second in Nanaimo during the 1986 election; this time their vote completely collapsed. In that worker's town, their candidate, a popular ex-pro hockey player, had been trounced by an unknown female student. In Point Grey, the Socreds were lucky to even finish second as the Liberals put on a stronger-than-usual showing. The Liberal support disproved another Socred theory: that any rise in Liberal fortunes hurt the NDP more than the Socreds.

The legislature resumed, and it was time for another Vander Zalm speech from the throne. In 1987 the speech had been full of ambitious promises about a new style of governing. His 1988 speech had been a bitter attack on the federal government.

The 1989 speech, however, did not sound like Bill Vander Zalm. It sounded like Bill Bennett's government reading an NDP policy statement. It was what throne speeches are supposed to be: bland, boring, vague, cautious, and diplomatic. (After all, the lieutenant-governor, a traditionally neutral representative of the Queen, reads it.) As well, what little content it possessed didn't resemble Vander Zalm's usual agenda: instead the speech called for a new ministry for women and increased emphasis on the environment and education.

Vander Zalm had said little about environment or education when he was campaigning. Those issues were thrust onto the government's agenda largely because of a practice Vander Zalm said he abhorred: polling. The polls showed that the environment was fast becoming the number one issue in B.C.

Vander Zalm had denigrated polls in favour of his gut instincts, but his instincts had led him to disaster. Also, his personal legislative agenda had pretty well ground to a halt while he had spent almost an entire year fighting a civil war in his party and government.

Reluctantly, he had had to turn to the polls, his main adviser being Eli Sopow, a former television journalist whom the premier's office had originally hired as a long-range planner. At BCTV, Sopow had enjoyed spending a dozen or so broadcasts a year analyzing the latest public opinion poll. He didn't lose his fascination for polling when he went to the premier's office.

Vander Zalm told Sopow he wanted to be "managed." Sopow dutifully tried to do just that; one of the first acts of the former reporter was to limit the media's access to Vander Zalm.

Vander Zalm needed more help than that, though. The principal secretary position left vacant by David Poole had yet to be filled. But Sopow did not have the necessary depth for the comprehensive position of principal secretary, so Vander Zalm turned to an old hand: political fixer Jerry Lampert.

In some respects, it was remarkable that Lampert returned. He and Vander Zalm had parted on cordial terms in 1986, but it was no secret that they were incompatible. Vander Zalm did not entirely trust him; Lampert was baffled by Vander Zalm's style and methods. But Vander Zalm was now desperate. He needed Lampert more than Lampert needed him.

The hiring was hailed by party supporters. At last, thought the Socred ranks, here was a person with experience and a track record. In fact, Vander Zalm now had two capable and experienced advisers: Lampert and his deputy, Frank Rhodes, the talented and respected bureaucrat who since his appointment a year before had brought direction and stability to the premier's office. If Lampert and Rhodes had been in those positions from the election onward, Vander Zalm might have spent the spring of 1989 confidently planning his next election campaign.

On March 24, Good Friday, Sopow phoned Vander Zalm in the early evening and told him of a giant oil tanker spill that had just occurred off the southern coast of Alaska. Sopow said B.C. was sending several key officials to view the spill and wondered whether or not a politician should accompany them. Environment minister Bruce Strachan was holidaying in Arizona and was unavailable. Vander Zalm decided to make the trip.

"That was my idea and I'm glad I went," Vander Zalm says.

The trip was hastily arranged, and it showed. No one in Alaska knew Vander Zalm was heading their way until he got off the plane (after a lengthy delay getting through customs). Alaskan officials, scrambling to find ways of coping with the disaster, didn't know what to do with him. A few state officials took a jaundiced view of Vander Zalm's visit, thinking he wanted only to look good on TV.

In the Valdez, Alaska, airport, Vander Zalm passed the time of day with a local fisherman. He later attended a public meeting to hear executives of Exxon Oil, owner of the tanker, try to explain why the disaster had happened. He sat in the audience like an interested bystander, flew over the oil slick, met briefly with the governor, and flew home.

All the time, he was in constant touch with Sopow, getting instructions and wondering what to do during the hectic, disorganized expedition. Little was accomplished, but the trip turned out to be a bit of a public relations coup for Vander Zalm. The government had been rightly blasted for its arrogant, uncaring attitude about a major oil spill off the west coast of Vancouver Island the previous December. Bruce Strachan had not even bothered to visit the site, and the government's response to the disaster had been pitifully slow and inadequate. In contrast, Vander Zalm's Valdez visit at least created the impression that the government was changing its attitude. (Some critics, however, blasted Sopow for his botched planning effort and dismissed Vander Zalm's visit as a cheap media stunt.)

Regarding what the NDP labelled his "born again" environmentalism, Vander Zalm told the authors, "I've always been an environmentalist. I'm a fuss pot, I can't stand to see a cigarette butt on the ground. If I see someone throw garbage out their window, I'll chase after them and get their licence plate number.

"I was never quite so concerned about oil tankers, I was never quite so concerned about clear cut logging. I'm definitely more aware and more concerned and that's growing every day."

The spring legislative session marked the end of the let's-all-be-pals behaviour that had existed, on and off, for two years. With an election looming, the two parties could hardly be expected to remain civil, especially in polarized B.C.

The government's chief hit man was attorney-general Bud Smith, who considered himself heir apparent to Vander Zalm's throne and who had little time for the politics of niceness. Like W.A.C. Bennett and Bill Bennett, Smith viewed every day in the legislature as another pitched battle in a long-running political war. He was the loudest, most vicious of the hecklers on the government side, he did not believe in taking prisoners, and he saw to it that few favours were done for the Opposition.

For example, the NDP did not receive its copy of the throne speech ahead of time, a courtesy shown to them the previous two years. When the B.C. Supreme Court made a ruling involving redrawing the electoral map, Smith did not notify his critic or provide him a copy of the ruling before he raised the issue in the legislature.

Smith baited the NDP MLAs, some of whom occasionally lost their cool. Smith admired the American style of politics, particularly its growing reliance on anything negative about an opponent. He was an ardent admirer of W.A.C. Bennett and had refined his own methods at the elbow of Bill Bennett, for whom he had been principal secretary.

He also wanted to raise his own profile for the day when he would once again seek the Socred leadership. He always made sure he was in the house to defend his cabinet colleagues from any Opposition attack and he coached the cabinet during question period. Clearly Vander Zalm was no longer calling the shots, since his efforts at maintaining good will in the house were over.

The NDP had changed too. Much to the displeasure of the party's left wing, leader Mike Harcourt steered the party toward the middle, aggressively courting the elite business community. One evening in mid-March, Harcourt and one of his lieutenants, MLA Colin Gabelmann, met with 120 top businessmen in one of Vancouver's swankiest hotels. There, the two men described the NDP's "new" philosophy, which involved the "creation of wealth," economic growth, and "sustainable development"–a balance between growth and environmental protection.

"The creation of wealth is what we think you have to do," Harcourt told his well-heeled audience. "You can't just redistribute a shrinking pie."

Gabelmann said the days of the NDP's "limited growth" strategy were over, and he publicly turned his back on the old Dave Barrett government, in which he had served as a backbencher.

"One of the mistakes some of us may have [made] in years gone by was that we assumed we knew what to do and how to do it and we would do it on our own without consultation," Gabelmann said. "Many of us in caucus have a very different view of the world now than what I think many of you fear–the one you saw in action in '72 to '75."

Already slipping in the polls, the last thing the Socreds needed was weakened ties to business groups. But that had already been happening for two years, NDP or no NDP.

Political donations continued to roll in during Vander Zalm's term, but they were small ones: $25 or $50 from the so-called grassroots. But the grassroots do not fund election campaigns.

The Social Credit Party spends about $4 million on each election in B.C., plus another $2 million running the party between elections. Membership donations only contribute about $100 000 a year, if that. Hence a confidential 1988 memo from Bob Ransford to David Poole. The memo dealt with party contributions from the forest industry, which was upset with the government's policy of collecting much higher stumpage fees, and which traditionally provides the bulk of the corporate donations to the party.

"Despite the industry's strong commitment in the past, there is a real reluctance to be involved now because they feel they are not being listened to and their involvement is not worth it.

"Actual numbers, comparing 1985 versus 1987 commitments to the party, show a 150 per cent drop in that sector. This sector has been very important to us on the corporate side."

Vander Zalm knew there was a serious problem, and in early 1989 he started to do something about it. "I'm attending more meetings, more luncheons," he told the authors. "I think we've had more $100 bills from more people. But we're not getting the big donations. I know you need big contributors too, who give $1000 or $2000. I've got to work on that."

He also knew he had to convince the business community that the NDP was simply the same old radical bunch. Harcourt, he claimed, was just a front man; the real leader was Bob Williams, the irascible veteran MLA from Vancouver East whom the Socreds loathed and feared more than anyone else in the NDP. Most government members withered under Williams's blistering, sarcastic attacks in the legislature.

The Socreds branded him a radical leftist, but Williams was actually a successful small businessman whose "radical" ideas consisted mostly of having tighter controls on resource industries and retaining public control of public land. He also wasn't well liked by many people in his own party. Bitter memories lingered of his role in the Dave Barrett government–he had been Barrett's arrogant and all-powerful lieutenant.

In speech after speech, Vander Zalm warned businessmen not to be "fooled" by Harcourt and his fellow socialists in disguise. It was, perhaps, one of the few strategies left open to him short of resigning.

Meanwhile, some old issues continued to come back to haunt Vander Zalm and his government. One reason for this was that there had been no fall legislative sitting, so the NDP had simply stored up all its ammunition for an all-out assault in the spring.

The NDP was quick to jump on the $172 000 severance package (which included a pension) for David Poole. The NDP knew they had a winner with that one. It was clear that the severance settlement offended many British Columbians. Vander Zalm tried to evade the constant questioning in the legislature, but one day he happened to blurt out that Poole had been fired and had not left voluntarily.

Ironically, Poole had been in Vancouver that day and had been intending to meet with his old boss. After hearing about the comment an incensed Poole flew home without talking to him. There had been an understanding between the two men about his departure: Vander Zalm would not say he had been fired, since he had resigned voluntarily (although Poole was aware that if he had stayed much longer, the axe would have fallen).

Another lingering issue was the sale of the BCEC lands. The NDP had spent much of the winter break researching title deeds and real estate purchases. An almost salivating Bob Williams was quick to jump on two BCEC sales of large valuable land tracts. He claimed that one piece of waterfront property in New Westminster had been flipped quickly for millions of dollars more than the government had sold it for. The minister responsible, Cliff Michael, maintained that the government had gotten the best deal possible, and he disputed some of Williams's facts. The truth lay somewhere in the middle, but Williams made mincemeat out of Michael in the house and garnered tremendous media attention with his attacks.

In another transaction, a chunk of a Vancouver suburb was sold to a single bidder, instead of being parcelled out and sold to several bidders for a larger total sum.

Williams was delighted to find some odd allies on this one. When the sale was announced, at least eight Socred backbenchers went through the roof in a caucus meeting. They knew the party had lost public relations points over the Expo lands sale because the site had gone to a single bidder, and they didn't want it to happen again. Williams was delighted.

Vander Zalm's reaction was another indication that he was listening to his backbench more. He agreed that the issue should go back to the cabinet for one more look, and he made his lands minister meet with the opponents of the scheme (the minister, Howard Dirks, had stormed out of an earlier caucus meeting when the questioning became too rough for him).

The other issue that would not go away was abortion. In March, an American anti-abortion group, which calls itself "Operation Rescue" and believes that the court system is "enemy territory," began blocking access to Vancouver's free-standing abortion clinic.

The clinic was granted injunctionary relief, but the protesters refused to leave; each day police would cart truckloads of them off to jail. Many returned to protest even after a judge warned them they would be held in contempt; scores were slapped with jail terms ranging from two weeks to three months. The anti-abortion movement took on the appearance of being led by religious zealots.

Vander Zalm would not be tempted into saying anything about the protesters. Yet just one year earlier, he had needed little prompting to discourse at length about abortion as an abomination.

At a Social Credit function in Nanaimo one evening in March, he was cornered by three reporters, all eager to pin him down on the Vancouver protests. But he wasn't even willing to passionately defend his views on abortion. He carefully referred all questions to his attorney-general, Bud Smith. It appeared he had learned his lesson.

However, in May, one John Huf and his group of ardent anti-abortionists were able to take over the executive of the Langley Social Credit constituency association.

Langley, one of the more conservative towns in the Fraser Valley, has a strong religious community. Its two Socred MLAs are Dan Peterson and Carol Gran, the Socred caucus chair. Gran came under fire from many of her constituents in 1988 for her public opposition to Vander Zalm's abortion policy. She recalls being booed at a breakfast meeting.

Vander Zalm's hard policy against abortion had cost the party votes; incidents like Langley were not bringing them back.

On a sunny May afternoon, Bill Vander Zalm stood among the mourners at the funeral of a long-time Social Credit politician, Alex Fraser. More than 1000 people had turned out in the northern interior town of Quesnel to see their beloved "King of the Cariboo" laid to rest after a lengthy bout with cancer.

But amid the large crowd, Vander Zalm stood alone, accompanied only by a single loyal cabinet minister, Neil Vant, whom he had plucked from the anonymity of the backbench less than a year earlier. Despite being premier and leader of the party Fraser had loved so much, Vander Zalm was not entirely welcome at the service.

In the two years before his death, Fraser had become one of Vander Zalm's most ardent critics. First elected in 1969, he had been one of the longest-serving MLAs in the legislature. Only Bob Williams and Grace McCarthy had been elected earlier. But since the 1986 election Fraser had rarely been able to take his seat in the legislature because of steadily worsening throat cancer.

As transportation and highways minister from 1975 to 1986, he was instrumental in continuing the Socred tradition of blacktop politics: paving, extending, and expanding Interior highways.

He was beloved in his Cariboo riding, a huge, sprawling northern Interior area filled with ranchers, loggers, and small towns.

Fraser was bitter at being left out of cabinet after the 1986 election. He became even angrier when the Coquihalla Highway scandal broke in 1987. It was revealed that the project was plagued by cost overruns and funded partly by some cabinet sleight-of-hand that reflected badly on Fraser, who saw the investigation as an effort by Vander Zalm to discredit the Bennett administration.

There was a dramatic and emotional moment in the spring of 1988, when Fraser stood in the house and defended himself. Cancer had robbed him of his larynx, so he had to use a synthesizer to speak.

Fraser was also angry that the government had privatized all the highway road crews, a move he felt was political suicide in the hinterlands of the province, where road safety in winter is vitally important. Fraser predicted that the Socreds would lose up to fourteen seats in the next election because of the sell-off, and he called his caucus colleagues "sheep" for blindly following their premier.

Now, at his funeral, an awkward Vander Zalm stood off to one side. The night he had been chosen leader of his party, Vander Zalm had dedicated a huge Lower Mainland bridge to the man who helped build it: Alex Fraser. Almost three years later Vander Zalm felt uncomfortable at the man's funeral.

As summer approached, speculation continued about Vander Zalm's future. Even his aides looked for small clues that might provide some indication of what he was going to do. But Vander Zalm kept everyone guessing.

One day, he was all fired up, blasting the NDP with antiquated and hollow anti-socialist rhetoric and vowing never to let them in power. The next, he was a gloomy, depressed man, brooding in his office. Aides said sometimes he seemed lost in his private thoughts.

"He was very moody. You could almost tell how he felt from the weather," one aide recalls. "When it's sunny, he's feeling great. When it's raining, he has no enthusiasm."

The polls showed that the government's chances for re-election if he were leader ranged from dismal to nonexistent.

But Vander Zalm didn't like quitters. He did not want to walk away. He wanted to show that no matter what the polls said, he could win one more time and charm his way into the hearts of British Columbians.

Many party people worried that Vander Zalm would lead them into a situation similar to that faced by New Brunswick Conservatives when their leader, Richard Hatfield, overstayed his welcome and lost credibility with the voters. The Conservatives lost every seat in New Brunswick's subsequent election in October, 1987.

Vander Zalm hung on, slowly building up his confidence once again. By June, it looked fairly certain that he intended to stick around, if he had any choice. Nervous government members kept telling themselves that nothing really bad had happened for a while. At least it wasn't like last year, they said, when resignations and scandals seemed to pop up every week.

But by the end of the month, disaster struck again. And, once again, it was Vander Zalm's "moral values" that landed him and his government in trouble. The *Sun*'s medical reporter, Anne Mullens, discovered the government had quietly withdrawn its support for an anti-AIDS rock video. The 60-second clip had been hailed by doctors and researchers as a no-nonsense, provocative, and much-needed message to young people. It was to be shown in movie theatres just before so-called "teen" movies, where it was thought the impact would be greatest.

Vander Zalm nixed the whole project. He felt the video promoted promiscuity and he also thought it was another advertisement for condoms (part of his attitude was based on a misunderstanding about the video; a fictional condom called "Always" is featured in it, and Vander Zalm actually thought it was a real brand-name).

The premier figured the best way to combat AIDS was really quite simple: stop having sex. Of course, that attitude was more in keeping with the 1950s, not the 1980s. Teenagers were much more sexually active now, and therefore more susceptible to contracting the killer virus. But Vander Zalm refused to accept that reality; instead, he tried to change it.

The health ministry—which paid about $100 000 for the production—withdrew its sponsorship and refused to distribute the film. Some ministry officials were shocked. They had been led to believe the premier's office had okayed the film; after all, the government's public relations bureau, headed by Eli Sopow, had overseen the production. The officials were fully aware of Vander Zalm's own feelings on the subject; he had made them abundantly clear over the past two years. But it was the way the decision was made that shocked them so much: Vander Zalm viewing it during a private screening, hitting the roof, and then hinting darkly to the officials that their careers would not be helped if word should leak out to the press.

But of course, word did leak out and Vander Zalm was vilified in the press once again. He was denounced for enforcing his own "moral values" on the populace; his attitude to AIDS was labeled "prehistoric" and his own caucus again found itself cringing. They had tired of running on the same treadmill for so long: one step forward, two steps back.

The episode again brought questions about Vander Zalm's future to the forefront and he was well aware of the damage it had caused. But like abortion before it, Vander Zalm refused to back down or apologize. And with each passing day, it became more certain he was going to stay at least a little while longer.

During seven hours of discussions in his office with one of the authors over pizza and milk, Vander Zalm appeared relaxed and he still got excited when talking about his continuing plans for B.C. He loved to talk about policies he considered to be successful, such as his labour bills, economic policies, privatization, decentralization, and the downsizing of government.

He had vowed to rewrite the labour law and had done so with a vengeance; he had promised to bring in a balanced budget and had done so in 1989; he had pledged to reduce the size of government, and his privatization program and early retirement incentives for civil servants had done just that.

By July 1989, Vander Zalm could also point to another accomplishment. He had promised during the 1986 election campaign to bring in electoral reform and introduce some semblance of fairness to B.C.'s electoral map. To the surprise of almost everyone, his government did just that shortly before the legislative session adjourned. The charges of Socred gerrymandering would now be a thing of the past, and the archaic dual-member riding system would also disappear.

Some sitting Socred MLAs, particularly those in two-seat ridings, were sure to be hurt by the new electoral map to be drawn up, which made Vander Zalm's decision to keep his promise all the more surprising. Of course, his hand was forced in a large way by a successful court challenge of the old system. The B.C. Supreme Court ruled a new, fairer map had to be drawn up soon, probably before the next election.

Vander Zalm had also succeeded in his life-long goal of inflicting damage on the labour movement. His legislation weakened some union rights and increased government power in the labour relations field. (Vander Zalm maintained that the labour laws worked because there were few strikes during his mandate; the labour movement said the new legislation was grossly unfair and anti-democratic, and that in any case it was impossible to gauge its effectiveness because there was a massive boycott against the new labour adjudication body. Still, the dire predictions of chaos in labour relations and large-scale and bitter strikes never material-ized, and that played right into the hands of Vander Zalm, who had promised peace on B.C.'s volatile labour front.)

The privatization program earned the government more than $300 million and shed 5000 or so workers from the government payroll. The government also got rid of highways maintenance crews, B.C. Hydro's gas and rail divisions, part of the Queen's Printer, an environmental testing laboratory, and a tree nursery.

However, the so-called "phase two" part of the privatization program had been stopped in mid-stream. There would be no second phase. And the government's sell-off of public land–handled by the B.C. Enterprise Corporation–had turned into a political disaster. The Expo land sale, plus the sales attacked by Bob Williams in the spring of 1989, were giant headaches for the government.

Also, by mid-1989, other problems with the privatization initia-tive began to emerge. Environment Canada assessed the privatized provincial environmental laboratory and found it inadequate. Critical deficiencies that hadn't existed when the government owned the lab now cast doubt on its testing quality.

The forest ministry's decision to shift much of the responsibility for checking logs onto the private scaling industry resulted in loopholes big enough to drive a logging truck through, according to an RCMP inspector's May 1989 letter to forests minister Dave Parker. Millions of dollars in stumpage fees were possibly not being collected, a criticism echoed by the government's own independent auditor-general.

The privatization program, coupled with the early retirement package, reduced the government's civil service size considerably. But many government jobs were now simply being done through often cheaper "personal service" contracts. Thus the government reduced the size of the government employees' union but made little dent in the size of government itself.

As well, early retirement incentives–which had cost the taxpayers $100 million–had robbed the government of many of its most experienced senior and middle-management employees. In the long run, the measure might pay off once the junior management people became more experienced. But over the short term, many government departments were without leadership and experience.

Vander Zalm considers his economic policies to be the great monuments to his leadership. But political leaders are happy to take all the credit for a boom economy, ignoring the effects of world and national policies and pressures. When the economy goes bad, though, it's usually everyone else's fault.

"I guess the biggest single accomplishment has been the turn-around of the economy and the diversification of the economy," he says. "I think we've been very effective in our fiscal management. Privatization and reducing the size of government in part helped. I think we've accomplished a tremendous amount."

His government had stabilized provincial finances, balanced the budget and reduced the cumulative debt. The first two objectives were accomplished within three years, which allowed the government to at least start on the third.

True, the personal tax rates had jumped dramatically while many corporate taxes had declined. And the forest industry was upset by hefty increases in stumpage rates (which resulted partly from the settlement of a trade dispute with the U.S.). But the net effect was positive for the government.

The NDP liked to talk of "average" British Columbians being hit hard by the budgets, but the effect was nothing compared to the Bennett budgets a few years earlier, budgets which led to wide-ranging cutbacks in government services, higher unemployment, and a general mood of economic despair. The NDP found it hard to score many points on the economic front.

Even the balanced budget in 1989 had been criticized as nothing more than some flashy Socred-style book-juggling that allowed the government to show a balanced ledger. The NDP claimed that the budget could have been balanced a year earlier, and in fact was, but for the creation of a strange rainy-day fund that kept hundreds of millions of dollars from appearing on the balance sheet.

The fund, called the "Budget Stabilization Fund" (or, as the critics were quick to label it, the "BS fund"), essentially socked away hundreds of millions of dollars in an account separate than all other government accounts. But the money wasn't really sitting in the bank somewhere, drawing interest, because the government actually "borrowed" it back to pay for various things. The money in the fund, therefore, never appeared on the government's bottom line statement.

As for the decentralization program, it was little more than window-dressing for some fancy economic development schemes. The program had never been adequately explained, and as time went on, the government talked about it less and less.

It is true that the list of scandals, crises, and controversies could be recited by many British Columbians as easily as their telephone numbers: the abortion debacle, the Toigo affair and the rest of the BCEC dealings, the resignations of two senior cabinet ministers, the split within the government caucus over Vander Zalm's leadership, the labour legislation uproar.

But, almost hidden from view because of all those events, lay one fact: Bill Vander Zalm had accomplished much of what he set out to do. Whether or not they were admirable goals, and whether or not he had actually gone as far as he would have liked, Vander Zalm could at least point to them and say, "I did it."

He had failed to deliver on some key promises, of course. Most notably, his pledge to be less confrontational and more conciliatory than his predecessor seemed laughable now, in the aftermath of his never-back-down attitude in the abortion episode, the Toigo–BCEC affair, and the Bill 19 controversy.

He was supposed to end the power of the "backroom boys," but then he brought in David Poole, the all-powerful civil servant who centralized more power and created more damage to a premier's leadership and his party than any so-called backroom boy had done in any previous administration.

Vander Zalm's new-found reliance on polls betrayed another key promise: to operate a less secretive, more "open" style of government. His idea of "openness" consisted mostly of allowing the media access to his own thoughts.

And, perhaps most important, Vander Zalm said that he had changed his ways. The old days of the shoot-from-the-lip Surrey redneck were supposed to be over. He was supposed to be conciliatory, willing to listen to other points of view. But, as he showed month after month and crisis after crisis, he was clearly the same Bill Vander Zalm.

Once again, it had all come down to personality, that great variable in B.C. politics. Vander Zalm had swept the province in 1986 largely because his personality–upbeat, positive, conciliatory, and friendly–was right for the times. His opponent at the time, Bob Skelly, was just the opposite–weak, indecisive, and uninspiring.

Almost three years later, Vander Zalm's personality was the major factor once again. But this time, the qualities that stood out seemed markedly different: he was now confrontational, zealous, and not credible.

It mattered little that the economy was in good shape, that labour peace had apparently arrived, that prospects looked good for the future. The polls showed that British Columbians were going to cast their ballots for a *leader.* It was personality that counted once again, and waiting in the weeds was the bland, boring, but capable Mike Harcourt, who appeared to be ready to win the next election simply by default.

Vander Zalm had become the worst of all possible things for a politician: an embarrassment. Leaders who are dull, dishonest, or even slightly incompetent fare better than someone who is simply an embarrassment. The voters had grown tired of his act.

In late summer 1989, Bill Vander Zalm was alone. The dream appeared to be over.

David Poole was in exile in Ontario, a symbol of everything that had gone wrong, wondering when he could come home.

Peter Toigo spent most of his time in Palm Springs or back

east. He and Vander Zalm, once close friends, now talked only occasionally.

Charlie Giordano, Vander Zalm's old campaign manager, was facing a criminal charge for allegedly lying to the ombudsman during his investigation of the Knight Street pub affair.

Bob Ransford, the young aide whom Vander Zalm regretted not making more use of, had quit government, fed up with the way things had been handled. Another young aide, Brian Battison, had left as well, discouraged and disillusioned.

The news reporters, the people Vander Zalm had once thought he could rely on to spread his message, were now waiting patiently for his departure.

His own caucus watched and waited. They hadn't forgiven his autocratic style; he could never understand why they did not stick by him.

And then there was Grace McCarthy, once his counsel and his ally, now his enemy. The two had disappointed each other so badly.

Only a few allies remained: ministers Rita Johnston, Jack Davis, and Bill Reid—and, of course, that loyal foot-soldier Bill Kay. They were Vander Zalm's last connection with the glorious summer of 1986.

While the public speculation on his future continued, Vander Zalm weighed his options.

The dog days of summer, when politics usually drift quietly out of people's minds, would soon be over. The fall would bring on another key challenge: the by-election to fill Alex Fraser's vacant seat in the Cariboo riding. It was solid Socred country, but then so was Boundary–Similkameen.

Victory in the Cariboo appeared essential to Vander Zalm's political future. If he won, it might just give him the momentum he so badly needed to begin the climb out of the political cellar. It would be a long journey. Trying to persuade the public, the media, and his own party to give another chance was a task to daunt even the greatest believer in the power of positive thinking.

If he lost, the pressure on him to quit would increase. The Social Credit party's convention was scheduled for late October, and the knives would reappear. If he quit, he could go back to a world where he still writes the rules, where reality really is what he says it is. Perhaps it was time to go back there, back to the Gardens, to the apartment above the drawbridge and moat, to the fantasy land he had created. The flowers would be in bloom and Lillian would be waiting.